# A HISTORY OF
# PHILADELPHIA
# SANDWICHES

*Steaks, Hoagies, Iconic Eateries & More*

## MIKE MADAIO

AMERICAN PALATE

Published by American Palate
A Division of The History Press
Charleston, SC
www.historypress.com

First published 2024

Manufactured in the United States

ISBN 9781467152020

Library of Congress Control Number: 2024941880

# CONTENTS

# ACKNOWLEDGEMENTS

Because so much of this story was hidden within the vagaries of oral history, I could not have possibly completed this project without the generosity of the many people who took the time to speak to me extensively about their experiences, families and businesses and/or provided photographs and artwork that helped make this story come alive.

This includes, in no particular order, Brandon Bartoszek, Bryan Kravitz, Cee Heard, Celeste Morello, Craig LaBan, Danny DiGiampietro, Ed Brennan, Elliot Hirsh, Frank Olivieri Jr., Gary Lane, Gene Blum, Hank Caratura, Howard Robboy, Jeff Vogel, Jesse Amoroso, Jim Pearlingi, Joe Nicolosi, Joel Spivak, John Bucci Jr., John D'Alessandro, John Scaltrito, Jon Vellios, Ken Silver, Larry Ricci, Len Davidson, Levis Kochin, Louis Sarcone III, Lou's Steak Shop, Luigi Lemme, Marc Polish, Megan Rose, Mike Campo Jr., Mike Campo Sr., Neil Benson, Nick Miglino, Peter Miglino, Peter Romano Jr., Raymond Ricci, Sallie Kochin Abelson, Tabachoy Philly, Texas Hot Dogs, Tony Luke Jr., Tracy Kauffman Wood, Trevor Kerin, William Woys Weaver and Yehuda Sichel. (If I left anyone out, the mistake is solely mine.)

Of course, thanks also to Arcadia Publishing and The History Press, particularly Banks Smither, for giving me the opportunity and all your help (to come, as of this writing) crossing the finish line.

Lastly, thanks to my family for putting up with my strange obsessions and for (begrudgingly) understanding that writing a historical book about sandwiches occasionally required more than just consuming the sandwiches we like to eat.

# INTRODUCTION

'm not originally from the Philadelphia area. I realize this is an odd way to begin a book about Philadelphia, especially a topic—sandwiches—so deeply woven into the fabric of the region's identity. But I state this boldly up front for two reasons. First, it illustrates that I am an outsider, or was at some point. So, when I proclaim that Philly is the greatest city for sandwiches in the world, it's not just some biased local viewpoint. I've seen other options and found them wanting. Second, sandwiches have always been important in my life, so having moved to this area against my will as a teenager surely qualifies as kismet.

My early memories of sandwiches are, like most Americans, of the school lunch variety: PB&J or simple cold cuts on bland bread. But I quickly learned to go beyond the basics. I was never one of those kids who separated the different types of food on his plate, insisting they not intermingle. I preferred eating them all together, discovering new flavor combinations, both good and bad. Thus, the main appeal of sandwiches has always been how these amalgamated meals can, in a single bite, unify a bevy of diverse ingredients. A worthwhile sandwich constructor understands how each flavor complements the others and how it all must come together as something greater than the sum of its parts. A sandwich is a canvas for food-related creativity, innovation and showcasing the maker's personality.

Growing up, I recall identifying the post-Thanksgiving sandwich as an art form and revering those who could construct it perhaps more than the chefs who made the meal these leftovers came from. Then there was my grandfather—who apparently willed me both his love for constructing sandwiches and writing—presiding over a family lunch, painstakingly constructing each sandwich with not only practiced technique but also pride and love.

Not to be outdone, my grandmother introduced me to the most important family sandwich, the *vastedda*. This name refers only to the bread in Sicily, similar to but much smaller than a New Orleans muffuletta roll. In Palermo, the former is used to create *pani câ meusa* (literally "bread with spleen"), a sandwich of fried spleen, ricotta cheese and grated caciocavallo cheese. Because spleen—which my nonna insisted on calling "the melts" for some arcane reason—wasn't easy to come by in the United States, my nonna substituted crispy bacon and (obviously) never went back. Though her "uncles" originally ate these sandwiches after midnight mass, they're now our Christmas breakfast tradition, always served with a side of arguing about whether we got the right rolls or used the right cheese. The fact that my Italian American family—who always held food traditions in the highest of esteem—could value a mere sandwich this much only served to further my personal belief that sandwiches are as important as any other foodstuff.

As an adult resident of southeastern Pennsylvania, I've relished exploring the wealth of sandwiches that the Philadelphia area has to offer. Although I learned relatively quickly after moving here that cheesesteaks would never be my favorite, as I dug deeper, it became evident that there was so much more to discover than the one sandwich anyone from anywhere else knows.

I'll never forget my first visit to John's Roast Pork, for example. I took the day off for my birthday—this was back when the shop's hours were painfully minimal for those outside the immediate neighborhood—so we made the day of it, sitting outside on a beautiful afternoon. The rich pork, the bright herbs, the savory greens, the sharp cheese, the crusty bread—it was a symphony. I've been back since, but I still think about how everything came together so perfectly on that first experience.

Or the time I popped into Paesano's—at the height of its initial run—and ordered the namesake brisket sandwich but had nowhere to eat it. I drove nearly an hour to my next destination, worried the entire time that the food—particularly the fried egg—would spoil, my mind in complete agony. When I finally did tuck in, however, I was shocked to be confronted with not only an egg that was still delightfully runny but also a revelation of balance and flavor, the beef offsetting the roasted tomato, the egg smothering the fiery horseradish. I still think about that day, too.

A Madaio-style vastedda. *Author photograph.*

Or my first visit to the Reading Terminal Market, before I even knew about the majesty of DiNic's. When I lined up at what was then called Rocco's, everyone else was ordering cheesesteaks, but a little sign taped to the cash register suggested I instead try the Chicken à la Rocco, a fried cutlet slathered in secret-recipe Dijon mustard sauce. "Long hots?" asked the sandwich man after I decided to go for it. At the time, I had no idea what he meant, but said, "Sure, why not." What I got was sweet, smoky, spicy, crispy, messy. What a sandwich. (Yep, I still think about that day, too.)

Those are just a few examples, moments of sandwich bliss that only existed because of the region in which I live. There were many others, of course, and there will be plenty more in the future if Philadelphia has any say in the matter.

# THE PHILADELPHIA STORY

Sandwiches, obviously, are eaten everywhere and have been for centuries. But there is something different, ineffable even, about Philadelphia that other places just can't claim. It's unlikely that this stems from one specific factor; rather, it comes from a combination of many forces—including industrialization, a neighborhood-based culture, a strong street food scene and immigrant culinary traditions—all leading to the perfect storm of sandwich perfection.

While sandwiches are by no means an American phenomenon, during the period of rapid industrialization and urbanization in the late nineteenth and early twentieth centuries, a strong sandwich culture established itself in many U.S. cities. As people moved from rural to urban areas to work in factories and other industries, this created a newfound desire for quick, easy meals that could be eaten on the go or packed for work. Though this was not unique to Philadelphia, the city—once known as the "Workshop of the World"—certainly has a strong working-class tradition, so it's no surprise that affordable, portable and satisfying sandwiches became popular among laborers throughout the region.

Even before sandwiches made their mark, Philadelphia's vibrant street food culture long thrived, tracing all the way to the city's founding in the seventeenth century. Back then, food vendors selling oysters, pepper pot soup, pies and other baked goods were a common sight in public markets and on city streets, catering to the needs of workers and travelers who sought both snacks and more substantial sustenance. As the city continued to grow as a commercial and industrial center, street food became increasingly desirable among workers who needed quick and inexpensive meals. German staples like soft pretzels and waffles emerged in the nineteenth century, and sandwiches—including hot dogs, steaks and hoagies—followed in the early twentieth century.

Immigrant culinary traditions also played a key role in the development of sandwiches as a Philadelphia staple, particularly those from Italian Americans who settled in South Philadelphia in the late 1800s and early 1900s. "The primary stream of Philadelphia sandwich history stems from the Italian American tradition," said *Philadelphia Inquirer* food writer Craig LaBan. "There are also Puerto Rican sandwiches, Jewish deli sandwiches [etc.], but they're far less synonymous with Philadelphia."[1] Considering the famous pizza culture of New York or the Creole-Italian fusion of New Orleans, this Italian influence could have gone in several directions here, but for many of the reasons mentioned herein, it manifested itself as delicious sandwiches.

"I had this theory," continued fellow transplant LaBan, "that until not long ago, the pizza was so bad in Philadelphia because all our Italian street food energy had been put in sandwiches.…It made no sense [that the pizza wasn't better] because it's such a great old Italian American community. Well, everyone was busy making hoagies and steak sandwiches."[2]

Although Italians certainly led the way in developing these famous Philadelphia sandwiches, other cultures played—and continue to play—a part in expanding the city's evolving multicultural mosaic. LaBan, citing one example, said, "In deep South Philly, there's a Mexican bakery, La Rosas, on South 8th Street. Before they took it over, it was a well-known Italian bakery that produced all the rolls for DiNic's. And before that, decades ago, it was a German bakery. There's still this historical brick oven in the basement. So there are these layers of bakeries upon bakeries that reflect the immigrant experience here."[3]

This cultural diversity also helped Philadelphia develop into a large city made up of distinct small neighborhoods, where pride and identity often align more closely with a specific block than the city as a whole. "I do think it was these strong neighborhoods, these old immigrant neighborhoods where there were corner bakeries," said LaBan. They were, notably, all walkable and accessible with shops that could provide fresh bread and other types of everyday food items. "They were very European in that setup," he continued. "There were also all these import/export shops that are often tied to immigrant populations.…But not every city has Italian shops such as [fantastic cheese purveyor] Di Bruno Brothers on every corner."[4]

There are, of course, plenty of similarities when comparing the evolution of Philadelphia's food scene—especially the Italian American one—to those in other cities in the Northeast and mid-Atlantic regions or to those with prominent Italian enclaves. Regarding this one specific foodstuff, however, it's also clear that none of those other places have developed the same widespread passion for sandwiches that still translates to everyday life here.

# BEST OF PHILLY?

Speaking of passion, Philadelphia is well known across the world for its *special* brand of passion for many things, and sandwich preferences—which are often rooted in neighborhood loyalty—are certainly no exception. As one amusing example, former *Philadelphia Magazine* publisher Maury Levy, while recalling "Best of Philly" sandwich choices under his tenure, noted how rare it was for their picks to receive reader praise. A much more common refrain was instead: "Are you guys out of your f—king minds?"[5]

Given that, I feel obligated to issue some caveats before we dive into the meat of this book. My main goal is to tell the story of how these sandwiches originally came to be and how they entrenched themselves in the cultural fabric of the city. This book is not meant to be, however, a compendium of every great Philadelphia sandwich that has ever existed. (That, of course, would be a thankless task.) Nonetheless, there are sure to be some readers who get through this book and immediately wonder how I could have left out this place or that person. I understand and respect that and welcome the hate mail that is sure to follow publication. (Contact me at https://lifeattable.com.)

It's also worth stating that I chose the shops and people to include in this book based on their historical impact or—for more modern shops—an interesting connection to said history, not *necessarily* due to quality. It's absolutely possible to use this book as a guidebook of sorts, to try Philadelphia's benchmark sandwiches and shops, but my intent was never to suggest that the sandwiches mentioned here are intrinsically better than any that are not.

When thinking about these sandwich stories, I'm also reminded of the surely apocryphal quote from Napoleon, Churchill or some other famous leader of the past: "History is written by the victors." Shops that were around at the beginning of the cheesesteak or hoagie (or any other sandwich) that are *still* around have an inherent advantage when it comes to crafting these legends. For any that have long since disappeared, on the other hand, their stories are more likely to have fallen through the cracks of time.

Not surprisingly, these sandwich origins often hide themselves among layers and generations of oral history. The immigrants who created these foods were concerned, primarily, with supporting their family's basic needs, so they didn't always prioritize writing down their recipes and stories or keeping detailed business records. As such, their successful modern descendants—even those with historical predilections—are often unclear about the differences between truth and folklore. (And the latter is often better for marketing.)

For contrast, when I was writing my previous book, *Lost Mount Penn: Wineries, Railroads and Resorts of Reading*, which covered the wine house culture of Reading, Pennsylvania, in the 1800s, the research was far more straightforward. The people involved were the intelligentsia of Reading, well-educated professionals, politicians, academics, etc. of that region. They liked writing things down and keeping track of their exploits, which made my job easy.

With Philadelphia sandwich-makers, however, this was far from the case. The truth was often buried in a wisp of a memory from someone who knew someone who might have been there without anything concrete to verify. Though current publications love to praise the sandwich artisan, that sort of coverage was relatively rare until at least the 1970s. Pat Olivieri originated the now internationally famous steak sandwich in the 1930s, for example, yet neither of Philadelphia's main newspapers even mentioned his shop until the 1950s. Nobody is actively disputing the story Pat told, but could he have been relied on to remember it precisely twenty years later?

Despite this challenge, I remained committed to separating fact from legend, determining what actually happened and how those events still resonate throughout the Philadelphia region today. If I didn't always succeed, chalk that up to my own limitations as a part-time researcher and writer and perhaps to the stubborn grittiness of the city itself, holding tightly to its mysteries with a shrug of its shoulders and a pinching of its fingers.

# 1

# COMBO

The first great sandwich of Philadelphia might be surprising—even to longtime residents—and initially seemed like it would be a mere footnote here. Nonetheless, the humble hot dog is where our story begins.

"This isn't a hot dog town," wrote Robert Strauss for the *Inquirer* in 2005. "It is a cheesesteak place, which is nothing to cry about," added the late hot dog guru and food writer Holly Moore. "There is not a Pat's or Geno's type of rivalry to have the best hot dog, like it would be in other cities from Chicago to New York to Cincinnati."[6] And yet…it used to be…and there used to be.

"The birthplace of that great American institution, the hot dog, celebrated its 75th anniversary this week," wrote the Associated Press in 1970, referring to the 1895 founding of Old Original Levis, a mainstay on 6th Street near Lombard Street in South Philadelphia. "The modern hot dog was supposedly invented by old Abe [Levis], who put his frankfurters in a long piece of bread to save on dishwashing expense," the article continued, though it provided no further detail about this claim.[7]

"[Abe Levis's] wife really made the introduction by putting sausages in Parker House rolls," read a different article in the *Inquirer*. "This combination, Abe quickly decided, was far from ideal. So he had special, longer rolls custom-baked for the frankfurters which he made in his own kitchen."[8]

The validity of these claims is shaky at best, and today, few outside Philadelphia give the Levises any credit for creating the sandwich version

The front of Old Original Levis, undated photograph. *Marc Polish.*

of a frankfurter. Considering, however, that mainstream folklore around the hot dog's invention most commonly references (a) the 1904 World's Fair, (b) a 1901 New York Giants baseball game or (c) early 1900s Coney Island, it's not shocking that a business founded around 1895 might claim credit.

All that said, there is ample evidence such sandwiches existed prior to when the Levises began selling them. As one example, an 1887 article refers to Germans eating "frankfurter sausage sandwiches."[9] Closer to home, in 1892, the *Paterson* (NJ) *Daily Press* offered perhaps the earliest written account of these sandwiches being called "hot dogs."[10] (Not to mention that sausages are centuries old, so the idea that nobody wrapped one in bread until the late 1800s seems far-fetched.)

Regardless, the Levises' impact on local hot dog consumption was substantial. As the *Inquirer* wrote in 1951, "The origins of the hot dogs are as misty as the remembered details of a late party, and just as frequently debated. But to Philadelphians with long memories, one thing is certain: Abe Levis had a large share in introducing this popular product to their hometown."[11]

Old Original Levis would go on to become a Philadelphia institution, a rite of passage for children and adults alike and an enduring hangout for countless shopping excursions, birthday parties and even dates. "God I miss Levis," recalled food writer Alan Richman in 2005. "To have a Levis dog with a cherry soda beat even a cheesesteak."[12] Yes, it was just a hot dog joint, but it was also so much more.

# Roots of a Legend

Abraham Levis came to Philadelphia—from Bialystok, now Poland—during the 1880s, as part of the large-scale exodus of Jews from the Russian Empire.[13] Per his great-grandson Levis Kochin, Abraham's family name in Europe was Meltzer, but at some point, he ended up with papers that said Levis.[14] Once Abraham arrived in the United States, various records from his early life here spelled his name Levi or Levy, but it is common to see such misspellings in documents from the era. The S matters though; Philadelphians properly pronounce the name to rhyme with *crevice* or the possessive to rhyme with *crevices*. (It should never be Levi's!)

Few who knew Abraham ever called him by his first name or even the nickname "Abe." To just about everyone—even his wife—he was simply Levis. (Which is also why Kochin's first name is Levis, not Abraham, in honor of his great-grandfather.)

In 1892, Levis married Anna Solominsky (also known as Annie Solo), and in either 1895 (according to a sign on the Levis building) or 1896 (according to a different sign on the same Levis building), they opened a small grocery store at 513 South 6th Street, where they also rented an apartment.[15] Listings from the *Philadelphia City Directory* suggest the store's focus may have varied in those early days, starting as "grocer" and transitioning to "mineral waters"—surely a synonym for a soda fountain, which Levis had purchased in those early years and would become a focal point of the shop—and eventually "restaurant."[16]

By 1911, the shop had moved to its longtime location of 507 South 6th Street—Levis bought the property in 1910—where it was mainly listed as "dining" or occasionally "soda water" or "ice cream."[17] This evolving definition at least appears to explain the inscription at the top of the building: "A.L. Levis, Est. 1896, Soda Water Ice Cream & Light Lunch." (Though one would probably not describe a hot dog as "light" today, this term likely equates with what we'd now call a "quick lunch.")

The cornice that appeared on the Levis building until it was removed in 2019. *Joel Spivak.*

"Stout, mustachioed, cigar-chomping" Levis was described as "gregarious," which will become a recurring theme in these sandwich stories.[18] "My great-grandfather was a showman," said Sallie Kochin Abelson, "and he attracted a lot of people. He did a lot of flashy things."[19]

"He brooked no nonsense from [employees]—or customers—insisting on strict adherence to the '10 Rules of Behavior' he posted on the wall," reported the *Daily News*. "Rule No. 10 was a personal credo and business success story rolled into six words: 'Talk less, eat and drink more.'"[20]

"He was also the quintessential businessman, one who apparently could leave his fingerprints on a penny," wrote the *Inquirer*'s Kathy Hacker. "When the Starr Gardens, a recreation center located across the street, asked him to chip in for athletic shirts, he refused—until the coaches agreed to decorate the backs of the jerseys with the words 'Eat at Levis.'"[21] (Did he also invent the idea of sponsoring Little League jerseys?)

"I've been coming here since I was 7 years old, and I sure do remember Abe," regular Levis patron Sammy Gansky told Hacker in 1982. "Had his legs amputated, you know. He used to sit there and watch the boys who worked for him and yell, 'Ring the register, you [expletive]!'" Now smiling, Gansky added, "He was a good man."[22]

After a dispute with the electric company over an unpaid bill, Levis told them to take a hike, instead installing a "wheezing, gasping gas-engine-

## ARE HOT DOGS SANDWICHES?

This debate has become particularly heated in the internet era, when strong opinions about unimportant topics are, of course, fiercely and frequently contested. More relevant here are reports that even the Levises considered their products to be in a separate category from other sandwiches (though that may have just been for marketing purposes).

From a semantics perspective, it would admittedly be odd for someone to say they were going to make a sandwich only to come back with a hot dog. That said, it is difficult to find a valid definition of the word *sandwich* that does not clearly include a frankfurter on a bun in its scope. If—and only if—one's definition *required two distinct slices of bread* for a true sandwich, perhaps hot dogs would not qualify. This definition, however, would also exclude hoagies, cheesesteaks, barbecue on a roll, etc. Alternatively, if we allow that the valid definition of a sandwich is a filling between two slices of bread *or* within a roll, it's absurd to argue that hot dogs don't fit this criterion.

(Thankfully, we don't have to figure out wraps here.)

The other relevant fact—that the historian author would be remiss to ignore—is that before this dish was so commonly called a "hot dog," there is ample documentation of it being called a "frankfurter sausage sandwich."[*] This is clearly because frankfurters can be sold and eaten without bread.

As such, as far as this book is concerned, a hot dog—when defined as the sausage and the bun together—is a sandwich.

_____

[*] Stevens, "Drinks of the World."

driven generator" in the store's basement.[23] When his neighbors objected to the noise, he bought the surrounding buildings so he could continue to produce his own electricity unfettered.

Levis also wreaked havoc on Philadelphia trolley schedules. The operators, it turns out, were regularly parking in front of the restaurant on 6th Street—not an official stop—while they (and passengers) took a leisurely trip inside for dogs and drinks, impervious to the honks of building traffic.

Though Abe Levis was clearly the front man for the family operation, drawing most of the attention, it is perhaps Anna Levis—once described

The famed Levis soda fountain. *Elliot Hirsh/Levis Hot Dogs.*

as "a sausage and fish cake maker of some skill"—who warrants further recognition.[24] Importantly, she was responsible for the recipes, the cooking, the food that brought people back to Levis time and time again. "I've always thought she should've gotten more credit," said Abelson of her great-grandmother. "But that wasn't unusual at the time. Women who were equal partners did not get equal credit."[25]

Writing reverently about Anna Levis's recipes, the *Inquirer*'s Robert Lasson remarked that a later incarnation of the shop still used her fabled originals. The "recipes were—and are—closely guarded secrets, kept from prying eyes for nearly a hundred years in a safe deposit box," he wrote. "The frankfurters are made by a suburban meatpacker, with the help of special spices that Levis sends to him. Over the years, competitive packers have tried to duplicate the succulent Levis dog, without success."[26]

Elliot Hirsh—current owner of everything Levis—didn't offer to share the secret recipe but did allow himself to say that it is a "garlicky, kosher-style…great hot dog."[27]

# THE (ONCE) LEGENDARY COMBO

Over time, Levis developed a following for its hot dogs, ice cream and sodas. For the latter, the shop produced its own carbonation in the basement and arguably became as famous for its Champ Cherry soda as it was for any food it sold.[28] That said, it was the fish cake—or, rather, its addition to a hot dog on the same bun—that cemented Levis's unique role in Philadelphia sandwich history. Though this rather surprising marriage of seemingly incompatible foodstuff has mostly disappeared from menus in the twenty-first century, it was once as important to many Philadelphians as the cheesesteak or hoagie is today.

Essentially a mix of whitefish (most commonly cod) and mashed potatoes, shaped into a disc and fried, fish cakes appeared on a variety of menus, from street food to haute cuisine—where the snootiest or most sarcastic people called them "piscatorial patties"—and were popular with home cooks. This dish also came to mean, to Philadelphians, something more than just a quick meal. Recapping some of his favorite vintage Philly-isms for the *Daily News* in 1992, for example, Ron Avery included the phrase "you can get it for a fish cake," used to indicate that something is inexpensive.[29]

As Levis built much of its reputation on the quality of both hot dogs and fish cakes, it's no surprise it also became the flagship location for the once-revered "combo," a frankfurter sandwich with a fish cake smashed on top. (Also known colloquially as the Philly or poor man's surf 'n' turf.) It's unclear if the Levises invented this dish or merely popularized it; though many give them credit for its origin, an 1891 *Inquirer* article describing a local hot sausage place as selling both items suggests that their association is perhaps older than the Levis shop.[30] A menu from the reincarnated Levis of the 1990s claimed the combo was "invented at Levis during the Great Depression," but a note on a modern menu is hardly proof.[31]

It's certainly an odd concept, this combo, that will seem absurd to anyone who hasn't been indoctrinated to its charms from an early age. But the fish cake—mainly potato, typically—is not strongly flavored and thus mostly adds texture, especially next to a robust beef frank. When cod is used, it can offer a lingering briny flavor, but this rarely overwhelms the sandwich. Add some zesty mustard and sweet and tangy pepper hash (see page 27), and the cake serves more as a canvas for the other flavors than one that takes center stage. In a way, it's the glue that brings the other disparate notes together and perhaps the key to making the combo more delicious than the sum of its parts.

*Top*: A homemade fish cake. *Bottom*: A homemade combo with pepper hash. *Author photographs.*

"Apart from nostalgia and Philly pride, it's easy to see why folks still order the combo," wrote *Philadelphia Magazine*'s Alexandra Jones after tasting one at Johnny's Hots—arguably the best of the few places that still serve it—in 2018. "The cake is very mild, crispy on the outside and tender on the inside from the potato that's blended in with the cod," she continued. "You'll get a pleasant hint of fishy flavor, but nothing like the Van De Kamp's fish stick flavor I grew up with."[32]

*For a fish cake recipe, see appendix.*

# FAMILY MEALS

Over the years, the Levis family would do more than make great food; they'd also take steps to build a community around their brand, which would in turn lead to lifelong connections with customer families over multiple generations. Early on, for example, Abe Levis developed an interest in the movies, eventually opening the first theater designed specifically for moving pictures in Philadelphia, at 508 South Street, which he purchased in 1908. More importantly for the combo lover, he regularly projected free movies on a giant screen hung from his 6th Street building's roof, with refreshments available to purchase from Levis, of course.

Though Abe and Anna Levis obviously laid the groundwork for what would become a Philadelphia tradition, it was their son David—who took over after his parents passed (Anna in 1930 and Abe in 1934)—who implemented many of the things people remember most about Levis.

David didn't get along with his father, so he was living in West Philadelphia and selling men's clothing when Abe Levis died. But since Abe's eldest son, Julius, was already a practicing lawyer and uninterested in taking over the shop, David came back to South 6th Street to become the new leader of the family business. Before he himself died in 1954, David would go on to create the soon to be well-known slogan "Levis: That's All," start the 50 Year Club and add the shop's famous neon sign.

The sign in question, designed by Joseph Feldman of the Ajax Sign Company in the early 1950s, became a beacon for all who passed on 6th Street. It was a symbol of not only Levis, but also the city itself. David likely commissioned it in response to the machinations of his brother Joe Levis, Abe and Anna's youngest son and the family's black sheep. Joe was "considerably younger than the other three," Kochin said, "and they had a problem with him. In particular, maybe that he raided the till, that he had gambling problems….So they bought him out."[33] But not, perhaps, before Joe had procured his own copies of the family's treasured recipes. After a brief stint slinging franks in Atlantic City, Joe returned to Philadelphia in 1952 to open a hot dog shop at 40th Street and Girard Avenue near Fairmount Park. He called it simply "Joe Levis," with the tagline "of 6th Street fame." This, in turn, led to the Levis at 507 South 6th Street adding the now-standard "Old Original" to its name with signage to match. This, of course, forced Joe to update his own shop's name to "Original Joe Levis."

In 1954, not long after David passed away, Joe opened another shop at 403 South 6th Street, just across Lombard Street from Old Original Levis.

The Levis 6th Street restaurant, circa 1961. *PhillyHistory.org, a project of the Philadelphia Department of Records.*

"For several years it was hot dogs at 30 paces," recalled Nels Nelson in the *Daily News.* "The two establishments sold essentially the same viands but made a couple of sign-painters rich enough to retire. 'The Only Living Son of the Original Levis,' screamed a sign at Original Joe's. 'This Is Our Only Store,' countered a large placard at O.O.L.'s. The signs got bigger and more contentious until Joe sold out to Society Hill redevelopment and hired himself to A.C. for good."[34]

Also in the early 1950s, David started the famed Levis 50 Year Club, a list of patrons who'd been eating there for a half century or more. It's unclear if this was in response to Joe's encroachment; regardless, it would become a lasting memory for many Levis regulars. Though, in design, it was not much to look at—the membership placards were essentially just handwritten lists of customers, framed once full—these honor rolls were a source of amusement for both old-timers and their descendants. When the rolls reopened in 1991, for example, Ron Avery described the following scene:

*Bessie Schwartz of South Philadelphia enters the historic hot-dog shrine… with an expectant expression on her face. "I want to find my husband, Harry, my brother-in-law, Isadore Schwartz, and my name should be up there, too.*

*"Oh, look! There's Nathan Merlinksy. He was a barber on the corner of American and Porter.…Oh, and here's Jack Terlitsky.…And there's my husband," she declares with a grin.*

*It takes a while, but eventually she locates a placard at the far end of the room containing her name and that of her brother-in-law. They're on the same list as Tommy Loughran, world light-heavyweight boxing champion in 1927. On the Levis roll, all eaters are equal.*[35]

Those who ran Levis after the family bowed out also witnessed the lasting importance of this club. Marc Polish, who owned the shop in the 1980s, said that he "could see it meant so much to people—the thrill of seeing a father's name after he's gone." Current Levis trademark owner Elliot Hirsh was blunter, quipping that "everybody wants a séance with their dead father."[36]

John Girardo of South Philadelphia, who was forty-two in 1991, filled out a card that year for the resurrected rolls, which had, by this point, long abandoned the strict fifty-year requirement. "It's going to be nice to come back 30 years from now and see my name up there," he said, not realizing Old Original Levis would be closed within eighteen months.[37] Thankfully,

A 1953 advertisement in the *Philadelphia Inquirer* for Joe Levis's first city location. *Newspapers.com.*

South Street historian Joel Spivak was able to salvage many of the old plaques, and they're still available for viewing on his website.[38]

"What Daddy had in mind for the 50 Year Club, we didn't know," said David's daughter Phyllis in 1970.[39] (David died shortly after he started the project.) After taking over from her retiring mother, Bessie, and uncle Harry in 1966, Phyllis Levis Kochin Wurtman ran the shop with her twin sister, Gladys Levis Litwin—who died in 1975—until 1979. Despite being in the dark about her father's plan for the club, Phyllis invited as many members as she could locate to the Levis Diamond Jubilee (seventy-fifth anniversary) in 1970. About this celebration, wrote Nelson, "how O.O.L. will accommodate the flourishing 50 Year Club and all manner of teeming public luminaries in the incommodious space behind its façade of bilious green tile, Yahweh only knows."[40]

Also in 1970—in perhaps a late attempt to capitalize on America's fast-food boom—Phyllis began to experiment with expanding the brand. First was a shop at Bustleton and Shelmire Avenues in Northeast Philadelphia. Not all of Levis's regulars bought into this idea, however, wrote Nelson. "Very difficult customers from the old neighborhood who order Levis hot dogs by phone for delivery to their new English Tudor split-levels insist the dogs be trucked in from 6th and Lombard."[41]

"The dogs at both places are the same," sighed Gladys, "but some people refuse to believe it."[42]

In 1975, Levis opened a third location, this time at 16th and Sansom Streets in the heart of Center City. To celebrate the occasion, which coincided with the shop's eightieth anniversary, they offered dogs at the "1895 price" of a nickel each during the grand opening. (Though it may have actually been *three* dogs for five cents in 1895.[43]) "She got a big line, offering those hot dogs for a nickel," said Kochin of his mother's promotion. "And she got a couple of local television stations to record it, to say on the evening news: 'what was that big line you saw downtown today?'"[44]

## They Reminisce Over You

Talking to people now about Levis, an interesting pattern emerges; while many recall the food as being good, the memories tend to focus more on the context of Levis visits versus any specific flavors. The most common recollection involves visiting Levis with a parent as a special treat. "Dad would take us there," wrote Marianne C. on Facebook, as one typical example. "Hot dogs, fish cakes, chocolate and ice cream. Nothing better! Sometimes daddy would just take me on a Saturday afternoon; he called it 'our date.'"[45]

"Best memories growing up!! My dad always took us," added Tracy T. "Chocolate Coke sodas & hot dogs, then to play in the park across the street!! I miss that place and him!!"[46]

"I remember going there on Saturdays for lunch after shopping on South Street with mom and aunts," wrote Peggy H., revealing another common storyline among these memories.[47]

Considering kids' palates are not necessarily the most discerning—and that so many of these memories involve visiting Levis as a child—it's logical to think that maybe the food itself was not the point. With due respect to the hot dogs, fish cakes and sodas, this deep connection was perhaps more about bonding with parents, the special treat after a (probably boring) day out or even the feeling of freedom that can come only from carefree youth.

"Playing at Stargarden [*sic*] all afternoon, then running across the street for a hot dog and a Cherry Champ soda," wrote Delores S. "YESSSS the good ole days!"[48]

*To read more great Levis memories, check out the bonus content at https://lifeattable.com/ phillysandwiches.*

## LENNY AND THE HASH

For many years, the only other place to get a combo was Lenny's, Philly's other twentieth-century hot dog behemoth.[49] (This includes Abie's, which, while technically independent, was an offshoot of the Lenny's empire.) Without any definitive origin story of the fish cake/hot dog conglomeration, some have even suggested—again, without definitive proof—that Lenny's may have invented it. Perhaps more importantly, it is almost certain that Lenny's introduced and popularized the sandwich's iconic pepper hash topping.

Around 1935, Russian immigrants Ida Bobis Kravitz and her husband, Max Kravitz, created the first incarnation of what would become Lenny's, then called Mom & Pop's Hot Dogs. "During the Depression, she had 10 children…and needed to do something, so she got somebody to build her this pushcart," said Tracey Kauffman Wood of her grandmother. "She went out on the corner of 4th and South and sold hot dogs....They had nothing; they were living in tenements....My grandmother came up with this [hot dog business] and was very proud of it."[50]

Wood continued, "She'd come home at the end of the day and line up her nickels and dimes on the kitchen table. Five dollars was an amazing day!"[51]

Ida Kravitz also had the idea of putting two separate steam ovens in her cart, something the family believes hadn't been done before. "She could have hot dogs in one and fish cakes in another, and also, they would steam the rolls. It just allowed for more product to be ready at once," Wood explained.[52]

More important was Kravitz's inspiration to add her own flavor twist to the hot dogs. "She couldn't afford to buy relish, so she made her own, called pepper hash, from Russia," said Wood, speaking of the sweet and sour condiment that would become Lenny's trademark. "She'd put mustard, sauerkraut, pepper hash and onion, all on a hot dog for five cents with an orange drink."[53]

Despite its misleading name, this pepper hash is mostly raw cabbage, chopped with carrots and, yes, bell peppers, mixed with vinegar, sugar and sometimes other spices. "When she used to make it," said Wood, "she would sit outside with [a mezzaluna wood chopping bowl] between her legs, just sitting and chopping. It's a lot of chopping when done by hand, because it's a whole head of cabbage. So, she would let the kids on the block come up and everybody would take turns chopping."[54]

Although Ida's pepper hash came from an old family recipe, when the Kravitzes arrived from Kyiv around 1908, the condiment was already well-associated with Philly cuisine, likely introduced by German (also known as Pennsylvania Dutch) immigrants in the 1800s.[55] "When Victorian Americans thought of pepper hash, they immediately thought of Philadelphia, much in the same way that a similar connection is made with hoagies today," wrote food historian William Woys Weaver, discussing a recipe he'd found in a local cookbook from 1855. "Like the hoagie, pepper hash had a working class appeal: it was an inevitable condiment in oyster and fish houses all across the city. Fish cooks paired it up with

Homemade pepper hash. *Tracy Kauffman Wood.*

fried oysters, soft-shell crabs, cod fish balls [similar to fish cakes], shad fritters, and grilled catfish."[56]

Ida's hot dogs, however, were new vessels for the hash. It seems the stuff also became sweeter over time, perhaps in response to its new foils mustard and beef. "It was not meant to be sweet but to take the place of the lemon juice," wrote Weaver, lamenting the fact that modern, sweeter hashes don't pair as well with fish.[57] (Though anyone who tries a fried fish cake with spicy mustard and Lenny's-style pepper hash might thoroughly disagree.)

"When my dad made the pepper hash for his luncheonette," said Wood, speaking of her father, Abie Kauffman, who married Ida's daughter Sylvia and opened Abie's Hot Dogs in 1947, "he would add extra sugar. His was sweeter because he loved it that way."[58]

"But there was never really an exact recipe, as far as how much sugar and salt and all that," added Wood. "My grandmother would just say '*shitarayn!*' ['throw it in' in Yiddish]."

"I do know it was something she brought from the old country," Wood continued. "She said that to me personally….I'm not sure if she was the first one [to make pepper hash], but I know she didn't copy it from anybody. The recipe was in her head."[59] Regardless of the hash's origins, Kravitz's version undoubtedly helped make a name for Mom & Pop's and would go on to become the signature flavor of the Lenny's Hot Dogs brand.

One of the curious aspects of having two similarly named hot dog empires in the same city is that confusion emerges within memories of the two places. In particular, many struggle to recall with certainty whether Levis also served pepper hash. When discussing Levis memories on Facebook, for example, one user wrote, "Never had/found the 'Pepperhash' like [they] had at Levis—it was great stuff." While another reported that they would "never forget [their] first hot dog with pepper hash" at Levis.[60] Others, of course, jumped in to point out that pepper hash was specific to Lenny's, but neither camp successfully built consensus.

"Old Original Levis never, to my knowledge, served pepper hash," said Levis Kochin. His sister Sallie Abelson couldn't remember either way. "No clue," replied Lenny's son Bryan Kravitz when asked the same question. Marc Polish—who owned Levis in the 1980s—said, confusingly, that they "had it from time to time, but it was not something we made." When Levis briefly experimented with franchising in the '90s (see page 34), they did carry pepper hash, but by that point, any connection to the original was tenuous.[61]

In sum, there does not seem to be concrete evidence suggesting Levis offered pepper hash during its heyday on 6th Street. And yet, Levis and

Ida Kravitz at her hot dog cart, circa 1946. *Tracy Kauffman Wood.*

Sylvia Kravitz serves a customer at Abie's hot dog cart, circa 1951. *Tracy Kauffman Wood.*

Lenny's are so connected in the foggy memories of former patrons that pepper hash has become an integral part of the combo, from either brand, in many people's minds. (It certainly improves the sandwich!)

*For Kauffman Wood's pepper hash recipe, see appendix.*

Leonard "Lenny" Kravitz—no, not that one—was born in 1921 in Philadelphia, the youngest son of Ida and Max. When he went off to fight in World War II, Ida "made a promise to God that if Lenny returned safe, she would give him the hot dog business," his sister Sylvia Kauffman once recalled.[62] Return he did, and sell him the business his mom did. (Lenny's obituary said he paid $2,000, while Wood suggested he paid a symbolic amount, like $1.)[63]

"Lenny was flamboyant," recalled his son Bryan. "He'd go out on the pushcart, and he'd wear a suit. He liked—they were incredibly expensive at the time—these *sharkskin* suits. They were made from this shiny fabric.... He would wear these suits every day! All the other pushcart guys, they'd wear blue jeans and a rag around their middle so they didn't get stuff on them. Lenny got stuff on him, and he'd throw the suit away! And he drove a Cadillac! He ran a hot dog stand and drove a Cadillac!"[64]

After about ten years of selling dogs on the street, a 1955 city ordinance banned pushcart vendors in the Fabric Row area of South Philadelphia—"except for the Italian Market…they had connections," Wood quipped—forcing Lenny to get creative.[65] He approached the owners of the Washington Inn, a bar at the corner of South Street and Passyunk Avenue, about making room for his hot dogs. They agreed, then carved a little space on the side of the building—maybe ten feet wide by four feet deep—with a window open to the Passyunk Avenue sidewalk. (This takeout-style window can still be seen in 2024 on the side of a bar currently called the Woolly Mammoth.)

It was around this time that Lenny began to think about expanding his business. "He went to a company that made these roach coaches," Bryan recalled, using a slang term for the early food trucks that eventually replaced pushcarts. "He had one made that was much more beautiful than what he was used to on the street. And he tried taking it out to conventions and shows, but it wasn't working."[66]

"My grandmother said to my father, 'Get your wife to work!'" Bryan continued. "My mother was happily raising two children in the Northeast. But [Ida] said, 'Put the roach coach on that nearby corner [Castor and Magee Avenues] and get your wife, Anita, who's not working, to stand inside of it.' So, my mother, who hadn't worked from the time that I was born and my sister was born, did it. She had a personality, so the second location became a success."[67] (They eventually moved into a storefront at 6620 Castor Avenue, near Fanshawe Street.)

By the early 1960s, fast food—in Philadelphia, primarily McDonald's and Gino's—was beginning to take hold in the market. "Coca-Cola came to Lenny and said, 'We want to use your name,'" said Bryan. "They started setting up Lenny's stands all over Philly. They were these white little trailers, no wheels, just something that's put on the ground, made of aluminum.… There was one at 41st [Street] and Lancaster [Avenue], 25th [Street] and Snyder [Avenue], on Wadsworth Avenue in Mount Airy, one up in Mayfair. He also put one down the shore in Margate, right next to Lucy the Elephant.…In my mind, there were seven of them."[68]

Like Abe Levis, Lenny was the frontman, the recognizable star of the business. But also like Levis, he was nothing without the women who supported him. "I want to make sure, if you talk about Lenny's expansion," Bryan said, "to say that Lenny could never have done it without my mother. She made him realize that he could have more than one location.…And then there's my grandmother, so it's two women really—Lenny got in the middle of it—and they called it Lenny's."[69]

"There was Jean and Bessie [Lenny's sisters] and Anita," added Wood. "They were the ones who manned the stores. He knew he could count on them."[70]

## The Future Ain't Hot Dogs

Thinking back to Levis, one story Levis Kochin shared stood out because it was so telling. Abe Levis, according to family lore, always dreamed of becoming a lawyer. "He felt that somehow fate had done him wrong," Kochin said. "That somehow, if he hadn't had to make a living from the age of thirteen, he would have become a lawyer."[71] It was, of course, not to be. And yet his firstborn son, Julius, did become a lawyer.

That's the thing with immigrants who came to this country seeking a better life: they often had limited options—in most cases, having no choice but to work menial jobs like slinging hot dogs—but if they worked hard enough, their kids would have better opportunities. To go to college. To get advanced degrees. To become lawyers, professors and the like. This is the American Dream, is it not?

And yet this dream can get in the way of keeping a beloved family business alive. When Phyllis Wurtman decided to retire from running Levis in 1979, for example, her son Levis Kochin was already happily working as an economics professor at the University of Washington. He declined his mother's offer to take over, as did his brother-in-law, who was also a professor. Similarly, when Lenny's was faltering in the 1980s, Bryan Kravitz was off in California, chasing his own American Dream.

Obviously, if these businesses were lucrative enough, someone in the family would have kept them going. Nowadays, however, selling hot dogs is not exactly a license to print money. The city has moved on; by the 1980s, the big street foods were cheesesteaks and hoagies. Healthier food was becoming more widely available and would continue to broaden its reach. People may have still been talking about the good old days at Levis or Lenny's, but they weren't buying enough combos to back up the lore.

Once any business is out of the family's hands, that connection to the past ceases to exist. Perhaps that's too harsh; obviously, the new owners can and do respect a place's history, but they're no longer connected by blood and thus can't be blamed if they want out when it's not profitable or life otherwise gets in the way.

Unable to find a member of the Levis family interested in taking over, Wurtman sold the business to her accountant Sid Goldstein and his niece Benay Birch. Despite promising the *Inquirer* that Levis would "never" close or change hands shortly after she took over in 1979, Birch ran the business for only three years before she sold it herself, this time to Marc Polish and Bill Goldberg.[72] ("I absolutely *hated* to do it," Birch said at the time.)[73]

By late 1982, Levis had seen better days. "The battered neon sign…seems a sorry beacon (its lights having blown out ages ago)," wrote Hacker. "The interior decor, done in fake-wood paneling and Day-Glo yellow paint, is perhaps a tad *outre*. And the furnishings, a collection of tiny tables and stiff-backed chairs set cheek-to-cheek, do invite one to ponder the advantages of standing while eating."[74]

That December, serial entrepreneur Polish was returning from a business trip with Goldberg when they saw a "for sale" sign at Levis. "We looked at each other like a couple of kids and started giggling," Polish told the *Inquirer*. "You wanna?" he asked Goldberg. "Why not?" They made a deposit the next morning.[75]

"Levis was always a very special place for me, although I grew up in Logan," said Polish of his new business. "I couldn't stand the thought of [it] going the way of H&H, Linton's, the Camac Baths, the Hot Shoppe at

Broad and Stenton. As a Philadelphian, I'm all too aware of all the places that have disappeared. I figured that since the place had a lot of meaning for me, it had to have the same meaning for others. It was time for someone to take a stand."[76] It seems, however, that Polish's entrepreneurial spirit could not keep him in one place for long. He was soon on to his next thing, while his wife, Max, took over day-to-day duties at Levis.

In 1989, Elliot Hirsh, the president of Jenkintown's Ginger Group Ltd., best known as the producer of Elliot's Amazing Juices, approached Polish about licensing the Champ Cherry name and formula. Hirsh, according to the *Daily News*, had "big plans" for the soda, lining up Canada Dry to bottle and distribute it, and was "hot to take Champ Cherry coast to coast."[77] (This never happened.)

Though Polish considered Levis "like a member of the family," he—and, most crucially, Max—didn't want to run the place anymore.[78] "We were in the beverage business and wanted to bottle Champ Cherry soda," Hirsh recalled. "We entered into a licensing deal, and within six months, [the Polishes] offered to sell me the whole business. So, I wouldn't have to pay licensing fees or royalties, and it was a relatively small amount of money [about $100,000]."[79]

This is, in short, how a man with essentially no interest in the restaurant business ended up owning one of Philadelphia's oldest and most beloved restaurants.

Though Hirsh originally attempted to keep the 6th Street landmark running, it closed permanently in 1992. "We had other things we were involved with, so [the restaurant] wasn't a very reliable situation," he said. "[With] three employees and overhead, you have to do a lot more business than we were doing. I reached out to restaurateurs in the area….Nobody was interested. They basically were joyful that there'd be one less eatery in the South Street area."[80] He ended up franchising a few locations for a short time, but those agreements eventually fell apart.

"I tried—believe me I tried," Hirsh told the *Inquirer*'s Clark DeLeon. "I wasn't going down without a fight. But I discovered tradition doesn't sell. What are you going to do when you get three old people walking into the store to order one fish cake that they want to split three ways? We were going after a younger, hipper crowd, and we found out that they don't eat hot dogs and fish cakes for lunch. They eat salads."[81]

After closing the flagship location, Hirsh attempted to keep the brand alive through a short-lived reboot of the restaurant concept in Abington and by selling the dogs in supermarkets, but neither proved to be sustainable

A retail box of Levis hot dogs. *Elliot Hirsh/Levis Hot Dogs.*

over time. With health problems mounting and his admittedly "prickly personality" causing too many lawsuits and broken deals, the brand has, at this point, essentially ceased to exist.[82]

"Now, we have the recipes, formulas and trademarks, but I can't find anyone that's interested in [running Levis as a restaurant]," Hirsh said recently. "It's out there if somebody wants to do something with it."[83]

As for Lenny's, the story isn't quite as contentious or drawn out, but otherwise, it reads almost the same. The business lost momentum in the 1970s, and nobody in the family was lined up to keep it going. By the late '70s, only the Castor Avenue location remained in Philly. Margate lasted until 1985, but when Lenny lost his lease down there, he closed up shop for good.

"I moved to California when I was eighteen and stayed out there," said Bryan Kravitz, who's back east now, running Philly Typewriter. "So, I wasn't part of Lenny's demise. I really don't know what happened to the business.…I think it just slowly ran out of steam, and he ended up selling."[84]

In 1986, Lenny sold the final location to Wayne Knapp and his partners, who ran a shop at 6620 Castor Avenue from 1986 to 1993. Once Hirsh started bottling Levis's Champ Cherry, the new incarnation of Lenny's sold

A combo with pepper hash from Lenny's in Feasterville. *Author photograph.*

that, too, along with chocolate soda and egg creams. A few years after the Castor location closed, in 1998—ironically, the very same month that Lenny passed away—Knapp revived the concept in Feasterville, where it continues as of this writing.

While researching this book, I visited this last bastion of true pepper hash on West Street Road. "You ever been to Johnny's Hots?" a gregarious fellow patron asked while I was waiting for my order. He was speaking of the hot dog joint on North Delaware Avenue in Philly, which also sells combos and pepper hash. "It's better than this. *Much* better."

"This place has the name," I countered.

"It ain't like the days on Castor Avenue!" he replied. Then he added, rationalizing aloud, "But I was driving by, so I figured I'd stop." We didn't speak further, but his assessment turned out to be spot-on.

## Greek-Texan Fusion?

While Levis and Lenny's typified—in the less politically correct world of yesteryear—the Jewish hot dog joint, a popular alternative for tube-based meat lovers was to go Greek, specifically the many incarnations of "Texas wiener," sometimes spelled "weiner." (The spellings are often used interchangeably by the same establishment and other times have the word "hot" included in various positions within the name.) Despite its moniker, this hot dog style was specifically associated with Greek immigrants who settled in Pennsylvania, New Jersey and New York.

A Philly-style Texas wiener is split lengthwise, charred on a flat-top grill, placed on steamed club roll and then topped with mustard, diced raw onions and, most importantly, the so-called secret sauce, also known as "Greek sauce," a thin, chili-style concoction. (Presumably, the "Texas" descriptor is related to the sauce's similarity to chili con carne.)

Like so many others, the origins of this hot dog style are disputed. Paterson, New Jersey—where these frankfurters are often deep-fried—makes the loudest claim, with mainstays such as Johnny and Hange's and Libby's Lunch leading the charge. Legend says that a Greek immigrant by the name of John Patrellis invented the dish in 1919 while working at his uncle's lunch place in the Manhattan Hotel on Paterson Street before opening his own stand around 1920.[85]

An older claim, however, comes from Altoona, Pennsylvania, where Texas Hot Wieners—today, Texas Hot Dogs—opened in 1918. Here, another Greek immigrant, Peter Koufougeorgas (also known as Peter George), is given credit for developing the signature sauce that turns these sausages from measly hot dogs into Texan wieners.[86]

A Texas wiener from A.P.J. Texas Weiner on 13th Street in Center City. *Author photograph.*

Regardless of which origin story is correct, it's highly unlikely this construction belongs to Philadelphia; rather, it probably migrated both here and throughout the mid-Atlantic during the 1920s. As such, it is probably less important to local sandwich history than the fish cake combo, but it nonetheless warrants mention as an important foil to the Levis/Lenny's style.

Of particular note is the shop called Texas Wieners that opened in 1923 at Broad Street and Snyder Avenue—it later moved a block away to Snyder Avenue and Carlisle Street—and was affectionately known as The Greek's, after its founder, Stephanos Mandrohalos (Americanized to Steve Miller), another Greek immigrant. Because the line between fact and folklore can be difficult to draw, even for dishes that didn't originate in Philly, it is probably not surprising that The Greek's secret sauce also developed its own local mythology.

"'The Greek' didn't talk much, and hardly ever cracked a smile," wrote Ron Avery in 1993. "But like other great Greeks of the past—Aristotle, Sophocles, Euripides—this one was a creative genius....Seventy years ago, 'The Greek' gave mankind the Original Texas Wiener with 'the Greek's Secret Sauce.'"[87]

Avery was less complimentary about the topping's aesthetic. "If truth be told, Greek's secret sauce isn't that great to look at; it's sort of a sickly brown mush, but it's the flavor that counts. It's not blazing hot, but it packs a wonderful tangy zing that leaves an afterglow in the mouth."[88] In 2011, when admitting to "sort of" liking the wieners, *Inquirer* restaurant critic Craig LeBan added that "something about the gray, gruel-like appearance of the special gravy...is a turnoff."[89]

This sauce does indeed lack visual appeal, and it's unlikely one would ever associate it with the vibrant, deep-red chili con carne if not previously conditioned to do so. That said, its presence has the ability to raise a mere hot dog to a higher level. As Avery noted, the hot pepper spice is there—but only subtly. The sauce also features warm layers of pumpkin pie–style warm spice, creating waves of complexity and flavor. The kick of mustard, if added, deepens this further, forcing the meat itself almost to the background. The Texas wiener, it turns out, is indeed an entirely different hot dog experience.

Much was made over the years about how secret the sauce truly was. Both Dick Britt, Texas Wieners' owner in 1993, and Russell Viggiano, who owned the shop in 2011—it changed hands a few times—boasted to interviewers that it was so secret that none of their employees were privy to its details. The recipe, according to Viggiano, passed from owner to owner on a little index card written in Greek.[90]

Artist Cee Heard's rendition of the old Texas Wieners at 1426 Snyder Avenue, circa 2010. *Cee Heard.*

As fun as it is to perpetuate these myths, a little bubble bursting is in order. This special sauce, it seems, is essentially a variation of *saltsa kima*, a Greek Bolognese-type ragu made from ground beef, tomatoes and spices that's often served over pasta. Beyond Greece and North Macedonia, similar toppings are used on Cincinnati chili (with spaghetti), Detroit Coneys and various other chili dogs around the country. (The Philly version does appear to contain less tomato than some others.)

Regardless of the sauce's uniqueness, Texas Wieners still holds a special place in Philly sandwich lore. "When Levis' famous hot-dog emporium at 6th and Lombard folded last year after nearly a century in business," Avery wrote, "Texas Wieners was positioned to claim the title of Philadelphia's oldest, most revered hot dog. Just as customers kept returning to Levis' long after they had left the neighborhood, they keep returning to Greek's Original Texas Wieners....Like other venerable South Philly eateries…[the shop has] a special place in the hearts of the populace."[91]

"Particularly on the weekends, we get a lot of people stopping in from South Jersey and the Northeast who once lived around here," said Britt.[92]

"I've been eating hot dogs here for at least 55 years," reported a customer named Albert Barbato. "It was originally around the corner on Broad Street. Everyone called it The Greek's. It had a low porch, and you could watch Steve the Greek on the grill through the window. He'd have a dozen rolls lined up on his arm."[93]

"The closer to the armpit," said Viggiano, "the better it tasted."[94]

The original Texas Wieners closed permanently sometime after 2017, but an unrelated shop, A.P.J. Texas Weiner on North 13th Street—which has been slinging this style of dog since 1927—remains a bastion of old-school Greek sauce, as of this writing.[95]

# 2

# HOAGIE

I t is natural to wonder whether there is any material difference between what Philadelphians call hoagies, New Yorkers heroes, New Orleanians po' boys and most of the rest of the country calls submarines, or subs. (Not to mention odd pockets of grinders, zeps, wedges, spuckies, torpedoes, etc.) Some local zealots will claim that the Philly hoagie is superior because it is always on hinged bread—as opposed to sliced-through—or that it is the specific mix of meats that makes all the difference. It is difficult, however, to put any validity behind these claims; every incarnation of the sub, no matter what it happens to be called, consists of the same basic ingredients. Yes, the well-crafted Philadelphia hoagie is unquestionably the world's best version of a submarine sandwich—but not because it is fundamentally different from others. Instead, a more compelling argument is that widespread local passion for hoagies encourages vendors to focus on key details: the best bread (see chapter 7); fresh, well-made ingredients; perfectly balanced flavors and textures; proper construction methods; sheer volume; etc. The variety and quality of hoagies found in the Philadelphia area is simply unparalleled elsewhere.

Also worth clarifying is that these sandwiches, when first developed, existed only in their *Italian* form. This means they had a base of cured pork—typically a mix of meats like ham, salami or capicola—alongside provolone cheese, vegetables (tomato, onion and roasted or pickled peppers, sometimes with lettuce, olives or pickles) and olive oil (occasionally mixed with vinegar). Only later, as the hoagie became more mainstream, did alternate stuffing options (turkey, roast beef, tuna, etc.) emerge, which, in turn, opened the door for further customization and creativity. Even today, some Philadelphians will insist that the only *true hoagie* is the Italian, implying that all others are something lesser, perhaps merely subs. For the most part, however, when someone orders a hoagie in the twenty-first century, they are required to clarify which type: an Italian hoagie or a turkey hoagie, or even the fantasy name (e.g., Daddy Wad, Godfather, etc.). In this chapter, hoagies from the early to mid-1900s can be assumed to be Italian, while more recent references will include the entire category unless otherwise specified.

# Origins

When it comes to the broader history of these long sandwiches, it is probably fruitless to search for a single point of entry. Obviously, Italians were already putting meat, cheese and vegetables on bread to some extent before they immigrated en masse to the United States in the late 1800s and early 1900s. Their meals, however—especially for those who lived agrarian lives, which was much of the southern Italian immigrant population—were generally more formal affairs, where they'd take a break from work and head home for lunch and dinner. In the United States, on the other hand, a growing industrialized job market created the need for quicker lunches that were still hearty enough to sustain energy over a long workday, which, in turn, led to the Americanization (i.e., super-sizing) of the Italian *panino*.

Just about every enclave of Italian immigrants has its own origin claim to these sandwiches. In New York, Angelo Basso began stuffing half loaves of Italian bread with ham, mortadella and cheese in the 1880s. In New Orleans, Sicilian street merchants reportedly began selling muffuletta in the 1890s. (These come on large round rolls, but they contain similar ingredients to an Italian hoagie, and the sub-like po' boy was not far behind, officially introduced in the 1920s.) Even remote Portland, Maine, where Giovanni Amato began selling his so-called Real Italian Sandwich on the fishing docks in 1902, warrants consideration.[96] In all likelihood, however, a shared background of southern Italian food, along with the changing labor market, led to a parallel evolution of these sandwiches throughout the eastern United States.

# CHEWY IN CHESTER

In the Philadelphia area specifically, most sources agree that DiCostanza's Grocery, originally located at 1212 West 3rd Street in Chester, Pennsylvania, was the first to introduce a commercial version of the sandwich that would become the hoagie in the mid-1920s.

 Of what she initially called her Italian sandwich, Catherine DiCostanza (originally written Di Costanza) told sociologist Howard Robboy that she created it one evening in 1924. A group of men were playing cards at nearby Palermo's Bar, she recalled, and one came in looking for something to eat. She split a loaf of Italian bread and piled different varieties of meat, cheese and vegetables inside. "A few weeks later," wrote Robboy, "Mrs. DiCostanza made a similar sandwich for a truck driver working in the neighborhood, who, amazed by the size and taste, proceeded to show the sandwich to other workers in the depot. They began eating [it], and by the summer of 1927, lines two blocks long were formed by people who craved this meal." Due to this great demand, DiCostanza began using an electric meat slicer, claiming to be one of the first users of this device.[97]

 It's fascinating how these stories tend to get warped and reinterpreted over time, even within a family. Looking at the same tale, as told on DiCostanza's website in 2024, for example, many of the noted details raise questions. Was it 1924 or 1925? Did the man who came in ask DiCostanza to put a little bit of everything in his sandwich, or was the combination her idea? Was it the smell of frying peppers that whet his appetite, or had he come in looking for food? Did she sell out of sandwiches that night, or did it take longer for the idea to catch on? These facts all seem to vary depending on which version of the story is told.

 Eventually, DiCostanza would partner with nearby Euro's Bakery to make special rolls for her sandwiches, about a foot long and two inches wide. This happened the *very next day*, according to one version of the story, though based on Catherine DiCostanza's first-person account of the truck drivers' gradual interest, it's far more likely this happened sometime later. Furthermore, in a 1947 interview, Catherine's husband, Augustine DiCostanza, recalled that business was, at first, slow, but gradually picked up over time.[98]

 This 1947 profile also described DiCostanza's Italian sandwich as having the following ingredients: cooked ham, salami, capicola, provolone cheese, tomato, onion, pickles, hot pepper, sage and oil.[99] On the modern DiCostanza website, the supposed original recipe is also said to have included "hamcudighino" (presumably an alternate spelling of cotechino sausage),

Joseph DiCostanza puts the finishing touches on the shop's signature hoagie, circa 1970s. *DiCostanza's.*

as well as oregano in place of sage.[100] (The latter is especially interesting, because oregano has become the default hoagie herb today. Did that, one wonders, evolve over time as well?)

# PHIRST IN PHILLY?

"There are heretics who say the first hoagies were made in Chester, about 10 miles south of [Philadelphia], but that doesn't bother Antoinette Iannelli," wrote William Robbins in 1984. "I don't know anything about that," said Iannelli at the time. "All I know is that I made the first hoagie in Philadelphia."[101]

Iannelli, a short but fiery dark-haired woman, presided over the long counter at Emil's, the self-proclaimed "Home of the Original Hoagie," at Broad and Moore Streets from 1945 until her death in 1992. Before that, she and her husband, Emilio, who retired to Italy on his own later in life, ran a grocery stand at Passyunk Avenue and Mifflin Street for about ten years.

"I made [Philadelphia's] first hoagie, back in 1935. Or maybe 1936," she told reporter Jim Quinn in 1983. "At the time it didn't seem like much, and it's not the kind of thing where you circle the date on the calendar."[102]

"I'll tell you the story of how the first hoagie was made," she continued, "if you don't mind a long story."

> *My husband and I came down from Maine, where I was born, looking for work during the Depression. And there wasn't any work. But in Maine, we were always in the food business, because that is all there is up there—no factories, nothing but tourists to keep you alive. So we opened a little grocery store around the corner from here on Mifflin Street, right between Broad and 13th. At that time, we had a police station at 15th and Snyder, where the Melrose Diner is now, and one day a police officer came and said, "Antoinette, I just had a fight with my wife and she wouldn't even pack my lunch. Make me up a sandwich, I got to get to work."*
>
> *Well, poor fella. I took a loaf of Italian bread and cut it in half and stuck in lots of meat and cheese and lettuce and tomatoes and sliced onions and roast peppers and pickles and olives and then made up a little sauce so it wouldn't be dry. Then the next day, that same police officer was back again, saying, "Antoinette, make me up another one of those sandwiches, please. And I want one for the captain, too." After that, we had a regular influx of*

*police officers—red cars, they had them lined up and down the block. And
then more people found out about them, and the war work came and I was
making a thousand hoagies a day.*

*During the war, the business kept right on. You couldn't get meat then, but
I used hard-boiled eggs—and peppers and olives and whatever you could
get. It made a good sandwich, too. I'd boil up crate after crate of eggs in
that little store, and we would sell so many egg hoagies to all the men down
at the Naval Hospital that the naval officer came in to inspect to make sure
everything was sanitary and clean. Which it always is. Then the little store
on Mifflin got so crowded we moved over here to Moore and opened up in
1945. I remember that, because it was VJ Day, and people were outside
yelling and dancing and singing in the middle of Broad Street.*[103]

Shortly after Iannelli's story appeared in the *Inquirer*, C.J. Cancelmo of
Havertown wrote a letter to the editor arguing that her recollection was
"about 10 percent true and 90 percent fiction."[104]

"These sandwiches were being made and eaten by many of the Italian
American shipyard workers at the Hog Island shipyard during the first
World War, long before Antoinette Iannelli came to Philadelphia or made
a sandwich of any kind," claimed Cancelmo. "I made one in 1925 when
I was going to William B. Hanna School at 58th and Media Streets. It was
almost identical to Mrs. Iannelli's, as this is standard procedure among the
Italian people."[105]

Iannelli's claims, however—which she reportedly stuck to throughout her
life—never suggested that she *invented* the sandwich. She merely said she
introduced it to Philadelphia. "I remembered seeing a sandwich like it made
in Maine, by a woman from northern Italy," she told Robbins.[106] It's unclear,
however, whether Iannelli was saying that no Philadelphian—not even C.J.
Cancelmo—was making these before 1935 or that she was merely the first
in the city to *sell* these sandwiches. (The latter certainly seems more feasible.)

Later in the interview with Quinn, when asked why she called them hoagies,
Iannelli explained that she did not, initially. "I called them *submarines* at first.
Because we made them on Italian bread and they looked like submarines,
and that's what everybody called long sandwiches up in Maine. You know,
today, they have those soft little rolls, but we never used anything but real
Italian bread. And then it seemed more and more people didn't understand
the word *submarines*, and they were all calling them *hoagies*. So I did, too."[107]

There are several details that don't add up in Iannelli's account; whether
these are enough to discredit her overall claim is difficult to say. For one, she

was born in West Virginia, not Maine.[108] (This isn't relevant to hoagies but is an odd error for one to make, even at the age of seventy-two.) She did live in Maine for a time, where, as noted previously, Giovanni Amato began selling his Italian sandwiches in Portland around 1902. That said, Amato's has never called them submarines, so in Maine, they were known—especially prior to 1930, when Iannelli lived there—primarily as Italian sandwiches.[109]

Digging further into the etymology of *submarine sandwich*, despite several legends claiming it came from various parts of New England, compelling evidence suggests the term originated in New Jersey and spread through the mid-Atlantic region before appearing in other areas. The most likely story involves an Italian immigrant named Dominic Conti, who opened a grocery store on Mill Street in Paterson, New Jersey, around 1910. According to his granddaughter Angela Zuccaro, Conti sold sandwiches "made from a recipe he brought with him from Italy" (specifically Campania, near Naples) on a long, crusty roll that was "filled with cold cuts, topped with lettuce, tomatoes, peppers, onions, oil, vinegar, Italian spices, salt, and pepper." So the bread would not become soggy, Conti buffered the filling on both sides with a layer of cheese.[110]

The *Holland I* submarine, located at the Paterson Museum in New Jersey. *Wikimedia Commons/Tom Sulcer.*

"My mother often told me about how my grandfather came to name his sandwich the submarine," continued Zuccaro. "She remembered the incident very well, as she was 16 years old at the time. She related that when grandfather went to see the *Holland I* in 1927, the raised submarine hull that was on display in Westside Park, he said, 'It looks like the sandwich I sell at my store.' From that day on, he called his sandwich the 'submarine.' People came from miles around to buy one of my grandfather's subs."[111]

The *Holland I* was indeed an experimental submarine, built in 1878 and then scuttled in the Passaic River after a series of tests, that was recovered and salvaged in 1927, corroborating this story at least somewhat. Further substantiation comes from a 1931 Paterson, New Jersey newspaper, which contained the first written usage of "submarine sandwich."[112] Following the literal paper trail south, this terminology next cropped up in print in Wilmington, Delaware, in 1936; Lancaster, Pennsylvania, in 1937; and, eventually, Philadelphia in 1939.[113] It took a few more years for the term to spread elsewhere, even in the northeastern United States, giving further credence to the idea that this moniker originated in the mid-Atlantic.

As such, it seems more likely that Antoinette Iannelli first heard about submarine sandwiches after she arrived in Philadelphia. This doesn't necessarily prove her story false; it's certainly possible others called her creations submarines and that she merely picked up on it but lost track of this detail over the years. On the other hand, this error further contributes to the perception that her recollections were at least somewhat unreliable.

## High on the Hoag

Moving from subs to hoagies, etymologically speaking, brings even less clarity. There is much folklore around the latter word's origin—which will be covered in this section—but far less corroborable evidence. "It may be we cannot *actually know* when Philadelphia's official sandwich was invented and named," wrote Temple history professor Ken Finkel in 2018. "What we do know is that the hoagie originated in South Philadelphia at some point during the first half of the twentieth century. Hard evidence is sparse, and there's [*sic*] conflicting verbal accounts shared decades later. Opinion and hearsay…lore yearning to be legend."[114]

If attempting to separate fact from fiction, a good starting point might be two things that are verifiable: (1) this word first appeared in print as "hoggie"

SANDWICH shoppe, steaks, hoggies, etc.
Good location. Very reasonable. Rent
cheap. 1442 W. Passyunk ave.
SANDWICH SHOPPE, Italian Submarine;
good bus. Unable to attend. 5339 Chestnut.

Classified advertisements mentioning hoggies and submarines in the *Philadelphia Inquirer*, November 1940. *Newspapers.com.*

(sometimes "hogie" or "hoggy"), with the variation "hoagie" (or "hoagy") coming later and (2) these appearances began in the early 1940s.

The first published usage—that has made itself known, at least—came in the July 20, 1940 issue of the *Pittsburgh Courier*, one of the leading Black newspapers in the United States at the time. As part of a column called "Quaker City Daze" (about happenings in Philadelphia), Lucille Gaines asked, "Have you noticed recent signs in eateries announcing 'Hogies, 10c.' In case you don't know they are oversized sandwiches with about a half a loaf of bred [*sic*] surrounding a variety of Italian delicacies. They're good when you're hungry and don't have much money."[115]

Later that year, the term—in this case, "hoggies"—was first used in the *Inquirer* classifieds, posted by an unnamed sandwich shop at 1442 West Passyunk Avenue.[116] For the next few years, usage of "hoggie" (and its variations) slowly increased in both newspaper classifieds and the yellow pages. The spelling "hoagie" did not appear in print until 1946.

According to Finkel, "hoggie" and "hoagie" showed up with approximately equal frequency in classified advertisements from 1946 to 1949. In 1950, however, the "hoagie" spelling pulled ahead for the first time, appearing 73 times compared to only 45 appearances of "hoggie." Between 1951 and 1955, "hoagie" became the clear favorite, appearing 565 times to just 44 for "hoggie."[117]

As stated previously, Philadelphia papers first mentioned the submarine sandwich in 1939, before any version of hoagie, and the now-taboo term lingered at least through the following decade. Gradually, however, as the preference for "hoagie" took hold, the "submarine" moniker would mostly fade away. (But "submarine" obviously remains the most widely understood name for these sandwiches nationwide, thus it is still used in certain contexts.)

Beyond the classifieds, *Inquirer* writers and editors preferred the spelling "hogie" in the 1940s and often used quotes around the word as if to indicate its dubiousness. In the early 1950s, they switched to "hoagie" and mostly stayed consistent with that going forward.[118]

There are two probable reasons for this early variability. Firstly, it seems natural that a new word—especially when people might have only heard it spoken before attempting to write it—would lack a standard, agreed-upon spelling. One example illustrates this well: "Recently, while I was in Philadelphia," wrote Robert Byrnes of Baltimore in a 1950 letter to the *New York Times*, "I noticed signs in many of the restaurants, taverns and sandwich shops proclaiming the excellence of 'Hoagies,' 'Hoggies,' 'Hogies,' and 'Horgys,' almost every sign being differently spelled."[119] (It is probably also safe to assume that the people making and selling hoagies had a less-formal education than, say, journalists.)

Secondly, the "hoggie" to "hoagie" transition should be obvious to anyone familiar with the Philly accent. This is not said in jest; most people who've done any research on this topic tend to agree that the way Philadelphians pronounce their O is directly responsible for the "hog" to "hoag" revision. Or as blogger Johnny Roosevelt put it, Philadelphians "brutally melded and morphed" the original term, "because, apparently, [they] used to be physically unable to pronounce words correctly," and "many native Philadelphians still can't."[120] (Come to Philly and say that to our faces, Johnny.)

## Hog Island Hokum

It is impossible, of course, to discuss this moniker's derivation without mentioning Hog Island (which has already been referenced once in this chapter). That the word "hoagie"—once "hoggie"—is directly related to the former shipyard at Hog Island is the most widespread of the etymological theories and thus has the most public backing.

Hog Island was a small piece of land in the Delaware River south of central Philadelphia, eventually filled in to make the spot that houses Philadelphia International Airport today. Beginning in the late 1600s, European settlers used the island for dairy and livestock farming, likely naming it after the plentiful pigs that were allowed to roam free there. Neglect in the 1800s, however, led to an ebbing of the island's natural fertility. In 1894, the owners contracted with the American Dredging Company, allowing them to use what was then barren as a dumping ground for dredge spoils from the river.[121]

An aerial photograph of Hog Island, circa 1922. *The Library Company of Philadelphia.*

In 1917, after realizing how underprepared they were, navally, to participate in World War I, the U.S. government chose Hog Island for what would become the world's largest shipyard. Though the project was complex—requiring more space to fully explain than this book can provide—it's safe to say that it was, in the end, a boondoggle. The facility cost upward of $65 million to construct (which translates to over $1 billion in 2024) and did not fully complete even one ship before the war ended in November 1918. This misuse of funds and possible collusion with private contractors became a scandal requiring special congressional committees and ample news coverage. "Hog Island is the most reckless waste of public funds which has ever come to my attention," said Senator Hiram Johnson of California, summing up the feelings of many at the time.[122]

In the postwar years, however, both the residual effects of patriotic propaganda and the fact that Hog Island was briefly the region's largest industrial employer suggest that, in Philadelphia, many might have seen the project in a more positive light. The 846-acre yard's infrastructure was an impressive feat in and of itself; it employed 36,000 workers at its peak and featured, for example, 250 buildings, including a hospital, a YMCA and a hotel; at least 18 dining facilities; 80 miles of railroad track, 20 locomotives and 465 freight cars; and 3 million feet of underground wiring, with telephone traffic equivalent to a city of 140,000.[123]

The facility did eventually become mildly productive, completing several vessels between late 1918 and 1921. After extensive discussions about how to maintain the shipyard going forward, however, the government eventually closed and abandoned it in 1921. In 1930, after the land sat idle for nearly a decade, the City of Philadelphia purchased it for a mere $3 million, paving the way for the eventual airport.

There are several hypotheses of how life on Hog Island led to subs in Philly becoming hoagies. Some say a common name for the workers themselves was "Hoggies," so the huge sandwiches these workers liked to eat eventually took on the same moniker. Others suggest the food's original name was the "Hog Island sandwich," which naturally evolved to "Hoggie."

One regularly referenced and almost-too-specific-to-be-made-up story that first ran as a reader letter in the *Philadelphia Evening Bulletin* in 1953 said, "In 1918, Italian workers at Hog Island shipyard used a train on Washington [Avenue] and used to congregate at 7th and Washington. Their lunches included long loaves of Italian bread filled with cold meat and the boys would shout, 'There's enough there to feed a couple of pigs.' The retort of the shipbuilders was 'That's what they are, Hog Islands.' The term Hog Islands was shortened to Hoggies…then to hoagie."[124]

Unfortunately, despite this legend's persistence in the city's oral tradition, concrete evidence that specifically connects Hog Island with the sandwich descriptor has yet to emerge. Neither is there any written evidence of the workers being called Hoggies nor that anyone ever used the phrase "Hog Island sandwiches" to describe these subs. Because, however, it is also impossible to prove definitively that this story is false—without a flux capacitor—it becomes, in a way, an article of faith; if one believes it with conviction, it cannot be disproven. (Though, obviously, the true burden of proof should lie with those pushing this hypothesis.)

When reviewing the circumstantial evidence on either side of the Hog Island debate, the biggest obvious flaw is timing. The facility operated only from 1917 to 1921, yet as previously noted, variations of "hoggie" did not appear in print until 1940. That's a twenty-year gap, compared to, for example, the less than ten years that it took for the "hoggie" to become the "hoagie." Furthermore, when Lucille Gaines wrote about hoggies in 1940, she referenced them as if they were a new development in the city. Is it possible that this name persisted only in the Italian American oral tradition for twenty years before finally expanding? Yes, but it seems unlikely.

This is, perhaps, also why Hog Island is sometimes misattributed to World War II in these legends: it fits the provable details better. It's also why that native Philadelphian who swears up and down that their grandfather confirmed the Hog Island story with a firsthand account is full of it. (Since the grandfather in question was born in 1930.)

The scope of the Hog Island project may also work against the hoggie hypothesis. If these sandwiches did exist at the shipyard—which is certainly plausible, even if people didn't call them hoggies—most agree it would have been Italian Americans doing the eating (aligning with the Italian sandwich origin stories previously discussed). And yet Hog Island was an enormous facility with workers of many ethnicities. Yes, there was a strong Italian contingent, but there were also Germans, Poles, Irishmen, Black men, Native men, etc. So, if the workers were collectively known as Hoggies, why would a sandwich consumed by only a subset have taken the name of the entire group? Or if only a small group of Italians ate this sandwich, why would it have become associated with the entire facility?

There is, incidentally, the persistent-yet-preposterous tale that an Irish Hog Island worker named Hogan (Or were all Irishmen called Hogans?) once took a liking to these sandwiches after being introduced by an Italian colleague and thus inspired the label. Perhaps the *hog* root here makes this hypothesis appealing to some, but it seems far more likely an Irish American came up with this story after a few beers just to mess with his Italian American friends (or enemies).

Rather than bring their own food, many Hog Island workers—including all the boarders—ate at the on-site dining facilities. The minutes from a 1918 United States Senate Committee on Commerce meeting, though early in the lifespan of the facility, offered some insight into these conditions. According to a statement from Hog Island worker Sheldon Vanderburgh, boarders—of which there were around five thousand at this time, with more planned—ate three meals a day in the mess halls, while many day workers also used the facilities for lunch. When asked what percentage of workers took their meals in the mess halls, Vanderburgh responded: "I can not say exactly, but there are thousands that eat there, and I have stood in the line for one hour at the mess hall."[125]

According to Dudley Reed Kennedy, a manager at the company that ran Hog Island, by this point, they'd served as many as seventeen thousand meals in a single day, with plans to expand that to forty thousand.[126] "I do not believe you can get as good food, as well cooked and as well prepared anywhere in the United States for the money," Kennedy said.[127] The workers,

Workers gather outside a canteen on Hog Island, 1918. *Library of Congress.*

however, didn't always agree with Kennedy's assessment. One Hog Islander, for example, told the Senate Commerce Committee that he could purchase "a better meal, a more wholesome meal and a cleaner meal also a more abundant meal in Philadelphia" for less.[128]

An interesting tidbit that came out of these conversations is that some of the camps of Italian boarders—workers apparently grouped themselves by ethnicity—ran their own commissaries. It is also possible, then, that these Italian American facilities, which were not described in detail in the committee report, served large sandwiches similar to hoagies. On the other hand, most of the hoggie legends talk of the Italians bringing these sandwiches from home, not purchasing them from the on-site facilities.

Unfortunately, this analysis fails to provide any irrefutable insight into whether workers ate sub-like sandwiches on Hog Island. It does, however, seem to disprove the legend that hoggies were widespread across the entire facility—workers everywhere chomping on huge loaves, as the story sometimes implies—to the point that the sandwich and the island would have become forever entwined. That said, it's still theoretically possible that there were enough small pockets of Italian workers eating these sandwiches that the name began to circulate within the region's tight-knit Italian American community.

The following sample menus are from mess hall No. 2, Hog Island, Philadelphia, where combination meals are served at 30 cents each:

JANUARY 14, 1918

| Breakfast. | Dinner. | Supper. |
|---|---|---|
| Oatmeal.<br>Liver or sausage.<br>Fried potatoes.<br>Bread and butter.<br>Coffee. | Pea soup.<br>Roast beef.<br>Steamed potatoes.<br>Beans.<br>Bread and butter.<br>Coffee. | Frankfurters.<br>Sauerkraut.<br>Steamed potatoes.<br>Bread and butter.<br>Coffee.<br>Bread pudding. |

JANUARY 20, 1918

| | | |
|---|---|---|
| Oatmeal.<br>Ham.<br>Scrambled eggs.<br>Fried potatoes.<br>Bread and butter.<br>Coffee. | Vegetable soup.<br>Beef stew.<br>Boiled potatoes.<br>String beans.<br>Cottage pudding.<br>Bread and butter.<br>Coffee. | Pot roast.<br>Steamed potatoes.<br>Bread and butter.<br>Hominy.<br>Apple sauce.<br>Tea. |

An example of the Hog Island cafeteria menu, featured in the 1918 text "Restaurant facilities for shipyard workers." *Archive.org*

On the other hand, when Catherine DiCostanza and Antoinette Iannelli, both Italian American food purveyors in the area, started making these sandwiches in the mid-1920s and mid-1930s, respectively, neither was familiar with the term. (Surely, at least Iannelli would've heard it by 1935, running a sandwich business in South Philly.)

In sum, the circumstantial evidence here—though hardly indisputable—suggests that a Hog Island–to–hoagie linguistic evolution is implausible. Did Italians eat large sandwiches at Hog Island? Probably—it's clear these sandwiches existed by the time the facility opened. And yet, when considered together, the available documentation pokes too many holes in the Hog Island hypothesis for it to be ultimately believable.

# HOKEY POKEY, MAN

If Hog Island is an unlikely origin point, could it instead have been the famed Gilbert and Sullivan theatrical partnership that led to the first hoagie? Some historians think so. Another popular postulate in today's thinking, the hokey pokey hypothesis appears to have first emerged with *The Larder Invaded:*

*Reflections on Three Centuries of Philadelphia Food and Drink*, a joint exhibition held by the Library Company of Philadelphia and the Historical Society of Pennsylvania in the late 1980s. In the companion book to the exhibition, authors Hines, Marshall and Woys Weaver wrote the following:

> *Since the Centennial, the hokey-pokey man has become a curbside institution in Philadelphia. In him the black pepperpot hawker was replaced by the Italian selling ices, sandwiches, sausages, fresh breads,* [animal crackers], *and little salads that were in fact miniature antipastos. Ever sensitive to the current fad, he became a barometer of shifting public taste. When "H.M.S. Pinafore" first played at Philadelphia in 1879, the city's Vienna bakeries cranked out a new loaf called the "Pinafore," while the confectioners busied themselves with new and trendy themes in chocolate in sugar. But the hokey-pokey man left the most lasting impression with a brilliant bit of street savvy, for when his antipasto went into the boat shaped Pinafore loaf, the hoagie was born, and with it all the spin-off sandwiches that have followed. In name, hoagie evolved from hokey-pokey; in New York and other parts of the country, the term meant a type of ice cream.*[129]

The rationale here seems sensible, with all the pieces coming together well. An explosion of street vendors—many of them Italian immigrants—came in the early 1880s, spurred on by the city's centennial celebration. The popularity of the Gilbert and Sullivan comic opera *H.M.S. Pinafore* led to the creation of the Pinafore roll, which indeed looks a heck of a lot like hoagie bread.

And yet this explanation relies on the supposition that, in Philadelphia, the term "hokey pokey man" became synonymous with "street food vendor"—a person who might sell salads, breads and sandwiches, etc.—unlike in every other city, where it meant a very specific type of inexpensive and questionably edible ice cream. This is, unfortunatcly for proponents of this hypothesis, demonstrably untrue; in Philadelphia newspapers, every available reference to "hokey pokey"—from the heyday of *H.M.S. Pinafore* through the first printed references to hoggies—strongly implied that the term was *always* associated with ice cream and only ice cream, just like it was elsewhere.

Typically Italian immigrants, these hokey pokey men arrived in, among other places, Philadelphia, New York, London and Paris all around the same time (1880s), though it is unclear if success in one place quickly led

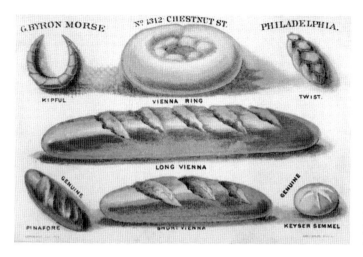

An advertisement card for G. Byron Morse bakery, featuring the pinafore roll. *Graf Brothers.*

to another or they descended on the world from Italy simultaneously. The name apparently derived from the traditional song of the Italian-speaking vendor, possibly *"o che poco"*—"oh how little," referring to the cost—or some similar dialectal phrase. "On the air now comes a cry long, resonant and appealing," wrote the *Philadelphia Times* of this phenomenon in 1893. "Out on the summer air it launches forth, 'Hokey pokey, hokey pokey,' and dies away in tremulous waves of sound as the queer little donkey cart and its burden of frozen delight passes from our view."[130]

Throughout this period, there were countless examples in local papers of "hokey pokey" referring specifically to the ice cream or its vendors. Despite the *Larder* assertion, then, it does not appear that journalists ever used this term to describe other types of food carts. Instead, they wrote of hokey pokey men *and* hot dog or sausage men, sandwich vendors, pretzel men, hot waffle wagons, peanut hucksters and those who sold doughnuts, crabs, candy, apples, etc.[131] This practice was consistent from the late 1800s to 1941, when the city council finally cracked down on street cart sanitary conditions, effectively ending the era of the hokey pokey man (and clearing the path for hoggie shops to become the city's next inexpensive food obsession).

Reacting to this crackdown, the *Inquirer* lamented what the city had lost, illustrating further the connection between the term "hokey pokey" and frozen treats: "How many a Philadelphia urchin, one eye watchful for the parent who painted dire pictures of the fate of the hokey-pokey eater has handed over his penny for the brief ambrosia of a dab of questionable 'ice-cream' between two slivers of cardboard!"[132]

HERE'S THE "HOKEY-POKEY"

The itinerant ice-cream vendor finds hot weather his harvest time. He and some customers are shown at Fifth and York streets. Business is brisk, but returns are small.

## HOKEY POKEY ICE CREAM

"NOVICE."—Four gallons of sweet milk, one box cornstarch. Take some of the milk and boil the starch. When done, mix it with the other milk. Add two pounds of sugar and sweeten to taste. The yolks of six eggs. Flavor with vanilla.

Place all in freezer and make same as ice cream. When frozen take out of the freezer and place in small pans or moulds; lay them on ice; cut when sufficiently frozen with thin-bladed knife. Wrap in paper quickly and pack in pan with ice. The pans should be placed in ice box to freeze solid—This recipe is an old one and was sent in by "Grandma."

*Top*: A hokey pokey man sells ice cream at 5th and York Streets during the summer of 1924. *From the* Philadelphia Inquirer/ *Newspapers.com.*

*Bottom*: A hokey pokey ice cream recipe printed in the *Philadelphia Inquirer* on October 15, 1912. *Newspapers.com.*

This is all a long-winded way of saying that, even if the already established hoggie-as-a-precursor-to-hoagie evidence is disregarded, between 1880-something and 1941, it's quite clear that the term "hokey pokey" meant only one thing to Philadelphians: cheap ice cream.

## Further Afield

While several other hoagie origin stories abound, they tend to get less attention than the two previous. Still, it is worth briefly covering a few more before eventually arriving at the most likely truth.

Responding to a query on the genesis of hoagies in 1953—the first known written discussion of this subject—the *Philadelphia Evening Bulletin* wrote that "there are several legends but the most probable says the origin of the huge 'hoagie' is found in 'hoggy' because it is clumsy and heavy and shaped something like a hog's back—drooping at both ends."[133] The fact that the meats featured in the original hoggie/hoagie were pork-based further contributes to the undeniable plausibility of this idea, though it is one of the less-commonly spread legends today. Perhaps it is too obvious and thus uninteresting.

Following the previous suggestion of hoagie etymology, a *Bulletin* reader named Fred P. wrote in with his own story. "About 1926 my mother had a grocery store in South Philly near a railroad and hoboes used to buy these large Italian sandwiches," said Fred. "Since all hoboes were known to be 'on the hoke' it became known as a hoke sandwich; later a hokie, and the name was finally changed to hoagie."[134] (It is certainly curious that two distinct theories exist with a "hokie"/"hokey" to "hoagie" evolution, even though written evidence of this word ever referring to these sandwiches has yet to emerge.)

Similarly told are the tales of children eating the sandwiches while skipping school or white people who just liked eating them, suggesting the name originally derived from "hooky" or "honky," respectively. (The latter seems particularly absurd but is nonetheless a real hypothesis that people have shared.) Lastly, according to Philadelphia historian and writer Jim Smart, "hoagie" may have evolved from the "hobo sandwich," popularized on Ditman Street in the Holmesburg section of Northeast Philadelphia.[135]

Aside from the pig's back suggestion, all these alternative stories lack one key factor: the *hog* root. Therefore, considering the verifiable fact that the term "hoggies" indeed appeared before "hoagies," any alternate spelling evolution becomes highly unlikely.

# Hoggie Royalty

The most plausible tale of hoagie history originates with Al DePalma, the self-styled "King of the Hoggies" (later "Hoagies"), who opened a store in South Philly in 1936 (or maybe 1937) and later ran another in West Philly for many years. In 1971, DePalma (originally written De Palma) told his story to Howard Robboy:

> *In 1928 when I was playing with a jazz group, I was returning home one night when I saw a couple of guys eating the sandwich which was then called a submarine. I said to my brother who was with me at the time that you had to be a hog to eat one of those sandwiches.*
>
> *During the Depression, when I couldn't get any work as a musician, I decided to open a sandwich shop. I wanted to do something different, so I remembered what I had said eight years before and decided to call the sandwich a hoggie. Business was good and I was able to start a chain of shops, all of them featuring the hoggie. I noticed that a lot of people would call them hoagies and decided to change the name to hoagie.*[136]

Aside from the fact that DePalma was born in 1906 and raised in West Philadelphia, not much is recorded about his early life. As a young man, he worked as a jazz musician and, during the Depression, in construction for the Works Progress Administration (WPA). In the mid-1930s, after saving $400 from his WPA jobs, he opened a luncheonette called the College Inn at 20th and Mifflin Streets, taking an apartment above the store with his second wife, Catherine, and young daughter, Rita. According to Rita, the College Inn was briefly a candy store before it shifted its focus to sandwiches.[137]

At first, DePalma's hoggies contained just lunch meat and tomato and cost fifteen cents, with the option of onions and lettuce added later, recalled John Scaltrito, who was married to Rita until her death in 2002 and occasionally worked at the store. Scaltrito and his former wife had slightly different viewpoints on the proper fillings, however. "Genoa salami, American salami, capicola, provolone cheese," said John. "That was standard."[138] Rita, on the other hand, said that a proper DePalma hoggie included Italian ham, Genoa salami, provolone cheese, shredded lettuce, tomatoes, onions, olive oil and a sprinkling of oregano. Although—and this is interesting when recalling DiCostanza's purported use of sage—she remembered her father using *thyme* as the hoggie herb in the early days.[139] Later, DePalma introduced a mushroom

A young Al DePalma. *John Scaltrito.*

and sweet pepper salad and cherry peppers as optional toppings.

Unhappy with the bread he saw others using for these gigantic Italian sandwiches—usually cut from larger loaves—DePalma went to nearby Buccelli's Bakery (21st and McKean Streets) to request a special eight-inch bun. "The roll really made a difference," Rita said. "People would come from all over the city, and there were lines of customers waiting for my father's hoagies."[140]

"I remember on a weekend there would be lines out into the street," said Scaltrito. "People would come to visit their relatives from other states, and they'd heard about the hoggies, and they wanted to take some home."[141]

DePalma's early success led to rapid expansion. According to Scaltrito, he opened a shop in the former Airport Circle area, as well as one on East Gay Street in West Chester. Classified advertisements also suggest one may have briefly existed at 5142 Market Street.[142]

"Right before World War II broke out," said Robboy, "[DePalma] and Pat from Pat's Steaks were going to open up King's Palace in Strawberry Mansion, around 33rd and Diamond....They were going to have DePalma's King of Hoggies on one end, and Pat's King of Steaks on the other. Then [the war] broke out and that was the end of that."[143]

As wartime took hold of the city, DePalma shifted his focus to the Navy Yard. "My father turned the restaurant into a hoagie factory," said Rita. "Since the Navy Yard workers worked in three shifts, we worked three shifts, making and delivering hoagies. We were so busy we had to expand to the second floor, which was the family apartment."[144]

A curious point here is that Antoinette Iannelli also reported doing a brisk hoagie business for the Navy Yard during World War II. Thus, assuming the timeline is indeed more connected to World War II than World War I, perhaps this association with the Navy Yard is what initially triggered the Hog Island hypothesis. Both were navy shipyards, but only one was around during a key period of hoagie evolution.

In the late 1940s, DePalma ran into some hard times, forcing him to briefly shutter his hoggie empire. After working for a short time as a cab driver, he saved up enough to open a new shop in 1950 at 62nd and Vine

DePalma's West Chester store. *John Scaltrito.*

Workers at DePalma's West Chester store display their uniforms. *John Scaltrito.*

Streets, close to his childhood neighborhood, where he made hoagies until his death in 1975.[145] (Non-hoagie people purchased this location after Al passed on.)

## Behind the Crown

DePalma's family remembered him primarily as a neighborhood philanthropist. "He was a generous man who would do anything for most people," said Scaltrito. "Just don't cross him," he added. "[Al] was good-hearted, but he also had a bad temper."[146]

During the war, continued Scaltrito, DePalma regularly sent food and cases of cigarettes to the soldiers. But he was always working an angle, a natural-born promoter. Rita remembered, for example, a block party on Mifflin Street where they put together an enormous sixty-foot hoagie and sold it off in pieces to raise money for care packages for the troops. In 1951, DePalma resurrected the giant hoagie charity promotion—this time benefiting a neighborhood church—creating the "largest hogie in the

A giant DePalma hoggie (*left*) on full display. *John Scaltrito.*

## Cold Cuts, Cocozza and Caruso

Shortly after DePalma started selling his hoggies, a South Philadelphia teenager named Freddy Cocozza appeared, becoming one of the nascent shop's best customers, loitering for hours and eating prodigious amounts. His penchant for volume grew to legendary status, with one report suggesting he regularly devoured four of the gigantic hoagies, five bottles of soda and three banana splits in one sitting, while another suggested he could down *six hoagies* before moving to dessert.*

DePalma told author Constantine Callincicos, "One night in 1939, a terrible snowstorm cleared the streets. But in walked Freddy, in his navy blue wool cap and turtle-neck sweater. He had his records and record player under his arm, and icicles on his nose and chin. Without a word, Freddy walked to the back of the restaurant, settled himself in a warm corner, and started to play his favorite Caruso and Tito Ruffo records. As he sat and listened, tears rolled down his cheeks."

Around 11:30 p.m., DePalma told Cocozza he was closing for the night. "But Freddy, still weeping quietly, didn't answer....When [DePalma] returned in the morning he found Freddy asleep, just where he had left him."

"The boy played his records all night, over and over," said DePalma. "Later when I asked him about it, he said he had just felt sad and that he found peace in my restaurant. I'll never forget it; it was kinda strange, the whole thing."

More commonly, however, Freddy would enter with a flourish, loudly singing his demands for food while DePalma tried to serve other customers, wrote Callinicos. "Once when he came in singing in that strident voice of his, Al threw his ice cream dipper at him. But Freddy only howled with delight."

"If you're the King of the Hoagies," he would yell at DePalma, "some day I'm going to be the king of the singers, like Caruso!"†

Cocozza would, of course, eventually adopt the stage name Mario Lanza and go on to widespread acclaim as a singer and actor.

---

* Constantine Callinicos with Ray Robinson, "'Hoagie King' Remembers Boy with Appetite," *Philadelphia Daily News*, December 17, 1960; Elaine Tait, "An Expert's Recipe for a Gen-u-wine Hoagie," *Philadelphia Inquirer*, April 9, 1972.
† Callinicos with Robinson, "Hoagie King."

world," which some reports claimed was as long as twenty feet and held as much as fifty pounds of filling. This mammoth sandwich reportedly included cotechino (amusingly spelled "godighin" in the paper), salami and capicola ("cupocoli"), along with the standard toppings.[147]

Later in life, while suffering from diabetes, DePalma had fourteen operations before eventually having both legs amputated. But that didn't stop the king; he walked with prosthetics and would drive around in a specially made car, with the brakes and gas pedal controlled from the steering wheel. This tenacity perhaps came from the fact that he was the DePalma family's

Al DePalma, later in life. *John Scaltrito.*

black sheep. (Both Scaltrito and Robboy used this exact phrase.) His elder brother, Louis, was a prominent orthopedic surgeon at Lankenau Hospital, and his younger twin brothers, Emilio and Attilio, both performed in the Philadelphia orchestra. "They were high culture–type people, and then he's in the sandwich business," said Robboy. "Also, he had mob connections, which the people in his family looked down on him for."[148]

DePalma's second wife, Catherine, was also a crucial contributor to the business, echoing several of these stories. "If he were alive today," read one of Al's obituaries, "he would be the first to admit that the success that came to him would not have been possible if it wasn't for his wife Catherine that worked beside him serving the customers and making the sandwiches until closing time which would be wee hours in the morning, but Mrs. DePalma thought her day was not done until she would scrub the counter and mop the floors only to get 2 or 3 hours sleep."[149]

## RITA'S RETURN

Despite having a strained relationship with her parents growing up, Rita Scaltrito was inspired to speak out about the DePalma legacy later in life. In the early 1990s, when she heard about Wawa's campaign to have the hoagie declared Philadelphia's official sandwich, Rita called Wawa headquarters to share the secret she'd kept "lo these past 55 years," as she put it. "My father," she said, "made up the word."[150]

"I'm almost sure my father was the original. I'm positive," she told the *Daily News*. "Pictures tell a thousand words."[151]

"And, indeed," wrote Becky Batcha, "what appear to be period photographs show De Palma overseeing sandwich assembly at his luncheonette, the College Inn, at 20th and Mifflin. A sign nearby proclaims him to be 'De Palma, King of Hoggies.'" Further down, the sign also reads: "When buying a hoggie, be sure to buy De Palma's original. Accept no substitutions." (A version of this photograph is available at https://lifeattable.com/phillysandwiches.) "The woman seems honest enough," continued Batcha.[152]

"My father didn't invent the sandwich. He invented the name," Rita said. "That's why I never bothered before."[153]

"He was hard on her," said John Scaltrito of Al and Rita's relationship. "But afterwards, she was proud of him, and of the hoagie being popular. She felt part of it. When the reporters came to interview her, she did all the talking. She was so proud to share it."[154]

There is—just as things were becoming clear—one glaring issue with Rita's story. The way she told it, her father got his idea for hoggies *at Hog Island*. (Here we go again.) In her memory—though she would have been a toddler at the time this was happening—he went to the famous shipyard looking for work during the Depression and saw men eating the huge sandwiches. Then, instead of applying for a job, he decided to start selling lunch.

This is obviously not possible, since Hog Island was not open during the Depression, and it's just too ridiculous that he would have seen them there and then decided to call the sandwiches hoggies for a completely unrelated reason. The good news here is that Al DePalma himself never made this claim. He told Robboy, of course, that he first saw the sandwiches (and made the now-famous hog comment) in 1928 on Broad Street, outside the Academy of Music. It is fascinating, however, that the Hog Island legend became so prevalent and influential that it even made it into the princess of hoggies' recollection of her father's backstory. As for whether it was folklore or truth that led to that alteration, that fact is likely lost to history.

Even with this unresolved detail, it does appear safe to say that DePalma was responsible for introducing the term *hoggie* from a commercial perspective. The question perhaps remains, however, whether he came up with the name on his own or if it was already informally part of the Philadelphia Italian American lexicon and he merely saw a business opportunity.

## No Sheetz

Wawa, the convenience store chain that has developed a cult-like following in the Delaware Valley, has a rich history that dates to the early 1800s. While the company has diversified its offerings over time, its hoagie counter has remained one of its most iconic and beloved features.

Founded in 1803 as a small iron foundry in New Jersey, the brand eventually transitioned into a dairy farm in southeastern Pennsylvania and began delivering fresh milk to customers' doorsteps. In 1964, recognizing shifting consumer demand, Wawa opened its first convenience store in Folsom, Pennsylvania, offering a variety of products, including grocery items, beverages and prepared foods. (It introduced premade hoagies in 1970.)[*]

Though locals have lamented the store's more recent trend away from quality sandwiches to a too-diverse-to-be-good variety of fast-food options, Wawa actually sold hot items like hamburgers and fried chicken before it ever offered hoagies, first introducing the former in 1969.[†]

That said, the made-to-order hoagie business, which began in 1984, was certainly crucial to the chain building its fervent following.[‡] With Amoroso rolls delivered each morning, fresh meats and cheeses and fast-but-personalized service, these hoagies may have never compared to the city's best, but for the price, they were difficult to beat.

An uninspiring Wawa Italian hoagie, modern day. *Author photograph.*

In late 1991, Wawa successfully campaigned to have the hoagie declared the official sandwich of Philadelphia, organizing a petition that gained over thirty-five thousand signatures.[§] In response, on May 7, 1992, then-mayor Ed Rendell held a noontime ceremony at city hall, confirming the first Philadelphia "Hoagie Day."

As of this writing, Wawa operates more than one thousand stores in seven states and continues to expand, spreading the Philadelphia hoagie gospel far and wide.

[*] Wawa, "Wawa: 50 Years & Counting," https://www.wawa.com/about/wawa-history.
[†] Wawa, "50 Years & Counting."
[‡] Wawa, "50 Years & Counting."
[§] "The Hoagie: A History," *Philadelphia Daily News*, June 23, 1993.

Robboy, who once testified in a federal court case about when the word *hoagie* came into use (an Arizona sandwich shop was claiming it owned it), believed DePalma's story. "He was a down-to-earth Italian guy, and I had no reason to doubt him," Robboy said. "It sounds more romantic to say it came from Hog Island, but that's obviously folklore. Still, some people are going to insist on believing it." Ever the academic, the retired professor's approach remained evidentiary. "I don't care," he stated plainly, about whether he had any personal investment in any of these stories being the correct one. "Why would I care?"[155]

## Commandments of Construction

A true Philadelphian will always have at least one hard and fast rule that must be followed in the construction of a hoagie. To break one of these rules is sacrilege, yet no one can fully agree on these rules. And so it goes.

When writer Tom Baldwin returned to Philadelphia in 1993, after fourteen years on the road, he lamented how these rules had changed since he'd left the city. "Time was we ordered hoagies and automatically got the whole garden," he wrote. "The only appurtenance left to choice were the peppers: 'Hot'r-sweet?' Those were 'real' hoagies. Nowadays we have to specify if we want an 'Italian' hoagie, which is the real thing, or a cobbled fraud."[156]

"In tailoring our hoagies we allowed them to be made plain," he continued. "What's next? Will our snapper soup lack the turtle? Will our pretzels break and not bend? We savants of the hoagie set get irked now when we place our orders, and Guido asks us, 'Oil or mayonnaise?' Ahem, mayonnaise goes on sandwiches. 'Onions on that?' Guido asks. Mio Dio. It's not a hoagie without onions."[157]

Perhaps the rules are ever evolving. Today, choice abounds. But these rules persist and are at least part of what keeps Philadelphia at the center of the hoagie universe. Without them, no sandwich can be trusted. They are what separates the religious experience from the mundane. Take this amusing anecdote, for example, of Philly expat and writer Stephen F. Friend trying to find a decent hoagie in Milwaukee:

> *I came across a restaurant advertising "submarines." What's in a name, I thought. A hoagie by any other name still tastes as good. A smiling waitress approached.*

*"I'll have a hoagie," I said.*

*Her expression immediately changed. "Watch your language," she snapped. "This is a respectable place."*

*Bewildered, I tried to explain myself.*

*"Oh, a submarine. Well, why didn't you say so?" she said, somewhat mollified. "Mustard and mayonnaise?"*

*That was a clue. Believe me, when someone suggests defiling a hoagie with mustard and mayonnaise, that's a clue. Within minutes, my worst fears were realized. The "hoagie" turned out to be bologna, cheese and tomato on an oversized hamburger roll! Despite my disappointment, I reacted in a manner befitting a rational, mature adult. I cried.[158]*

Mayonnaise is probably the strictest hoagie rule; simply put, it has no place on the Philadelphia Italian. On a turkey or roast beef hoagie, sure, mayo is fine. But on an Italian, only olive oil is acceptable, though today, many places—even in Philly—use an inferior olive and vegetable oil blend.

Hoagie lovers diverge on whether vinegar should also be added alongside the olive oil. The DiCostanza and DePalma stories specify only oil, while Iannelli's recollection of making "a little sauce" for her first rendition suggests she may have included vinegar. And if evidence from New Jersey is allowed, submarine-namer Conti also used vinegar in his creations. Although this is clearly not enough evidence to change anyone's mind about *the right way*, it's probably safe to say that vinegar is an acceptable optional ingredient but never required.

Onion is another divisive topping; some find that its flavor overwhelms the rest of the sandwich, yet others won't eat a hoagie without it. (Al DePalma fell into the first camp, as does this author.) DePalma also spoke of the importance of impeccably fresh bread (see chapter 7) and provolone that is sufficiently sharp, not the soft, flavorless version he once compared to a potato.[159] His daughter also emphasized how important it is to shred the lettuce before adding, but this was likely for better construction as opposed to flavor.

Speaking of construction, experts insist that a hoagie roll be *hinged*, or cut most of the way through, but never split into two pieces. This allows the bread to wrap around the sandwich, keeping the filling intact. (If a long roll is cut through, it's clearly a sub.) Some also like to *scoop* their roll, removing some of the excess bread interior, while others argue a proper roll does not require scooping.

In contrast to the standard hoagie construction of cheese, then meat, then vegetables, there's also the "Delco meat wrap" style, where vegetables are wrapped inside the cold cuts, resulting in a layer of meat appearing through the opening of the roll. Per the name, this format is associated with—but not limited to—Delaware County, just outside of Philadelphia. Fans argue this ingenuity keeps the sandwich together and creates a better meat-to-vegetable ratio in each bite, while opponents find these hoagies aesthetically displeasing and difficult to eat.

A turkey hoagie made with the meat wrap style from Our Deli in Paoli. *Author photograph.*

After LaBan highlighted this style in an article about the top Delco hoagie spots, he was delighted to receive spirited feedback from several colleagues who were born and bred in the county. "Wonderful that you extolled the virtues of what I call the 'right side up hoagie,'" wrote Anthony R. Wood in an email, as one example. "With the meat on top, gently encasing the innards, properly sliced, the roll became an archeological dig. That's the way they were made in Chester. We used to laugh at what Philadelphians called the hoagie."[160]

When it comes to which combination of cold cuts is ideal for an authentic Philadelphia Italian hoagie, the various examples already included in this chapter illustrate how this definition is ever-changing and how difficult it is to pin down one *correct* recipe. It's probably safe to say, however, that a proper Italian hoagie should include at least three different types of meat, with options including prosciutto crudo, ham, cotechino sausage, hot or sweet capicola, soppressata, pepperoni and various types of salami. The exact combination is a matter of taste, though freshly and thinly cut meat is always going to be superior.

At the end of the day, despite the protests of Baldwin and others, a hoagie is a customizable sandwich on a long roll. Like with many other food items (Hawaiian pizza, anyone?), it's fun to argue about which ingredients combine to make the finest product, especially when living in a place where there are so many amazing options. The true answer will, however, always be a matter of personal taste.

# 3

# STEAK

While the hoagie may be the city's official sandwich, the cheesesteak is, worldwide, the sandwich most associated with Philadelphia. Whether one considers it the pinnacle of sandwiches featured in this book—as stated previously, this author does not—the steak holds a special connection to the populace that no other foodstuff can duplicate. Though the idea that one must scarf down a cheesesteak to fully experience Philadelphia is cliché by this point, it nonetheless remains undeniably true. "It's one of those foods that cut across all classes and generations," Craig LaBan once said. "There's something that will be forever local about it, that gets to the heart of its greatness, because it's a sandwich that speaks to this place, and regional foods are so rare now in America."[161]

"It's the same as team spirit, when you talk to people about their favorite cheesesteaks," added Holly Moore. "It's like being a Phillies fan, or graduating from Cardinal Whatever high school. It's very much a part of being a Philadelphian."[162]

Maybe this connection is created by simplicity. Philly is a gritty town that wears its heart on its sleeve and thus appreciates a sandwich that does the same. There's no secret here: it's just steak, onions and cheese on bread, with barely any seasoning on most versions. And yet there's a magic created by this combination that (literally) courses through the city's blood.

Beyond the well-known places—the ones covered by Food Network or *Bon Appétit*, etc.—it's perhaps more amazing how one can walk into pretty much any sandwich shop or pizza joint in the greater Philadelphia region and get a decent cheesesteak. And yet, beyond this area, anything dubbed a "Philly cheesesteak" is likely to be trash.

# The Story

Like the combo and the hoagie, there are various similar but different versions of the steak sandwich origin story—cheese didn't come until later—although, in this case, most tellers generally agree that brothers Pat and Harry Olivieri were the first to serve it during the 1930s. It's a story that pretty much everyone who's interested in Philadelphia food has heard, but it can't be left out of a book about Philadelphia sandwiches.

Even considering the knowledge that memories and legends can shift over time, especially within the family that recites them most, it seemed prudent to start with Frank Olivieri Jr., Harry's grandson and current owner of Pat's King of Steaks. In a 2022 interview, Frank recounted the now-legendary tale:

> *The version that I've been told all my life is that my uncle Pat, my great-uncle, my grandfather's older brother, and* [my grandfather Harry] *were selling hotdogs during the Depression at an open-air hot dog stand basically right across the street from where the store is now. And every day, they had hot dogs for lunch.*
>
> *My uncle Pat got tired of eating hot dogs, so he wanted to make a sandwich he used to make for himself. When he had some extra money, he would go to the butcher shop and get some chopped trimmings, and he would cook them on his hot dog grill. The condiments at the time were onions, and he would get a loaf of an Italian bread and make the steak with onions and put it on the Italian bread, and that was his lunch: a steak sandwich with onions.*
>
> *One day, he sent my grandfather to the butcher to get the meat, and then he made the sandwich. At that time, a cab driver who ate hot dogs every day stopped by. This guy saw Uncle Pat making the sandwiches* [and] *said to him, "That looks really good—make one for me." And Pat said, "I only have enough for myself, but I'd be more than happy to give you half." So, he broke the sandwich in half and gave it to the cab driver, and after eating it, the cab driver said, "Forget about hot dogs. This is the sandwich you should start making."*[163]

As should by now be expected, the details of any such story differ slightly depending on who is talking. Pat and Harry are both deceased, but there is one surviving written record of the story Pat himself shared. "Hot dogs and pork," he recalled in 1951 of the inspiration day. "That's all I see, and all I eat. For once, I'm going to live a little."[164]

Pat Olivieri, undated photograph. *Pat's King of Steaks.*

"Here," Pat said, flipping a coin to his brother Harry, "go over to the butcher shop and get me a hunk of steak." Pat grilled the steak and, according to his story, put it between two slices of bread. A man approached the stand. "Whatcha got there," the man asked. "I guess you'd call it a steak sandwich," Olivieri said he replied. "Never made one before."

"Looks good," said the man. "Gimme one."

"You got this one," Pat replied. "I was gonna eat it myself, but the way business has been lately, I can't quibble. Gimme a dime."[165]

As much as this story has been told and retold over the years, one perspective that remained mostly overlooked was that of the lucky cabbie who supposedly enjoyed the first steak—until 2016, that is, when writer Danya Henninger shared Dave Kohn's story. Kohn died in 1992, but his nephew Ken Frank filled in. "Uncle Dave got a lot of hot dogs at the stand; he would go there almost every day," said Ken. "One time, Pat was grilling some meat, and says to my uncle, 'taste this.' 'That's fantastic,' my uncle says. 'You should put this on a roll.'"[166]

"The story is well known to everybody in my family," added Diane Schwartz, Ken's daughter and Kohn's grandniece. "Uncle Dave would bring it up all the time."[167]

Though it is, at this point, virtually impossible to resolve the minute details that differ in these three accounts, it is worth examining the bread in particular. Most versions of the story have Pat putting the steak into a hot dog bun—a sensible assumption for a guy running a hot dog cart—and yet when Pat himself told the story, his recollection was that he put the meat "between two slices of bread." (One thing is sure: the idea that the original Philly steak sandwich might have appeared on flimsy Wonder bread—if that's even what Pat meant—is highly disturbing.)

"From what I understand," said Frank Jr., trying to help clarify this mystery, "[Pat] was using the hot dog bun for the single hot dog, and then he would sell a large hot dog that was three hot dogs on a half a loaf of Italian bread. So that's how the steak sandwich got to be on Italian bread."[168] This does seem to fit with the fact that other sandwiches served on Italian loaves—the hoagie, perhaps, but also inexpensive meats like tripe (see chapter 6) and even one where the *only* filling was *meat drippings*—gained popularity during the Depression, especially in South Philadelphia.

## Promotion of Invention

The combination of fried steak and onions was not at all novel in 1932. Even then, it was an obvious and long-used pairing, as was the idea of a steak sandwich, both of which regularly appeared in print prior to the existence of Pat's version.

The Tun Tavern—reportedly the first brew house in Philadelphia, having opened in the 1680s—served a similar sandwich starting around 1745. According to the tavern's history, Peggy Mullen (who ran the place with her husband, Thomas) discovered that by "thinly slicing and grilling beefsteak, then serving it on a bread roll, she could produce a delicious, satisfying meal." Once established, these sandwiches reportedly sold by the thousands, perhaps foretelling how quickly they move at Pat's today.[169]

Local historian Woys Weaver also wrote that, in the 1800s, German settlers of southeastern Pennsylvania commonly served "shaved beefsteak browned on a grill with onions" over toast or waffles.[170]

Broaching the topic of prior invention with Frank Olivieri Jr., some Philly attitude initially emerged. "There's *no* debate!" he exclaimed. "Who else made the first cheesesteak? Tell me right now. Who?"[171] It's hard to fault this kind of reaction; after all, Frank needs to protect the brand he now presides over, which has been so bolstered by this legend for so long.

When historian Celeste Morello wrote the text for the historical marker erected outside Pat's in 2008 (which is not an official marker, rather something sanctioned by the business), she included the phrase "from a centuries-old recipe used in American homes." Morello later recalled telling Frank Jr. that she wasn't comfortable writing that Pat *invented* the steak sandwich, though she did acknowledge that he put his own spin on it. "Frankie understood that," she said.[172]

Unlike with hoagies, however, the community at large has widely accepted that the first steak sandwich in Philly belonged to Pat's and Pat's alone. When asked if he's ever heard an alternative version of the origin story, Ken Silver, the current owner of Jim's Steaks on South Street—another institution in the city—said, somewhat cagily, "No. And even if I had, I probably wouldn't tell you."[173]

While being occasionally obtuse helps perpetuate the lore, Frank Jr. does begrudgingly acknowledge that it was mainly Pat Olivieri's relentless pursuit of publicity that made the brand into what it is today. "Pat was *the person* who promoted this sandwich," he said.[174]

"Many people think cheesesteaks became famous because of their taste," wrote Carolyn Wyman in *The Great Philly Cheesesteak Book*. "No, the cheesesteak became famous because of Pat."[175] Thus, like Abe Levis and Al DePalma, Pat Olivieri was, in many ways, himself the product, quickly becoming the boxing-style promoter, the propagator of truth and legend, the one who turned a simple steak sandwich into *the* icon for an entire city.

## THE MAN, THE MYTH, THE LEGEND

Though many sources claim Pasquale "Pat" Olivieri was born in Philadelphia, immigration and naturalization records suggest he likely took his first breath in Italy, in the Apennine province of L'Aquila, in May 1907. He first came to the United States at the age of six, but his family also lived in Italy for extended periods during his youth. Unlike many Italian immigrants during this era, Pat's father, Michele, had a quality job in Italy and left only for political reasons. As such, when he had difficulty securing a good job in Philadelphia, Michele sent his wife and children back to Italy while he attempted to build a better life. Pat himself settled in Philadelphia permanently—after completing his schooling in Italy—in 1924.[176]

Then seventeen, Pat looked for employment to help support his family. He took a job as a blacksmith's helper, eventually working as a drop forger at the Flexible Flyer sled factory. Unsatisfied with this trade, Pat followed in the footsteps of many immigrants who struggled to find work they enjoyed: he invested in a hot dog cart that he could run on his own, without the need for oversight from more established ethnic groups or the restrictions of a factory schedule. His younger brother Harry, who had picked up the carpentry trade, also joined the business. For a time after starting the cart, the brothers continued to toil at their day jobs—or perhaps night jobs (accounts conflict about whether their hot dogs were aimed at the lunch or dinner crowd).

The exact date when Pat made that first steak remains disputed. Many now follow the restaurant's lead and say 1930, as claimed on the Pat's sign and merchandise. This, however, seems unlikely, as that's also reportedly when Pat first acquired the hot dog stand. In addition, older newspapers that covered the story mostly stated 1932, and Herbert Olivieri, Pat's son, confirmed 1932 in a 1980 letter to the *Inquirer*.[177]

Regardless of the specific early '30s year in which the sandwich was first made, this was a time when most families still made daily shopping trips. Wisely, Pat situated his stand just across from the busy trolley stop for the 9th Street Italian Market at Wharton Street. In addition to slinging dogs for a nickel each, the brothers sizzled piles of chopped onions on the grill, creating an intoxicating aroma to lure tired workmen, hungry shoppers and cranky children alike.[178]

The stand was not an immediate success; in fact, Pat planned to ask for his factory job back shortly after trying to briefly go all in on sandwiches. "On his way to see the boss, so many of his former coworkers came up to him to congratulate him on the new stand and getting out of there that he left without doing it," recalled Pat's third wife, Evelyn Olivieri-Cirillo.[179] Harry, on the other hand, being the younger brother, worked at the Navy Yard during World War II to help subsidize the family.

The brothers' contrasting personalities, which complemented each other perfectly, also played a key role in building the business. While Pat was "exciting" and "a true showman," for example, Harry was "down-home" and "modest."[180] This meant the elder Pat could get out from behind the grill and become the cheesesteak promoter that only he knew Philadelphia needed, and Harry would happily hold down the fort at 9th and Wharton Streets.

Pat would regularly take steaks to local theaters and nightclubs, especially the old Earle Theater, and give them out to celebrities in exchange for a photograph that he'd proceed to blow up and hang at the store. Though a relatively common practice among famous cheap-eats places today, Pat was likely a local pioneer of this tactic to drum up sales, and it worked wonders.

"He met Humphrey Bogart one time," said Frank Jr., "and Uncle Pat pulled out his .38-caliber revolver and asked Bogey to hold the gun on him while he held his hands up. Uncle Pat was crazy."[181] Other celebs immortalized on Pat's wall included the Three Stooges, Louis Armstrong, Benny Goodman, Jimmy Durante and Tony Bennett, to name just a few.

Frank Jr. colorfully described Pat's vivaciousness: "I heard stories of him bending railroad spikes with his bare hands. He loved horses, so he would ride his horse over there. We had friends that had Cadillac dealerships, so he would drive over with new Cadillacs. And people would gather around Pat's new Cadillac, and then he would literally sell them the Cadillac in front of the store. He bought mansions up on the Main Line. He parlayed the money he made at the sandwich place into his real estate ventures."[182]

Humphrey Bogart holds
up Pat. *Pat's King of Steaks.*

"Uncle Pat was bigger than life," Frank Jr. continued. "He was the beginning and the end. People adored him—and he used that to sell [sandwiches]."[183]

Another often told but difficult to substantiate story is the rumor that Pat was supplementing his beef with horse meat during a time of meat rationing—either the Depression or World War II, depending on who is telling the story. (This does seem to be a fair question considering the context: *Where was all that beef coming from?*)

"He put $10,000 in a mason jar and offered the money to anybody who could come down and prove he was selling horse meat," said Frank Jr. "People came from all over the country to Philadelphia to try a sandwich because they wanted that ten grand; back then, that was like $1 million! But nobody could ever prove that he was selling horse meat." After a surely rehearsed but excellently executed pause, Frank Jr. added, "Because my Uncle Pat started the rumor."[184]

# Cheese + Steak

Relatively early on, the owner of the building in which Pat's currently resides—a guy named Joe Butch—offered Pat the warmer-than-outside upstairs space to continue selling his sandwiches through the winter months. Though Pat couldn't afford this initially, a forgiving Butch agreed to hold off on rent until the food started making money. "Well," said Frank Jr., "he started making money pretty quickly. More people were coming into the bar to eat sandwiches than to drink."[185] So, Butch cut a hole in the side of the building, instructing patrons who wanted to drink to come inside and eaters to use the window. Before long, the bar was forgotten.

Pat's opened a second location at 33rd and Dauphin Streets in Strawberry Mansion in 1938. Around 1951, they moved into a new "steak emporium" just up the block, which included an eight-thousand-square-foot dining room that seated more than four hundred people and featured a $2,800 crystal chandelier as its centerpiece. Though the South Philly location was still going strong, shortly after opening, the newer place was reportedly serving upward of forty thousand customers each week. Amazingly—considering the production line of the surviving Pat's location today—the new spot also served pizza and pasta.[186]

Pat's emporium may be long gone, but it served a crucial role in Philadelphia history: this is where cheese first appeared on a steak sandwich. "They had a manager there, 'Cocky' Joe Lorenza," said Frank Jr. "The guy was a complete waste of time. He was always sloshed, [a] real sloppy guy. He was one of those people who liked to give people a hard time, fight, things like that. This was the guy who added the cheese."[187]

A torn newspaper clip shows part of an advertisement for Pat's Ridge Avenue location in Strawberry Mansion. *Pat's King of Steaks.*

78

In the 1980s, Pat's son Herb Olivieri told the *Inquirer* that he remembered the March 1951 day vividly. Just like Pat at his hot dog stand in the early days, Lorenza—a longtime employee, despite Frank Jr.'s less-than-flattering description—supposedly got tired of eating steaks the same way every day. So, he put some American cheese on the grill, which melted and mixed in with the beef. Pat, who was apparently watching all of this, simply said, "Joe, do that again."[188]

When Frank Jr. tells the story, he's more prone to say the cheese was provolone. Lorenza, apparently, was "100 percent Italian" and loved the stuff. But he admitted, "I'm not exactly sure what kind it was....*Probably provolone.*"[189]

One thing is certain: it was not Cheese Whiz.

While there isn't anyone else suggesting they invented the Olivieri-style steak sandwich, others have insisted they added cheese first. As one example, Michael Morroney—the son of Larry, who opened Larry's Steaks in 1955—told Wyman that when he experimented with cheese allocated for burgers on a steak sandwich in 1957, he believed he was the first to do so.[190] Nonetheless, more people give credence to the Olivieri/Lorenza claim. "There seems to be no indication of cheese on the sandwich before Pat's," said historian Morello.[191]

The circa-1950s Pat's King of Steaks sign that sat atop the Strawberry Mansion location. *Neil Benson.*

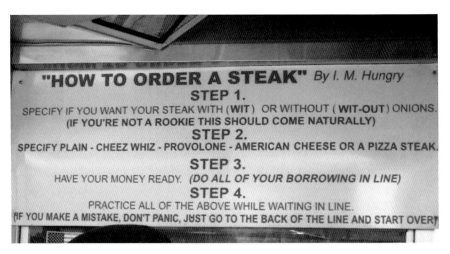

Helpful tips on how to order at Pat's. *Wikimedia Commons/Nymfan9.*

Even as this newfangled modification was growing in popularity in the mid-1950s, Pat never wanted cheese at his original shop because he worried about keeping the food kosher for his Jewish friends in the neighborhood. (Mixing cheese with meat on the same grill would have been a problem.) Then, in the late '50s, Harry's son Frank Sr.—who had recently completed high school and come to work full time at the 9th Street shop—had a revelation. He was aware of Cheez Whiz, a processed cheese product that had entered the market in 1953 and could be spread without requiring melting on the grill. He wondered whether it would work on Pat's steak sandwiches. Curious, he bought a couple of cans and began to experiment covertly.

"My grandfather would've freaked out if he saw the Cheez Whiz," said Frank Jr. But the canned cheese, he continued, "was perfect…because [my dad] could just hide the can at the edge of the grill where my grandfather wouldn't see it. [192]

"People freakin' LOVED the Cheez Whiz," he added. "They were like, 'Holy moly…this is great stuff.'" [193]

## Is Whiz Authentic?

There's this idea that perpetuates in and around Philly that a cheesesteak requires Cheez Whiz to be *authentic*, the real thing. And yet the historical

80

exploration here has hopefully illustrated that Whiz was neither part of the original recipe nor even part of the initial consideration set. (And of course, the true original had no cheese at all.) Whether credit belongs to Cocky Joe, Michael Morroney or someone else, it is quite safe to say the first cheesesteaks were nowhere near a can of Whiz.

So, how is authenticity determined? On one hand, it can be established that Whiz was not part of the original cheesesteak and that Frank Olivieri Sr. initially added it to help the production line, not to improve flavor. On the other hand, most of the cheesesteaks at the city's most well-known shops today—such as Pat's, Geno's and Jim's—contain Whiz. (In 2015, Frank Jr. said about 60 percent of Pat's customers chose Whiz, followed by provolone, then American.) Obviously, the fact that more people order Whiz does not make it superior. But does it make Whiz more authentic? Maybe.

It's also worth thinking beyond the well-trod spots. Any place that is primarily a steak joint, has the word *steaks* in its name or considers cheesesteaks a specialty of the house will likely have some sort of Whiz as an option, though it won't necessarily be the default. Another important part of steak culture in and around Philadelphia, however, is that one can walk into just about any pizza place or deli and walk out with a decent cheesesteak. (Not always, of course, but often.) And most of these places *don't serve Whiz.* Typically, they don't even offer a choice of cheese, with American being the common standard. If one requests a specific type of cheese—and the place carries it—then sure, it's probably feasible. But don't expect them to ask.

This, in turn, suggests that a cheesesteak with Whiz is perhaps a specialty product itself, that one must go to a place that takes their steaks seriously to acquire it. Whereas, on the other hand, a steak with American or provolone cheese is available far more widely throughout the region.

Obviously, those who live in an area with easy access to quality cheesesteaks are going to order whatever cheese they like, perhaps without even giving much thought to whether they are behaving authentically. And yet eating a cheesesteak is also a key part of the experience of visiting Philadelphia. From that perspective, it's worth stating, as clearly as possible, that American and provolone are, at the very least, just as authentic as Whiz. (Perhaps even more so, for the history lovers out there.) For those trying their first cheesesteak, then, feel free to give the alien oddity that is Cheez Whiz a try. But don't feel pressured; it's also totally fine to stick with the less processed, more natural provolone. (Just don't think that makes the sandwich healthy.)

# The Cooper Amplification

The most obviously associated cheeses with Philadelphia are probably Cheez Whiz and Philadelphia cream cheese, yet neither has any roots in the region. On the other hand, Cooper Sharp—a cheddar-influenced, processed American cheese—has a long history here. After founding the company in New York in 1893, former banker I.C. Cooper moved his operation to the Philly area in 1918, where it was exclusively available until around 1970. Though Cooper Sharp is now owned by Wisconsin cheesemaker Schreiber Foods, the original recipe is supposedly unchanged.

While similar to most deli-style American cheeses, Cooper's distinctive sharp flavor comes mainly from being aged for 100 to 180 days. *Bon Appétit* once described this unique taste as being "completely different from any [other] American cheese," featuring "the sharpness of a cheddar and a hint of salty Parmesan" with a texture that is "impossibly creamy."[194]

Although Cooper Sharp had surely been used as the house American cheese for countless Philadelphia delis and sandwich shops for decades, only recently has it come to be associated with cheesesteaks and, perhaps more importantly, marketed as the key ingredient in special ones. This resurgence can almost certainly be attributed to Angelo's Pizzeria, which opened on South 9th Street in 2019 and proceeded to sing the praises of Cooper Sharp as the ultimate cheesesteak cheese to its cult following. Others soon followed, and now, anyone who wants to make a splash in the cheesesteak world is offering a Cooper Sharp option.

"Nobody knew what Cooper Sharp was before I opened in Haddonfield," said Angelo's owner Danny DiGiampietro, referring to his shop's precursor located in the New Jersey suburbs from 2014 to 2019. "Nobody. I mean, in delis, of course. But nobody was putting it on cheesesteaks, I can promise you that."

"Before then, my wife and I would always ask for cheesesteaks with Cooper Sharp," he continued. "And people would have no idea what we were talking about. So, I always said, if we ever open a shop, we're going to do Cooper Sharp. It's the f—ing perfect cheese for cheesesteaks."[195]

On whether Schreiber Foods officially recognizes his efforts, DiGiampietro is skeptical. "I'm still working on getting my royalties," he quipped, "but I feel like it's gonna be a while before that first check comes."[196]

# THE STEAK GOSPEL BEGINS TO SPREAD

Considering the virtually endless competition among cheesesteak makers today, it's difficult to fathom that, for a brief period, Pat and Harry had the market to themselves. Early on, according to Wyman, a few stands cropped up nearby to target Pat's overflow traffic, but that was about it.[197] The first major development then—at least in terms of the popular names today—was the opening of what would become Jim's Steaks in 1939.

The most important thing to understand about Jim's history is that the flashy, unforgettable South Street institution of modern times—which suffered a major fire during the writing of this book but has since reopened—has only a tenuous connection to the original operation. Although, in fairness to the current owners, it does appear that they have remained faithful to the original recipe and technique.

In 1939, Millie Pearlingi (née Marie Carmella Morrone) began selling candy and soda out of a house she shared with her husband, Jim (Vincent James Pearlingi, sometimes written Perlingi) at 62nd and Noble Streets in West Philadelphia. Soon thereafter, Millie added sandwiches and started calling the place Millie's Steak Shop.[198] By the late '40s, the shop had become so successful that Jim retired from his day job as a roofer, and they changed the name to Jim's & Millie's Steaks & Hoagies. (It's unclear whether the name was more or less of a mouthful than the sandwiches.)

Jim's & Millie's developed a reputation for quality beef, sourcing it from Cross Brothers, a famous meatpacker of the day. (Incidentally, boxer Joe Frazier claimed to be the first cattle puncher at the meatpacking plant, and Cross Brothers was also where Sylvester Stallone punched sides of beef in *Rocky*.)

Upon their 1965 retirement, the Pearlingis sold the business to William "Bill" Proeto, who eventually simplified the name to Jim's Steaks and opened a second location in Upper Darby (which, like Pat's emporium, briefly flirted with being a full-fledged Italian restaurant).

Proetto became friends with Abner Silver, a Main Line lawyer who handled the Jim's real estate transaction in 1965. Silver, according to his son Ken, loved Philadelphia but didn't really care for being a lawyer and was looking for a career change. So, when Proetto approached him about partnering on the next Jim's location at 400 South Street, Abner jumped at the opportunity.

The new, soon-to-be-flagship Jim's opened in 1976 with "a sophisticated black and white rendering in the manner of art deco," including striking

Jim's & Millie's celebrates at the Cross Brothers Meats holiday party, circa the 1950s. On the left, cook Henry "Geech" Caratura with his wife, Ida. On the right, Jim and Millie Pearlingi with their son and daughter. *Hank Caratura.*

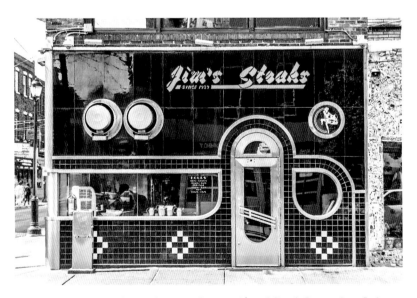

The famous Jim's Steaks art deco storefront at 4th and South Streets (pre-fire). *Flickr/Brandon Bartoszek.*

floor tiles, a stainless-steel ceiling and deco lighting fixtures that continue to wow tourists and local visitors alike.[199] On the style of design, which he would also install at 62nd Street and future Jim's locations, Proetto said, "I don't just *like* it. I'm an art deco *freak*."[200]

Though Jim's was ready for South Street, at first, South Street may not have been ready for Jim's. "It was just hippies and beatniks and Fabric Row down there then," said current owner Ken Silver.[201]

"South Street was literally at a crossroads in the 1970s," recalled Proetto, "as plans for a crosstown expressway had been scuttled shortly before and businesses catering to young people—such as J.C. Dobbs and the TLA—were moving in." The area, he added, "was very dangerous at the time."[202]

After a slow start, however, in 1977, *Philadelphia Magazine* surprised many by selecting relative newcomer Jim's as the "Best of Philly" cheesesteak. Business immediately took off, and Jim's was on its way to becoming the beloved institution it is today.[203]

Beyond Jim's, steak joints began to proliferate throughout the region during the post–World War II period. Though it would surely be impossible to list every decent steak maker, a few still-legendary institutions warrant a quick mention here.

While Camden, New Jersey's **DONKEY'S PLACE** was founded as a bar in 1943, it is unclear exactly when it started selling its trademark cheesesteaks, which—unlike those from South Philly—are seasoned heavily and served on poppy-seed kaiser rolls. (If that sounds strange, it's worth adding that a sandwich on a poppy-seed kaiser roll has no business tasting this good.)

"There was a Polish bakery that sold kaiser rolls right up the street," said the late Robert Lucas Sr. of his father's cheesesteak innovation, "and being Polish, he liked a lot of onions."[204] (It's said that if one eats Donkey's for lunch, they ought to hang out exclusively with other patrons for the rest of the day.)

Despite persistent rumors, the tavern's name does not derive from the type of meat it serves. It comes from founder Leon "Donkey" Lucas, a former boxer whose punch supposedly matched the kick of a mule. (How convenient.) According to his wife, Alice, Leon tried some other sandwiches at the bar—including a cold ham and a hot roast beef with mushroom gravy—before eventually settling on the now-signature steak.[205]

Donkey's achieved newfound acclaim when, in 2015, Anthony Bourdain visited and proclaimed to the nation that "the best cheesesteak in the area might well come…from New Jersey."[206] Being featured in a 2018 episode of ABC's sitcom *The Goldbergs* further raised its profile.

In 1949, **Chink's** opened in the Torresdale neighborhood of Northeast Philadelphia; Samuel "Chink" Sherman (who learned the trade at Pat's) indeed continued to use his childhood nickname, despite it being a slur. After years of controversy over the moniker, in 2013, current owner Joseph Groh—a longtime employee who purchased the place in 1999—changed it to **Joe's Steaks + Soda Shop**. (Sodas, milkshakes and egg creams were always an important part of the menu.) The original location closed in 2022—Groh cited pandemic-related market forces—but another location lives on in Fishtown at the high-traffic intersection of Girard and Frankford Avenues.

**Larry's Steaks** first opened in 1955 at 60th Street and Lancaster Avenue, though today, it operates at the St. Joseph's University–friendly location of 54th Street and City Line Avenue. It is best known for the "belly filler," one and a quarter pounds of ribeye on a three-foot-long roll, that it's served since 1959. (And maybe for inventing the cheesesteak; see previous.)

Other mainstays that debuted during this era include **Thunderbird Pizza** in Broomall (1956), **Mama's Pizza** in Bala Cynwyd (1958) and **Dalessandro's** in Roxborough (1960).

# The Ribeye Rivalry

It is of course impossible to discuss modern cheesesteak culture without mentioning Pat's nearby rival Geno's Steaks. Though located within spitting distance across the strange, triangular intersection of 9th Street and Passyunk Avenue, the two places are strikingly different upon first view. In contrast to Pat's blue-collar, spartan design, Geno's neon palace "rises up tall from the surrounding squat, dull row houses like Vegas in the desert."[207] That said, the steaks themselves are relatively similar, simple versions churned out for customers who are probably there just as much for the scene as for the sandwich.

"If it wasn't for the rivalry between Pat's and Geno's, the world would not know that the cheesesteak even existed," said the owner of another popular steak shop. "They led the way for all of these new cheesesteak places to do what they do."[208]

Although the two shops are today inexorably linked, seemingly since the beginning of time, locked in a McDonald's/Burger King–style battle of proximity and foot traffic, Geno's first opened quite a bit after Pat's, in 1966. But its story starts well before then.

In the early 1940s, James Vento opened Jimmy's Steaks—no relation to Jim's—just across the street from Pat's, and after dropping out of the ninth grade in the early '50s, his son Joey came to work at the stand. But the two disagreed on how to run the business; "I would tell him how to beat the guy across the street," Joey recalled, refusing to speak Pat's name.[209] But James didn't agree, so in 1957, Joey packed up and joined the army.

Meanwhile, crime was leaving its mark on the Vento family. In 1960, James was convicted of first-degree murder for inducing another man, Rudolpho Dominguez, to kill numbers writer Frank Agnella. (The victim had apparently accepted but failed to carry out a contract from James to kill a third man, Joseph Petruzzi, who had reported Jimmy's Steaks to the health department for selling horse meat.) After James went to jail, Joey received a hardship discharge and came home to run the shop.

From the ordering window of Jimmy's and, later, a nearby shop where he worked after Jimmy's failed (Joe's, no relation), Joey could see the building where Geno's would eventually reside. When the stores in that building closed, Joey procured a $2,000 loan from his father-in-law (who was, of course, a bookie), and—the story goes—with two boxes of steak, some hot dogs and a cardboard Pepsi sign, founded Geno's. Since there was

Geno's at dusk, circa 2007. *Wikimedia Commons/Bobak Ha'Eri.*

already a Joe's, Vento used the name he found painted on the door of his new space: Gino's. (He eventually changed the spelling to avoid confusion with Gino's Hamburgers, a popular local fast-food chain at the time.) This time around, without his father's legacy hanging over his head, Joey Vento's steak shop blossomed. "My family history wasn't that great," he said in an uncharacteristic understatement. (Aside from James, Joey's brother Stephen and nephew Stephen Jr. both amassed long rap sheets.) "But I reversed it. I brought the respect back."[210]

Beyond the steaks themselves, Joey Vento—who died in 2011—is perhaps most remembered for his controversial "This is America: Speak English" signage that went up in 2005 at the Geno's ordering window amid a nationwide debate about immigration policy. But dissecting Vento's personality is far more complicated than that. There's the family crime for one, while Vento himself was a law-abider who regularly supported the police and their charities. His time as an evangelist for many conservative causes began with the aforementioned sign in 2005, yet that same year, he donated $100,000 to an AIDS awareness concert put on by the publisher of the *Philadelphia Gay News*. "Like most stories," wrote the *Inquirer* in 2006, "Joe Vento's is one of contradictions."[211]

The grill man makes a steak at Geno's, 2011. *Flickr/Shinya Suzuki.*

As for the rivalry with Pat's, Vento is probably more responsible for stoking its flames, which makes sense considering he was the upstart. "That guy across the street," Vento said in 2008, veering into his standard schtick. "He claims he invented the steak sandwich. I'll give him that. He claims he invented the Whiz. Okay. I'll give him that. All I did was come along and perfect it."[212]

"It really was [a rivalry] at the very beginning, when my dad and Joe Vento were running the businesses," said Frank Olivieri Jr. "But it turned out to be the best thing, because people will go across the street to check out their stuff and then come back to check out our stuff. And the media was the whole brainchild behind that, without knowing that they actually did it. 'Pat's and Geno's, blah blah blah, you have to try one, you have to try the other.'…It's perfect for business.…The competition really keeps us going."[213]

When asked what he would do if Geno's—which Joey's son Geno, who was named after the shop, now runs—ever closed, Olivieri admitted it would create a major void. "I'd buy the place and open it up again," he said. "And call it Geno's. And fight with myself."[214]

# I Like the Cut of Your Steak

In today's cheesesteak marketplace, ribeye is typically considered the cut of choice, the highest quality and most loved option, noted for its fat and flavor. In fact, all the places mentioned in this chapter thus far—apart from Jim's—reportedly use ribeye. That said, a wide variety of cuts, including top round, sirloin and loin tail, can produce a delicious steak sandwich. (And Pat Olivieri likely made his original from undefined meat trimmings.)

An outlier in the realm of iconic steak joints, Jim's cooks exclusively with top round. "The nice thing is that it doesn't have any sinew, so there's no fat grain going through it," said Ken Silver of Jim's preferred cut, which it has apparently used from the beginning. "You don't bite into it and get that stringy gristle or anything like that in the top round. It's solid beef. And when it's well marbleized, we don't have to add a whole lot of oil to the grill to give it flavor. It's got its own flavor because the fat is in the muscle itself."[215]

At John's Roast Pork, owner John Bucci is one of the iconoclasts who prefers a third cut, loin tail. "It has a richer flavor, and it chops better," he said. This choice does come at a literal price, with the JRP steak often costing slightly more than other nearby ribeye peddlers. "We put a ton of meat and we use a better cut," added Bucci with an implied shrug.[216]

Aside from choosing the cut, an aspiring cheesesteak maker must also decide whether to serve their beef in the chopped or slab style. In the former—which is far more popular nowadays—the steak is broken apart into small pieces on the grill and then can be mixed with onions and cheese. This is the most likely style to be found in pizza shops, food trucks and the like throughout the region, but many famous spots—most notably Jim's—are also choppers. Highly regarded Dalessandro's, where the ribeye is minced so finely it resembles ground beef, is another interesting adherent to this method.

The slab style, on the other hand—in which thin slices of meat are cooked flat on the grill and mostly retain their shape—remains truer to Pat's original and most early imitations. (Though more difficult to find, shops that still serve the slabs include Pat's, Geno's, Donkey's, Steve's Prince of Steaks, Joe's and Philip's.) "Back in the day," said Nick Miglino, the current coproprietor of sandwich shop Dolores' 2Street and another slab devotee, "there were no steak shops in South Philadelphia that chopped their steaks. It was unheard of!"[217]

Miglino believes that a big difference between then and now is the phasing out of USDA prime beef, the best available grade after the meat is assessed for both maturity and fat marbling. Unfortunately, in recent years, skyrocketing prices for prime cuts have led shop owners to look elsewhere. "There's fat there, but it's just not enough," Miglino said of today's cuts. "It's full of gristle, and doesn't melt nicely on the grill....A lot of it is imported

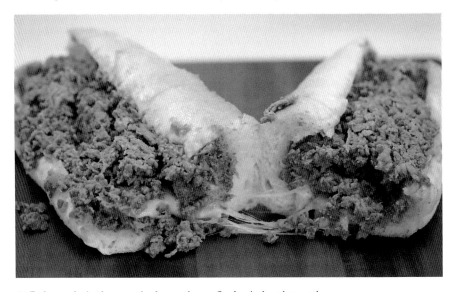

At Dalessandro's, the meat is chopped very finely. *Author photograph.*

The ribeye at Pat's is cooked in slabs that fold in the bun but are not chopped. *Pat's King of Steaks.*

from Australia and isn't even graded....So, if they didn't chop it so much, it would probably be inedible."[218]

Another reason the chopped style has taken over so thoroughly is that many lesser places (e.g., pizza shops and delis that don't specialize in steaks) now use formed meat products, in which smaller pieces of meat are conglomerated—sometimes with added marinades—into thin slices of steak primed and ready for the flat-top grill, where they'll surely be slashed beyond recognition. This obviously leads to a lower-quality product, though it's not as bad as the truly horrifying emulsified pink goo options that also exist (e.g., Steak-umm).

It can be, unfortunately, difficult to know which meat is being used in any given shop without further inquiry. As Wyman suggested, however, "the price and cooking presentation can offer clues. If the cook is chopping the meat like crazy and the shop is charging $4.50 a sandwich, it's a safe bet the place is not using [high-end steak restaurant] The Palm's meat purveyor."[219]

## BEYOND BEEF

The basic cheesesteak is simply beef, cheese and onions. That's it. But over time, a variety of additions and variations have been introduced or created.

A mushroom pepper cheesesteak from Pat's. *Pat's King of Steaks.*

In true Philly style—and depending on who is asked—some are considered permissible, while others are abominations.

Although it is unclear exactly when and where a steak-maker first used them, **BELL PEPPERS** and **MUSHROOMS** have been accepted as *optional* inclusions for decades. Interestingly, however, adding these by default is one of the most common mistakes one sees when restaurants outside this region try to serve so-called Philly cheesesteaks. This is, perhaps, the fastest way for a place to out itself as inauthentic. If a customer requests peppers or mushrooms, by all means add them. Otherwise, they don't belong.

There is also the oddity known as the **CHEESESTEAK HOAGIE**, which includes cold lettuce and tomato on top of hot beef, cheese and onion. Maybe this is the great unification of two iconic sandwiches—or maybe it belongs in the dustbin of history with the McDLT. And yet enough places include this menu variation that it must have at least a minor following.

Speaking of tomatoes, the original **PIZZA STEAK** came with pan-fried plum medallions topped with oregano, not the slathering of sauce so common today. Likely the invention of Anthony Milano Sr. at Milano's Luncheonette (11th and Morris Streets) in the 1950s, this throwback style is still available at a

## THE TONY LUKE METHOD

When Tony Luke's opened at Front Street and Oregon Avenue in 1992 (see chapter 4), it employed a different method for cooking steaks that helped differentiate it in the early days of the now-legendary restaurant. "We never used high heat," said Tony Luke Jr.

*You want crusty and brown on a thick steak, but not on the thin steak we use for cheesesteaks, because it gets cardboardy and dry. When cooked at a lower temperature, it takes longer to cook, but all the juices from the steak stay in, and they tenderize the steak as well.*

*And we never ever, ever, ever put salt on the meat until the steak is done. When you add salt to a raw piece of meat, it draws the moisture out and it dries up the steak. This of course helps with a thick steak, because it draws the moisture out and helps create the crust that everyone likes. But don't do that with thin steak, because you don't want it to crust or dry out.*

*Of course, this meant people had to wait five or six minutes. And a lot of people told me, "You gotta turn that grill up high, cook that steak in thirty seconds and get it out the door." I get it, but we were worried more about quality and flavor than time, because I believe that when something is good, people don't mind waiting.*

*Most people throw the cheese on top of the steak on the grill and then either put a lid on it or wait until the cheese melts. But by the time that cheese melts, the steak is overdone. And then, once they scoop it up and put it in the roll, there's just cheese on one side and steak on another. Well, at Tony Luke's we flip it so the cheese is directly on the grill and the meat is sitting on top, which creates a barrier between the grill and the meat so that the steak doesn't overcook. But more importantly, all the juice from the steak will drive itself into the cheese. So now the flavor of the steak is incorporated into the meat, the cheese and the bread. It makes a huge difference.*[*]

---

[*] Luke Jr., phone call.

*Above*: Dolores' 2Street's take on the steak Milano. *Author photograph.*

*Left*: An advertisement featuring pizza steaks from 1962. *Newspapers.com.*

SEASON'S GREETINGS
TO ALL OUR
FRIENDS & PATRONS

SONNY'S
STEAK-A-ROMA

★ PIZZA STEAK and
MUSHROOM STEAK
★ STEAKS COOKED WITH
WINE GRAVY

CURB — BOOTH SERVICE
S.W. Corner 11th & Tasker Sts.

few spots, including John's Roast Pork and Geno's, and is often called a STEAK MILANO, an OLD-FASHIONED PIZZA STEAK or similar.[220]

Of particular note is Dolores' version, which LaBan called "a subtle beauty by brash steak standards" that's "pure harmony…the tomatoes adding to its juicy savor."[221] According to Dolores' Miglino—who has fond personal memories of Milano's and thus strives to recreate their sandwich with painstaking accuracy—Milano also used a specific cheese that perfectly enhanced the sandwich's flavor and texture. "He had his friend [at a nearby cheese shop] make a certain type of provolone," Miglino recalled. "It wasn't so mild or sharp, it was somewhere in between. But it was soft." This allowed the cheese to feature ample sharp notes yet also melt nicely, something extra-sharp provolone often struggles to do. "Cheese like that isn't really around anymore," continued Miglino, though he attempts to emulate this bygone specialty by mixing shredded sharp and melty mild provolone together.[222]

All that said, today, the term *pizza steak* typically indicates a cheesesteak with tomato sauce and provolone. While it is unclear who was the first to make this version, it seems safe to say Dalessandro's helped establish the city's taste for saucy steaks. When Philomena D'Alessandro (the mother of founder William) died in 2001 at the age of ninety-seven, the *Inquirer*'s obituary celebrated her contributions in this area. "Mrs. D'Alessandro was best known for her cooking, especially peppers, whose smell made neighborhood nostrils flare and stomachs rumble, and a tomato sauce used on steak sandwiches that became the shop's signature."[223]

Though in Philadelphia a standard steak never comes with pizza sauce, in the Lehigh Valley (about an hour north of the city), many places add the region's unique version of tomato sauce by default, unless the customer requests to omit it.

# BEYOND BALBOA

Even as many Philadelphians will claim blasphemy at the smallest change to their beloved cheesesteak, today there are quite a few interesting alternatives. More recently, a global flair appears to be both prevalent and (gasp!) appreciated.

One of the first alt-steak pioneers was a colorful character of The Strip, an area along 52nd Street that made a name for itself as "home to the liveliest jazz scene, the most iconic 1950s-era urban shopping, and eventually Philly's best soul food."[224] It was here—on Locust Street, between 51st and 52nd Streets—that James "Foo Foo" Ragan set up his steak house, which would become a fashionable stop after a day or night out on The Strip.

Aside from being "a well-known numbers writer," Ragan was known for being injured in a notorious shootout in 1970; having connections to the local Black mafia; and going down for conspiring to sell heroin in 1979.[225] Before that, however, he created the **Mammer Jammer**, a cheesesteak topped with a ground beef sauce laced with hot peppers. (Which was probably at least somewhat like the Greek sauce of Texas wiener fame, if potentially spicier.)

FOO FOO RAGAN'S
STEAK HOUSE
242 S. 52d Street
(Cor. 52nd & Locust Sts.)
"THE MAMMER JAMMER IS
OUR SPECIALTY"
STEAKS-HOAGIES-HAMBURGERS
GR 2-9611

An advertisement for Foo Foo's from 1964. *Newspapers.com.*

So popular was Ragan's sandwich that Sammy Davis Jr. would reportedly send out for one every time he came to town for a show.[226] Hoagie writer Robboy shared another amusing anecdote. "I started grad school at Emory in Atlanta in '67," he recalled. "One day I was down on Auburn Avenue—it was a poor Black section of Atlanta, right near the center of town—just driving along, when there it was, on the right-hand side of 13th Street: Mammer Jammers! So I parked the car, walked in there and said, 'I'm from Philadelphia and I want a Mammer Jammer.'"

"You know Foo Foo?" The guy exclaimed. "You know Foo Foo!"[227]

In more recent years, St. Louis restaurant Mammer Jammer—named for its specialty of the house—carried on this tradition, but it closed in 2012. It is unknown if anyone is still making these sandwiches in the Delaware Valley.

In modern Philadelphia, an emerging trend integrates both regional U.S. and global flavors into the classic cheesesteak. This is a particularly heartening development, showing that creativity and cheesesteaks are not mutually exclusive and that, as palates change over time, the Philly icon can do the same. A few examples include:

- The **Train Wreck** from Beck's Cajun Cafe, which brings New Orleans influence by combining steak, andouille sausage, salami, American cheese, caramelized onions and Creole mayo, then serving it on a crispy French baguette.
- The **brisket cheesesteak** at Mike's BBQ, which tries to out-Texas the wiener by topping smoked brisket with Cooper Sharp whiz and onions.

*Right*: Tabachoy's Bistek Chistek. *Tabachoy.*

*Below*: A double Schmitter, served on a long roll. *Unbreaded.*

- Tabachoy's **BISTEK CHISTEK**, a Filipino-inspired sandwich made with soy and citrus–marinated, thin-sliced flank steak, white American and grilled onions, then topped with atchara (pickled unripe papaya) and green onions.
- The **ETHIOPIAN CHEESESTEAK** at Gojjo, which kicks things up a notch by adding the classic berbere spice mix.
- **INDIAN-STYLE STEAKS** from Little Sicily II and mini-chain Al Sham, which incorporate masala spices and chili peppers of various heat levels. (Al Sham also serves **LAMB CHEESESTEAKS**.)

# THE SCHMITTER

There's some debate among Philly sandwich enthusiasts about whether the Schmitter, created at McNally's Tavern in Chestnut Hill, qualifies as a cheesesteak. On one hand, it features thinly sliced beef, onions and cheese, all fried on a flat-top. On the other, it also contains salami and "Schmitter sauce" and comes on a kaiser roll. (For the record, the *Inquirer* included this sandwich in a 2022 article titled "The Best Cheesesteaks to Eat in Philly Right Now," calling it a "cheesesteak variation.")[228]

The tavern's story starts back in 1921, when Rose McNally opened a stand—McNally's Quick Lunch—in Chestnut Hill, across from the end of the trolley line (where her husband worked as a driver). In this posh neighborhood, word quickly spread among the working class about the quality food Rose was offering. Six years later, the McNallys purchased a newly constructed building across the street, and the place has been there ever since, today run by Rose's granddaughters Anne and Meg.

The Schmitter came along in the 1960s, invented by Hugh James McNally, the son of Rose and Hugh Patrick. There was apparently a regular customer at the time, Dennis Krenich, who worked at the nearby hospital and would often come in after his late shift for some beer and a bite to eat. One night, said Meg, Krenich told Hugh he was in the mood for something different and asked for a cheesesteak with some marinara sauce. (Aha! It *is* a cheesesteak!) "We're not Italian, so we don't have red sauce, but I'll make something up," Hugh replied, according to Meg. He put together a mayonnaise-based sauce—similar to Thousand Island dressing—added some tomatoes and, in another twist, fried salami, then served Krenich his sandwich.[229]

The following night, the legend goes, Krenich was back, asking for the same sandwich. After this occurred a few more times, the McNallys figured they ought to give the sandwich a name. Since Krenich drank only the local beer Schmidt's—and presumably because his last name wasn't all that appealing as a food moniker—they dubbed the sandwich the Schmitter. (It's unclear what happened to the D.)

To construct this now-classic sandwich, McNally's starts with thinly sliced bottom round, adding it to the grill on top of a pile of onions. "We take a fresh cut of beef that we [slice] here every day," said Anne. "It's a very high-end, quality beef…[the same cut] that we use on our roast beef sandwiches." Once the onions cook down, the mixture is flipped and then topped with a thick slice of tomato, some American cheese and, lastly, two pieces of cooked, soft salami. After another flip, the salami is seared until it "gets burned just a little bit," adding another layer of flavor complexity. Finally, everything is crammed into a Conshohocken Baking Co. kaiser roll and covered with a hearty dollop of sauce.[230] (A double Schmitter comes on a long roll, more like a traditional cheesesteak.)

It's "crispy, crunchy…meaty, rich and gooey," said Duff Goldman, lovingly, on the Food Network show *The Best Thing I Ever Ate*. "It's got a lot of sweetness going on from the onions, which are nice and caramelized, and also from the Schmitter sauce."[231]

Though McNally's remains a tiny pub in Chestnut Hill known for its lack of obvious signage, stints at the Philly ballparks have increased the Schmitter's stature in the city. While currently available at Eagles' home games at the Linc, the sandwich first became associated with the Phillies, sold from the opening of Citizens Bank Park in 2004 through 2016. But "the sandwich got its name," quipped Anne, "long before Mike Schmidt and long before we started selling [them] at the ballpark."[232]

# CHICKEN HAS JOINED THE CHAT

The most popular alternative meat used in steak sandwiches is, unsurprisingly, chicken. Some cheesesteak purists, of course, disregard the chicken version as illegitimate; "real Americans don't eat chicken, they're beef eaters," claimed Frank Olivieri Jr., for example, when asked about the rise of chicken steaks in 1994.[233] And yet even the most ardent beef backer can't deny how widespread poultry has become in the cheesesteak scene. Apart from a few diehard traditional spots, most steak joints—even longtime holdout Pat's, which added it in 2024—now serve a chicken version.

Unlike the regular steak, origins of the chicken cheesesteak are disputed, with three separate places—two of which have permanently closed—making a claim.

At the corner of 3rd and South Streets, a large sign above the now-defunct Simon's Steaks once declared the shop "Originator and Pioneer of the Chicken Cheesesteak." As the story goes, the first Simon's opened in 1978 in Germantown, and according to owner Ben Goff—nicknamed Simon—they sold chicken steaks from the start. "A lot of people at that time stopped eating red meat," said Goff. "[Chicken steaks] were one of my main features. That's what I was known for."[234] (Simon's expanded to Broad Street and Fairmount Avenue in 1988, then 3rd and South Streets in 1991.) The style of Simon's chicken steaks, however, was different from what is typical today. They fried a boneless breast whole, then cut it into smaller pieces on the grill once ordered, resulting in a chunkier final product.

At Ishkabibble's—which opened in 1979, ironically less than a block from Simon's eventual South Street location—they also use the chunky style. The now-iconic eatery, with its hot pink, black and yellow branding, proclaims "the original chicken cheesesteak" on its menu, but there's no one left to dispute this statement. And the similarity to Simon's style is certainly fascinating, considering their past proximity.

More commonly, chicken steaks are made from thinly sliced meat that's chopped finely on the grill until it resembles a chopped beef cheesesteak. This method traces back to the also defunct Billybob, which resided at 40th and Spruce Streets near the University of Pennsylvania campus and also once had a sign naming themselves "Home of the 'Original' Chicken Steak."

Billy Schoepe, who owned the place with his brother Bob, said he came up with the idea while traveling in Florida after seeing chicken-fried steak on a local menu. Not realizing this was a popular southern dish in which steak is prepared like fried chicken, Schoepe thought he was ordering a new twist on his beloved steak sandwich.[235]

Though this was obviously not the case, the idea stuck with Schoepe, and he brought it back to his restaurant, working with then-employee Bill Schultz to perfect this new creation. After some trial and error, they came up with a method of stacking skinless, boneless chicken breasts in stainless steel pans, freezing them into blocks and then slicing them thinly with a meat slicer.

"The chicken took off immediately," said Schoepe of its introduction in the early 1980s. "The first week we did 30 pounds. The next week 60, then

80, 90, 150, 250. We had to bring in people just to do chicken."[236] Within three months, Billybob's chicken steaks were more popular than their beef steaks. "It was a monster," Schultz recalled.[237]

While Simon's was likely the first and Billybob the creator of the more prevalent style of chicken steak, credit—or blame, depending on one's perspective—for propagation should belong to Ed Cohen, a former food supplier to Billybob. Perplexed at the restaurant's increasing chicken orders, Cohen asked Schultz, "What the hell are you doing with all this chicken breast?"[238]

After Schultz showed Cohen the process, the latter "was amazed," recalled Schultz. [239] He was so amazed that, a few years later (in 1988), Cohen founded his own company, Red and White Steak Co., with the express goal of spreading the chicken steak gospel through wholesale customers. At first, however, it was a difficult sell. "I was scoffed at, ridiculed, and laughed at," said Cohen. "I can't tell you how many people threw me out. It didn't fit the Philly macho image."[240]

"But after everyone tasted it," Cohen continued, "they thought it was great."[241] He eventually partnered with Alvin Shipon to create Shipon's Chicken Sandwich Steaks, a product targeted to area supermarkets. Meanwhile, other steak shop wholesalers jumped on the bandwagon, and chicken steaks eventually became a regional staple.

## Swimming Upstream

Perhaps the most fascinating alternative cheesesteak invention is that of the salmon cheesesteak. Yes, it's a real thing, and believe it or not, has become quite popular outside the mainstream. This oddity won't be found in South Philly or even Center City, wrote Matthew Korfhage in the *Courier-Post*, but "in North and West and Southwest Philadelphia, in the western suburbs and the urban centers of South Jersey, the salmon cheesesteak thrives."[242]

"The sandwich is a paradox," continued Korfhage, "so popular it inspires pilgrimage and half-hour waits on the sidewalk, yet largely unchronicled by food media and unknown to half its home city."[243]

Though they are certainly less prevalent than beef or chicken steaks, the salmon steak has occasionally found its way into the limelight. When Jimmy Fallon and the Roots' Tariq visited a Philadelphia family as part of the *Tonight Show*'s "Surprise Dinner Party" series in 2018, for example, they ate salmon cheesesteaks. In addition, rappers Meek Mill and Wale have both promoted the sandwich online. When the latter tweeted about it in 2019, local writer Jason Peters spoke for many area residents when he replied, "I live in Philadelphia. If anyone order[s] a salmon cheesesteak, they are getting roasted immediately. No hesitation."[244] Beyond that, however, the replies generally contained more love than skepticism.

The spot most aficionados give credit for starting this perplexing trend is Bella's Restaurant and Grill in North Philly. According to Bella's owner Albert Alwyn, a local barber named Marvin used to come by the shop regularly, but he didn't eat red meat. He was "a gregarious type guy, liked to try different things," described Alwyn.[245] One day around 2010, Marv asked Alwyn's late sister Tracy (Bella's chef at the time) to make a cheesesteak he could eat.

"If you wanted something special," Albert said, "she would make it for you." Tracy proceeded to put some salmon and broccoli on the shop's well-seasoned flat-top, and the Philadelphia cheesesteak scene would never be the same. "It just took off," Albert said. "All of a sudden everybody was serving them."[246] Bella's had to lengthen its hours to accommodate demand and would eventually count among its new fans hip-hop artists Meek Mill, Nicki Minaj, Doug E. Fresh and Charlie Mack.

The earliest mentions, in August 2009, of salmon cheesesteaks on social media, however, both referenced a different spot: North Philly's now-closed Cheesesteak Factory. (Love for Bella's, on the other hand, didn't reach social media until mid-2010.) In addition, chef Hannah Ahzai of Ummi Dee's—another place known for its salmon steaks—believes she had one in Southwest Philadelphia even earlier at the now-defunct Samiches Deli (whose 2011 menu, found online, lists several salmon dishes but no cheesesteaks).[247]

"People get really sensitive about who's the originator," said Jeff Lek, also known as YouTuber JL Jupiter, who has become an evangelist for the salmon steak through his popular videos. Lek is not convinced, however, that any professional chef was responsible. "It's something that we've enjoyed within the hood for a while," he continued. "Whoever first got the idea to put it in their restaurant, there's a good chance that it's been kicking around at cookouts and elsewhere for longer. Meaning whoever claims it can't even claim it."[248]

A scofflaw by its very nature, the main rule of salmon cheesesteaks seems to be that there are no rules. Though, in many ways, they're made similarly to regular cheesesteaks—meat chopped on the grill (sometimes finely, other times kept in larger chunks), topped with cheese (typically

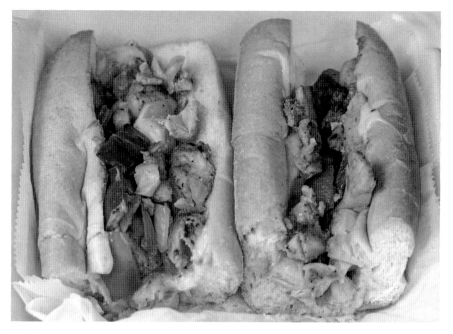

Marv's salmon cheesesteak with stir-fried vegetables from Bella's. For a recipe, see appendix. *Author photograph.*

American), then inverted onto a hoagie roll—a variety of other additions quickly expand the possible flavors of this sandwich. Heavier seasoning, first of all, is a must, with Old Bay or similarly flavored spice rubs liberally added. (At Harvinskins in Camden, New Jersey, they call their house spice mix "Crack."[249]) Onions, peppers and mushrooms are common, of course, but broccoli, spinach and cherry tomatoes are also regular mix-ins. And then there are the sauces; at Cafe II, also in Camden, they blend béchamel with tomato and seasonings to create a creamy condiment, while Lee's Deli in West Philly offers a sweet chili sauce. Others experiment with similar ideas, including, believe it or not, mayo. (Remember the main rule of salmon cheesesteaks.) Lastly, for added decadence, a popular trend is to top the entire sandwich with fried or grilled jumbo shrimp.

There's no doubt that some readers are questioning whether this salmon sandwich is technically a *cheesesteak*. At what point, in other words, does this become something distinct that belongs in its own category? On the other hand, if cheesesteaks can be made from chicken or lamb, why can't they be made from salmon? The technique is similar enough, as is the final presentation.

Either way, don't expect Pat's or Geno's to start serving salmon cheesesteaks anytime soon. (For one, fish and cheese in the same dish breaks Italian culinary law.) Beyond the soul food kitchens already mentioned, however, the sandwich is also growing in popularity at halal eateries, likely because Islamic guidelines are less complicated regarding fish than they are with land animals.

Perhaps the last word on salmon cheesesteaks should come from chef Kurt Evans, who made them for several years at Route 23 Cafe. "A lot of it," said Evans, referring to ignorance of or opposition to this version of the Philly icon, "is just people not being aware of the whole landscape of the city they live in."[250]

# 4

# ROAST PORK

After all that investigation into the cheesesteak, it's time to declare that the Philadelphia roast pork sandwich is, undoubtedly, the best hot sandwich style in the city. Yep, much better than the cheesesteak. Not to mention older than the cheesesteak, more complex than the cheesesteak and far more digestible than the cheesesteak. If these are controversial statements, that does not make them any less true. (Blame marketing.)

This isn't just one author's opinion. "The roast pork Italian with aged provolone and broccoli rabe is one of the finest treats the culinary world has to offer," wrote the *Inquirer*'s Karen Heller. "This is what Philadelphia should be famous for."[251]

"This is a cheesesteak town, or so you would think if you had not had the considerably greater pleasure of roast pork with [greens] at John's Roast Pork," added Rick Nichols.[252]

In an article about how the cheesesteak *isn't* the city's best sandwich, the *Washington Post*'s Tim Warren wrote of the roast pork, "It's filling and tasty, like a cheesesteak, but the subtle interplay between the pork and the tart greens, between the provolone and the spices in the juices, is heaven compared with the sledgehammer-like cheesesteak. (Sharp provolone versus Cheez Whiz? Please.) And you don't go away feeling you've ingested a grease bomb."[253]

National headlines have included: "The Roast Pork Sandwich That's Better Than Any Cheesesteak" (Eater), "Roast Pork Is Philadelphia's Real

Signature Sandwich" (Insider Food), "The Best Sandwich in Philly Is Roast Pork" (Tasting Table). This list could go on.

"When people think of Philadelphia, they think cheesesteaks," said Tony Luke Jr., one of the city's most well-known sandwich ambassadors. "But locals, they think [pork]."

"It's more comfort food than anything else," he continued. "It was a very big part of my growing up. Holidays. Christmas banquets. Birthdays. Confirmations. Baptisms. Roast pork was always there."[254]

"We would have christenings or holy communions and events like that," added John Bucci. "We wouldn't serve steaks; we'd serve roast pork sandwiches. That was the celebratory staple."[255]

These traditions, logically, came over from Italy, evolving from the *porchetta*—or, in Philly slang, "porkett"—of central regions Lazio, Abruzzo, Tuscany and Umbria. Though Italians still enjoy a spirited debate over where exactly this famous dish originated, it seems likely that the Philly version is mostly Abruzzese, as such a large portion of the area's immigrants hailed from the region formerly known as Abruzzi (today, Abruzzo and Molise).

"And midnight came, when a 'porchetta' made its appearance on the table," read the description of a 1921 New Year's Eve celebration in the local Italian-language paper *La Libera Parola*, "a custom from Abruzzi, because most of the newly arrived colleagues with whom we greeted the new year were from Abruzzi."[256] (As just one example.)

Anyone who has had the good fortune to experience Italian porchetta in all its glory will know that it is made from a whole pig, deboned but cooked with its skin, which becomes crackly, juicy and wonderful. In the Philadelphia area today, it is more common to find skinned picnic hams, sliced and served in a rich gravy, though the seasonings—garlic and herbs like rosemary, sage and fennel—are similar.

# The Shack

The oldest and most venerable Philadelphia brand of pig-based sandwich meat is undoubtedly John's Roast Pork, located on Snyder Avenue in South Philly since about 1930. Of the now-iconic sandwich at this now-iconic sandwich joint, Craig LaBan, who played a key role in putting the place on the food map in more recent times, had this to say about his first experience:

*As the juices dripped down my chin, I suddenly knew how a pork sandwich could become a legacy. Flavor filled my mouth like a cascade. The layers of finely shaved meat snapped between my teeth with tenderness, springy and lean, unlocking from beneath each layer the nuances of rosemary and bay. Intoxicating juices swirled like a whirlpool with each bite, washing across the farthest-flung taste buds with the essence of garlic and something more. Something more elusive. A hovering shade of clove was flowing through this river on a bun.* [257]

Despite this historic and flavorful pedigree, however, John's was, until relatively recently, a "hidden treasure," a tiny spot known only by those familiar with the deepest reaches of South Philly. [258]

In or around 1918, John's progenitor Domenico Bucci immigrated to Philadelphia from Abruzzi. "He came here," said the shop's current owner, John Jr., of his grandfather, "and what he knew how to do was cook. So, he became one of the first caterers in Philadelphia. It wasn't catering like what we think of now, just christenings and neighborhood events, serving roast pork, roast beef, meatballs." [259]

Although the business operated primarily out of his South Philly home, the elder Bucci would also occasionally park a bus at Delaware Avenue and Reed Street, where he could hawk sandwiches to stevedores, truck drivers and other workers at the busy port. [260]

Around 1930, according to John Jr., Domenico decided it would be better to sell his sandwiches out of a permanent location. He found a small triangle of land near the train tracks, at a busy junction where trains and trucks often passed by. After renting this spot from B&O Railroad, he constructed a "tiny wooden shanty that fit no more than two or three people," which locals would lovingly call the "Pork Shack." [261]

"It was just roast pork and meatballs," said John Jr., "and then he had an old-school Italian combo, which was roast pork with a meatball on top.… When someone asks for that today, I know they're either an old-timer or have a connection to one because it's not even on the menu." [262]

"There was no running water," he continued. "It barely had an address! It's not like today with all the health department stuff—it would have failed every friggin' code that exists." [263]

When Domenico and his wife both passed away in 1967, their youngest child, John Sr., with his wife, Vonda—after withstanding a brief court battle from his older siblings—took over the business. The Buccis brought in Vonda's brother-in-law (and carpenter) Ferruccio "Ferry" Ciccotelli to

John's Roast Pork's namesake sandwich. *Author photograph.*

redo the property, upgrading from the tiny wooden shack to a slightly larger cinderblock shack. "It was a disaster," said John Jr., "with paneling on the walls…but we were still known for having great sandwiches."

"They started selling cheesesteaks and hoagies," he continued. "All different sandwiches really, because regulars would come every day for lunch.…We became known a little bit around the Eastern Seaboard, just because of truck drivers. But 99.9 percent of our clientele was blue-collar men. Stevedores, dock workers, truck drivers, police and firefighters."[264]

In the 1980s, as the Goldenberg Group planned to build the strip mall that would become Snyder Plaza across the street, the developers approached the Buccis about moving into new digs. Though business was steady, the Snyder Avenue Lunch Bar (as John Sr. and Vonda had named it when they took over) was still just a little neighborhood joint, so an increased rent and 18 percent profit sharing did not appeal. They declined.

Shortly thereafter, John Sr. was diagnosed with terminal lung cancer. John Jr. was in his third year at St. Joseph's University, working on a degree in sports psychology, when his mother made him an offer: leave school, come to the shop full time and we'll get a loan to fix the place up. Otherwise, she said, they'd sell the business. "You gotta remember the context at that time; we were still just a neighborhood place," John Jr. recalled. "But I had always worked at the shop and…it came second nature to me, to make sandwiches."[265]

"I went to my counselor at school; I wish I remembered his name because he changed my life," John Jr. continued. "And he asked, 'Well, is your family's business established?' I told him it wasn't Pat's or Geno's or anything, but it had been there since 1930. His advice was to go for it, because I could always come back to school and finish later. When I started working at the shop, I realized, hey, I'm really good at this."[266]

They still, however, didn't own the land where the shack resided. "For years and years, we rented [from B&O, which became CSX] month to month. We had a thirty-day lease for nearly fifty years, so at any time, they could have told us to get off their property!" John Jr. said. He made it a priority to change that before they invested more deeply in the business. "I would call literally every day and try to get in touch with somebody," he recalled. "I'd always get the runaround. And then one day, I got through to a guy named Jim Weetencamp. I'll never forget his name."[267] Bucci was perplexed as to why a company that was dealing in multimillion-dollar real estate transitions—in the '80s—was playing hard to get, but eventually, he felt like he got a good deal on the land. They closed for three months, gutted the building and remodeled it completely.

Success was not immediate. "They were building the mall across the street around the same time," John Jr. said, "so all the laborers would come here, and we started to slowly make a name for ourselves. But it really took a good thirteen, fourteen years for us to get noticed."[268]

The true turning point for John's Roast Pork, ironically, came because of their cheesesteak. "My dad made the worst cheesesteak," John Jr. said. "When I came to the shop, I told him, 'I can't make this cheesesteak. It's terrible.'" The younger Bucci had worked briefly—much to his father's chagrin—at Larry's Steaks near St. Joseph's while attending school there and used that experience to inspire something new. "I put a spin on Larry's steak. Not exactly, but I took some of his ideas, mixed them with my own and came up with my cheesesteak. It was twelve ounces of meat and six slices of American cheese. I fried the onions with it, not on top but folded into the meat."[269]

One fateful day in 2002, the Buccis spotted four kids carefully plating and measuring their sandwiches at tables outside the shop. Striking up a conversation, Vonda learned they were working on their senior high school project at Lower Merion, which was to determine who made the *ultimate cheesesteak*. "Fast forward three weeks," recalled John Jr., "and this cameraman came in, a professional photographer, with all his equipment, and he said, 'I'm here for the cheesesteak thing.' And I replied, 'The kids sent you for their high school project?' He told me no, he was with the *Inquirer*." It turns out these resourceful students had contacted Craig LaBan for advice, and the writer had liked their idea so much that he'd joined in, with a plan to publish the results. Bucci, of course, asked the cameraman if they'd won. "They didn't tell me," the guy replied. "But I figure, why send someone to take photos of the loser?"[270]

LaBan had sung the praises of John's pork previously but hadn't been as familiar with their steaks. "I remember coming across John's in 2000," he recalled, "and looking through our archives and finding that nobody had ever written about them, as far as I could tell, for either the *Inquirer* or the *Daily News*."[271] So, he published the first article to feature John's, "Pork's Place," about the role of pork sandwiches in city sandwich lore, in April 2000, coincidentally nine years to the day after John Sr.'s death.

LaBan said, "[John Jr.] told me that he knew how good the roast pork was but that he loved making cheesesteaks. And that he made a great cheesesteak. So, I threw them in [the contest] as this wildcard when these kids wanted to do their senior project. I thought, 'John has really been bragging about his cheesesteak, so let's check it out.' And of course, he blew it out of the water."[272]

Nowadays, cheesesteak competitions are a dime a dozen. But back then? "There was Geno's and Pat's and then every other place," said Bucci. "There were no lists of the best cheesesteaks, no cheesesteak tours or anything like that."

"I got a call from LaBan on Sunday afternoon," Bucci continued, "and he said, 'Congratulations,' and then, 'I hope you ordered extra bread.' Boy, I thought, this guy's kind of full of himself." But, sure enough, the next morning, there were people waiting outside before the shop even opened. "We had a line down the street for like three months...and quite frankly, our lives were never the same."[273]

By 2008, the James Beard Foundation had also taken notice, choosing John's for that year's American Classics award. "They called at lunchtime on a Friday," recalled Bucci, "and I didn't know what James Beard was. I'm not a trained chef. I figured it was one of those scams to sell plaques. So, I'm blowing off this woman, and she said, 'John, do me a favor. You have friends that own restaurants. Call them and ask them about the James Beard Foundation. I'll call back tomorrow.' So, I asked my buddy, and he told me they're like the Oscars of the culinary arts, that they're as big as it gets."[274]

The Buccis went to New York City for the awards ceremony. "I had Giada sitting next to me," John Jr. gushed. "Emeril Lagasse, Tom Colicchio. And I'm a stupid sandwich maker. It was just—it was crazy, man. So,

The now-famous John's Roast Pork sign. *Wikicommons/Eric Kilby.*

that was kind of like our coming out party, which led to us being on the Travel Channel, the Food Network, in *Bon Appétit*, etc."

He continued, "I never thought in a million years that this place would have ended up like it did. We used to have the same thirty-five customers every day, and now, we get people from all over the world. I'm just so proud of our business. I always would work here when I was younger, and I would think, 'We have the best sandwiches, but no one's ever going to know.' And now people know. It's a shame, though, that my father never got to see it."[275]

Once renowned for its South Philly attitude, John's has become a kinder, gentler sandwich shop in the aftermath of John Jr.'s 2008 battle with leukemia. "The *South Philly Review* once called me the 'Pork Nazi,'" he recalled. "Like the guy in *Seinfeld*, because I would yell at customers who held up the line."[276]

Bucci doesn't consider himself a particularly religious man, but when he was in the hospital recovering from the bone marrow transplant that saved his life, he thought, "God, just get me out of this, and I'll let the Pork Nazi die right here at Fox Chase. I'll come back, and I'll be much nicer. So, I survived and went back, and I was saying 'thank you' and 'may I help you,' and my regular customers friggin' hated it! I told them, 'This is the kinder, gentler me.' And they said, 'We don't want that—we want to be hollered at.' It was hysterical."[277]

The angry persona is kind of hard to believe, considering how effusive and gregarious John Jr. is today, especially when talking about the impact his customers have had on his life. He lights up when telling stories about all the things he's seen because of this little shop.

"We had [TV star] Andrew Zimmern in," he remembered, "and he was sitting at the table with my mom, pork in one hand, and a cheesesteak in the other, and he said to us, 'This is definitely the best cheesesteak I've ever had. But this roast pork, this is one of the top three sandwiches I've ever eaten in my life.' And dude, I was crying. Tears were coming down my cheeks."[278]

"One day during the height of COVID," he added, "a couple came in, she in a wedding dress and he in a tuxedo....They couldn't have a big wedding, so they just went to city hall. And they both loved our sandwiches so much, they came here to celebrate right after they got married!"[279]

"The craziest story," he said, "is that one guy's dying wish was to get buried with one of our sandwiches....I went to the wake, and they had all these John's T-shirts and hats. It was just so unbelievable. There are so many fond memories like that, you know?"[280]

## Terminal Titans

"It's rare to find a credible rendition [of the roast pork sandwich] north of Christian Street," wrote Rick Nichols in 2004, "which is what has made Tommy DiNic's stand in Reading Terminal Market [a food hall in Center City] so special."[281] And while additional quality versions have surfaced since Nichols published his article, only DiNic's can compete with John's as the sandwich's true torchbearer. Rewinding a bit, however, it's probably not surprising that this other bastion of pork greatness also has deep roots in South Philly.

The story starts with teenager Gaetano Nicolosi (later Americanized to Thomas), who emigrated from Sicily in the early 1900s. In 1918, he opened a butcher shop at 8th and Reed Streets, which later moved to 7th and Reed Streets. Nicolosi's Butcher Shop was a true family affair; over time, his five sons not only joined their father and eventually took over, but they also lived with him, sometimes even after they were married, and never moved more than a mile or two away. (Only Felix, a middle child, left the brood to start his own meat market.)

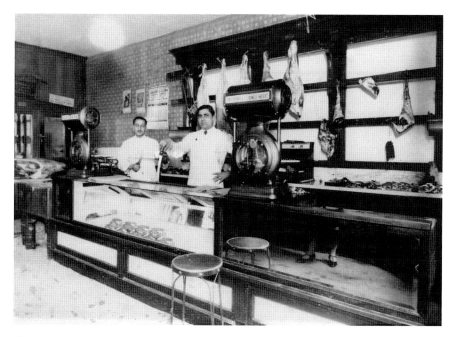

Gaetano Nicolosi poses behind his butcher shop counter, circa 1919. *Tommy DiNic's.*

Around the holidays, the Nicolosi brothers began to offer an extra service: they would cook roasts that customers had purchased in a garage adjacent to the store. This led to the idea of cooking their own meat—pork and beef—and selling sandwiches out of the same garage. The exact timing of this development is unclear. On one hand, Tommy Nicolosi—Gaetano's grandson and longtime proprietor of the Terminal Market shop—recalled this starting when he was a child in the '50s.[282] (He cemented this claim by celebrating the shop's fiftieth anniversary in 2004.) On the other hand, the *Inquirer* once reported that Nicolosi Bros. Roast Beef and Pork had officially opened in 1972.[283] Regardless of the exact date, the sandwich shop eventually made a name for itself beyond the already well-established butcher shop.

In a glowing description of Nicolosi's sandwich prowess from 1981, the *Inquirer*'s Mystery Muncher wrote:

> [I] *learned a valuable lesson this week: When in South Philadelphia, do as the South Philadelphians do and head for Nicolosi Bros., where the sandwiches are great. It's the kind of place that is easy to miss. Just a hole in the wall, really a converted garage adjoining the Nicolosi family's meat market. Follow your nose to the smell of roasting meat.... This is a strictly*

Dominic (*left*) and Anthony Nicolosi show off their wares, mid-1970s. *Tommy DiNic's.*

*no-frills operation. Behind the counter, one of the Nicolosis usually can be found dishing up warm roast beef or pork, lean and tender, with plenty of natural gravy, into a crusty Italian roll ($1.75). That's it. No other choices. But that's enough.*[284]

"They had no bags, nothing to really wrap up the sandwiches," added Joe Nicolosi, Gaetano's great-grandson and the current owner of the Terminal Market store. "Maybe just one little piece of wax paper that they would kind of half wrap this thing up with and hand it over to you....It was all very simple, very minimalist. It was like, 'This is what we have. Here, take it.'"[285]

When Gaetano's grandsons Tommy Nicolosi and Frankie DiClaudio (who'd both been born and raised at 7th and Reed Streets) came of age, they learned the sandwich trade hands-on, at some point taking over cooking in the garage. Eventually, the cousins decided to embark on their own venture, launching DiNic's—the new brand a portmanteau of their surnames—in 1977.

The first DiNic's opened at 10th Street and Oregon Avenue, but "that neighborhood started to go downhill fairly rapidly," noted Joe.[286] So, they opened a second shop at 10th and Reed Streets—just down the block from the Pat's/Geno's triangle, interestingly—and then, in the early 1980s, a stand at the Reading Terminal Market. After closing the original, they settled into Tommy running the Reading Terminal shop and Frankie focusing on 10th and Reed Streets, though the latter eventually moved to 15th Street and Snyder Avenue. "Finally," said Tommy, "Frankie and I, still friends, split up."[287] Both would continue to use the DiNic's name and recipes.

"Frankie passed away a few years ago," said Joe. "His son Frankie Jr. would be my [second] cousin, and I've only met him once in my life. He took over the DiNic's in the Navy Yard and had another one in Montgomeryville that didn't make it through COVID. So, long story short, he still runs the business in the Navy Yard, and we don't have a relationship…but he is the son of Frankie and I'm the son of Tommy, the two guys who started this business and came up with the name. So, his right to it is the exact same as mine."[288]

Asked about what transformed his shop—sometimes called Tommy DiNic's to distinguish it from Frankie's—from local delicacy to iconic tourist destination, Joe credits three specific developments: (1) the evolution of the Reading Terminal Market, (2) increased interest from the local press and (3) a feature on Food Network.

Reading Terminal Market "was on the cusp of being closed down in the '80s," Joe said. "It was a decrepit building with no air conditioning or heat. There were tarps on the ceiling because it would rain inside. It was truly a warehouse, and the customers were all locals—there were no tourists." Then in the early 1990s, the city built the Pennsylvania Convention Center right next to the market. "Every year, there were new conventions, and the flower show and the car show, all bringing people to this area of the city. That was the first stage. The second stage was local press, when we started getting some recognition in the *Inquirer*, *Philly Magazine*. This would have been mid- to late '90s."[289]

The original DiNic's location at 10th and Oregon Streets in the late 1970s. *Tommy DiNic's.*

DiNic's sign in the Reading Terminal Market. *Unbreaded.*

"But the thing that really put us over the edge," Joe continued, "was the first time that we did *Man vs. Food*. Not the best sandwich thing [see following paragraph], but we were initially on one of the segments before the main challenge. This was when the show was at its peak of popularity, when the fans were pretty crazy." The season two episode aired in September 2009. "The next weekend, it was like the flower show; there was a line around the store," he recalled. "We figured it would eventually calm down, but it kind of never did. I mean, there was a frenzy that doesn't exist anymore, maybe because we've adapted, but [that level] became the new norm. So, when I look back, that really was the breakthrough moment."[290]

Adam Richman and *Man vs. Food* would soon be back, leading to even more national notoriety for DiNic's. In 2012, the Travel Channel show crowned the stand's roast pork with sharp provolone and broccoli rabe the *very best sandwich in America*. Philly being Philly, this accolade, of course, sparked more local debate than consensus, but it cemented DiNic's as *the place* to go for tourists craving an authentic taste of the city beyond the cheesesteak.

## PUTTING IT ALL TOGETHER

Compared to many of the other sandwiches in this book, roast pork is likely the most challenging, or labor intensive, to prepare. In contrast to the short-order style of cheesesteaks and hoagies, the three-day process here is staggeringly long.

"One of the things that makes pork so difficult to cook," said Bucci, "is that it's such a fatty meat. It secretes a lot of grease." Roasting is important, of course, but for a practiced shop, that is the easy part. "We have to put the gravy in the fridge overnight, let the fat congeal at the top, skim that off and then do it all over again," Bucci continued. "And then put it on the stove with bones and skin in there and cook it for a while and then skim it again. So, while we could slice the pork the next day, the gravy won't be ready for two more days."[291]

DiNic's process also takes three days, though there are some differences. "On day one," said Joe Nicolosi, we prep, season and tie the hams, put them in pans and store them in the walk-in box. So, it's a twenty-four-hour dry rub. And then the second day, they come out of the fridge and are cooked. Then they have to be cooled down, so on day three, they can be sliced and put into the hot stock and served."[292]

Another key factor is the herb and spice mix that has been passed down from generation to generation. "Which is no secret at all," said Tommy Nicolosi before he retired. "Garlic, basil, oregano, black pepper, and a pinch—just a pinch—of salt. I chop my own garlic fresh every day, of course. I love garlic too much to buy garlic beads. But I am not a garlic snob. I do rub the outside of the roast with a little garlic powder."[293]

Bucci is cagier, refusing to share the name of the spice company they've used since the early days. "Continuity is very big in this business," he added. "People that have been coming for years, they want the same thing they've always had. So, when our spice company, for instance, began to narrow down their business to where they only have a few customers left, I started to get concerned."[294] (Thankfully, they're not changing anything when it comes to John's.)

Other than all that, it's all about freshness and quality ingredients. "I roast everything here myself, fresh every morning, from scratch, out in the open where anybody can see," said Tommy Nicolosi. "We give you fast service, not fast food. I never open a can of anything. No canned stock, no powdered stock, no chemicals, no preservatives, no junk."[295]

"We do not use slicing provolone," he continued, with a gesture of disgust. "Slicing provolone is just lunchmeat. It tastes like turkey breast! This is real aged provolone cheese we use, like we use real peppers, real garlic, real meat....The rolls are shaped by hand, not punched out of machines like the big bakeries. They have a crust, they have a bite to them—old-style, like my sandwiches."[296]

Aficionados will notice something missing in Tommy DiNic's screed above: the greens. It turns out, in fact, that one of the key ingredients in a Philly Pork Italiano—bitter greens like spinach or broccoli rabe—is a relatively recent addition to the canon.

"My dad started doing spinach in the mid-'90s—maybe?" said Joe. "The people in Center City at that time and the tourists (of which there were far fewer then) did not know or did not want broccoli rabe....He said he tried on more than one occasion over the years to serve it, and there were no takers. And then it was just an idea whose time had come at some point. We tried it again in maybe 2001, 2002, and it took off."[297]

Today, DiNic's offers a choice of rabe or spinach, but the former is twenty times more popular. "These things, for better and for worse, take on a life of their own," said Joe. "The people—especially tourists—have this idea that they're supposed to get this green stuff on a roast pork sandwich, and so that's what they get."[298]

At John's, the only green available is spinach. "I've often been asked about broccoli rabe," said Bucci, "but I just think it is so bitter. Why would I hide my grandfather's terrific recipe with such a bitter taste? That's why I use fresh leaf spinach, because it's complementary, as opposed to masking the flavor."[299]

Greens also entered the picture at John's around 2000. "It's not the way I was raised to eat it," said Bucci. "That only came in later. My grandfather and my dad would add mustard and onions. I gotta tell you, if you've never had it with mustard and onions, you've got to try it.…It's a unique combination of flavors with the vinegary mustard. We put that on the menu as Pop-Pop's Special."[300]

That unique take aside, roasted "long hot" peppers are the more traditional vegetable accompaniment—if there was one at all—to roast pork. At DiNic's, that goes all the way back to the Nicolosi days, when they simply used jarred vinegar peppers. In the 1980s and 1990s, DiNic's would offer "a slippery pile of homemade spicy-hot garlicky roast peppers," for anywhere from thirty-five to fifty cents extra.[301] At John's, they've also always offered long hots, which Vonda would fry up daily in big cast-iron pans.

So, where exactly did the idea for mixing in greens come from? Well, first, the concept is nothing new and likely came from the old country with waves of Italian immigrants. (Even today, broccoli rabe with pork is a common pairing in Central Italy.) "On New Year's Day," said Dolores' Miglino, "My mother, many Italian Americans, always made pork and always had broccoli rabe or spinach on the side. More than likely, that's where this stems from."[302]

In terms of restaurants, it was likely Shank's & Evelyn's, a luncheonette at 10th and Montrose Streets, that began adding greens to Italian sandwiches in the 1960s. Though these greens were reportedly first paired with chicken cutlet, Shank's eventually offered them as a side with their roast pork. Customers then began to request the side on top, and the rest is history.[303] (See chapter 5 for more on Shank's & Evelyn's and chicken cutlet sandwiches.)

## THE NEWBIE

Closer to the time DiNic's and John's adopted this practice, Tony Luke's opened on Oregon Avenue near Interstate 95. It's almost funny to think about Tony Luke's as a newcomer to the city scene because of how iconic the place became so quickly after it opened. Yet it's only been around since 1992. "People are always telling [Tony Luke's] they've been coming for decades," wrote Karen Heller in 2005. "Like many great things, it just feels as if it's been around forever."[304]

Founded by Anthony Lucidono Sr.—whom a pronunciation-challenged former boss nicknamed "Tony Luke"—and his sons Anthony Jr. and Nick, the joint was an immediate success. In October 1992, the *Inquirer* reported that there was "almost always a line" and in 1994 referred to it as "the major sandwich spot at Front and Oregon."[305]

Though by all accounts the food was a big reason for the shop's early success, the outsized personality of Tony Luke Jr. also played an important role. While Tony Sr. and Nick manned the store in the early days, Tony Jr. went to every radio and TV station he could find to try to drum up publicity. "I did this every day," he said. "I just kept pounding the door until someone would answer and give me a chance."[306] At first, he could barely get past the front desk, but he took that opportunity and converted the front desk people with free sandwiches. Then on the next visit, he'd get a little farther, until eventually, the people making the decisions started to take notice.

Once people were talking about the sandwiches, Tony Jr. continued, "I needed them to start talking about Tony Luke's when they weren't hungry—when they didn't even know what the hell Tony Luke's was."[307] Building on his background in acting and music, Tony Jr. began to create TV commercials that he wrote, produced and starred in during the early 1990s. Goofy but charming, they developed a cult following and helped quickly increase the brand's reach (and Tony Jr.'s profile) throughout the region.

"The first commercial was me playing a convict breaking out of jail during the work detail, risking getting more time in prison, but he just had to get a Tony Luke's sandwich," he recalled. "They didn't show anyone making the sandwich or the food on the grill. It was just me running up, saying, 'Gimme a roast pork Italian!' It was funny, it was stupid."[308]

The people at Prism, with whom Tony Jr. worked on the project, thought he was crazy. "How the hell do they even know what you're doing or what you're selling?" they said. "But I didn't want viewers to know," Tony Jr. said. "I wanted them to be curious about what Tony Luke's was."

"I knew two things would happen," he continued. "People were gonna love it…or they were gonna think it was the dumbest thing they had ever seen in their entire life. But either way, we'd get the same reaction: people talking about this shop they didn't know about."

"If they came up and said, 'We hate you and we just wanted to see you in person and tell you how much we hate your commercials,'" he added, "I would say, 'Yeah, but you're here buying food, right?'"[309]

By 1994, Tony Luke's had bagged a "Best of Philly" prize in *Philadelphia Magazine*.[310] A second location came in 1996, and by 2000, Tony Luke's had made it onto the America's Best Restaurants list in *Gourmet*, which wrote, "It's the Italian pork sandwich we dream about, a transcendent mess of garlicky pork, chewy roll, and soft, pungent masses of broccoli rabe cooked down until it reaches the consistency of heavenly sludge."[311]

"If you asked me how it happened so quickly," Tony Jr. said, "I'd say it was the perfect marriage between really good food and great operators like my brother and my father—and me just being a completely out-of-the-box thinker and being the face of the brand that made people want to come and try. It was the perfect scenario."[312]

Tony Luke's rise to fame was perhaps also the key factor in bringing the idea of bitter greens to the mainstream. "They were doing broccoli rabe before us," admitted Joe Nicolosi, "perhaps because, in South Philly, it worked."[313] Initially, these customers were—at least somewhat—people who frequented Shank's & Evelyn's, who shopped for fresh produce at the Italian Market and had likely grown up with rabe.

"Broccoli rabe with pork and with chicken was everyday food for [South Philly] Italians," said Tony Jr. "At that time, it was only unique to people who weren't Italian. For an Italian, it was like, 'Do you make good broccoli rabe, or you make bitter broccoli rabe?' Eating roast pork with broccoli rabe and sharp provolone was just an everyday thing. And back then, it was a lot of Italians. They'd try our roast pork, and then they would spread the word to people who weren't Italian, and then those people would come and try it and love it."

"Our broccoli rabe in the heyday, it was not bitter at all," he continued. "Because when we made it at home, we figured out how to get rid of the bitter flavor. I never liked it as a kid because it was so bitter, of course, but there's a way to cook it that removes the bitterness but keeps the great flavor. That was from my father, who was a great cook."[314] (For a recipe, see appendix.)

Today, after a reportedly acrimonious split, Tony Luke Jr. runs the eponymous brand as a franchised mini chain, opening in far-flung locales like New York City and Bahrain, while Tony Sr. and Nick still run the original location as Tony and Nick's Steaks.

# Back to Basics

Although most Philly roast pork has moved away from the traditional Italian porchetta, Luigi & Giovanni's in the western suburb Newtown Square still serves its phenomenal rendition of this delicacy. Located within a mile-long stretch of Route 3 (also known as West Chester Pike) that also houses A Cut Above Deli and Soprano's—two other shops that make a variety of excellent Italian sandwiches—Luigi's stands out for its weekend patio sandwich stand and centerpiece porchetta Abruzzese.

Cofounder Luigi Lemme learned the craft of porchetta as a teenager in the 1960s—using a five-hundred-year-old recipe—while working at Willie's Butcher Shop at 64th and Callowhill Streets in West Philadelphia. A decade later, partnering with John D'Alessandro (also known as Giovanni), he opened several Colonial Meat Markets and started the catering and specialty food business Luigi & Giovanni's.

"The difference in preparation between porchetta and roast pork is huge," said Luigi, who still offers both. "The roast pork is simple and easy to prepare. It weighs 7–10 lbs. and consists of 3–5 muscles….The porchetta, on the other hand, consists of 35 muscles, and requires a more detailed preparation: deboning, seasoning and tightening the whole pig in its natural form, then slow cooking for 8–12 hours."[315]

After being seasoned liberally with six fresh herbs, Luigi's porchetta is roasted (with skin intact for extra flavor) overnight in a brick oven rotisserie, then mixed with an Italian-style gravy. The cooking method for this pork renders the fat slowly, creating meat that is tender, juicy and extremely flavorful. It can then be shredded for sandwiches or sliced and finished off with a piece of edible roasted skin. On the patio, a sesame semolina roll is scooped (to remove excess insides, if desired), layered with piquant sharp provolone and house-made roasted red peppers, then piled high with steaming pork.

"We find broccoli rabe to be strong and bitter in flavor, in comparison to roasted peppers," said Luigi. "However, I could live with either and still enjoy the sandwich."[316]

Pulling the meat instead of slicing it gives Luigi's sandwich a texture more like Carolina barbecue, which is perhaps what makes it extra tasty. DiNic's also now serves an Italian pulled pork sandwich, introduced around 2004, "which is what you should get," wrote LaBan, "as opposed to the regular old sliced-down roast pork."[317]

The full Luigi & Giovanni's porchetta, ready to be served. *Luigi & Giovanni's.*

For its preparation, DiNic's uses pork shoulder, then braises it in a combination of the stock from their roast pork and red wine, along with caramelized onions and garlic. "So, we take our pork stock, which is pretty rich, with good flavor right out of the gate and then cook that for another six, seven hours to further develop those flavors. It's like if we took the original roast pork and amplified it."[318] (For a recipe, see appendix.)

Today, roast pork, in a variety of styles, has become a mainstay across the region, appearing more broadly than at just the big three shops mentioned in this chapter, at places like Woodrow's and Lil' Nick's, Dolores' 2Street and even Porco's, which has been serving traditional porchetta since 2019. It still lives in the shadow of the cheesesteak, of course, less known and understood, but thankfully, it's always there for those smart enough to seek it out.

# 5

# CUTLET

Of all these iconic Philly sandwiches, the most overlooked is the chicken cutlet and its primary form, the Italiano (which, like the roast pork, comes with greens and sharp provolone). *Philadelphia Magazine* echoed this sentiment in 2013, describing the wonderful concoction as a "dying Philadelphia tradition…that deserves a permanent spot in the pantheon of Great Philadelphia Sandwiches."[319] In the ensuing decade, however, a new crop of sandwich artisans—such as Angelo's and Dolores' 2Street—have given the modest cutlet more love, perhaps introducing it to a new generation of eaters.

Like others discussed previously, the idea of a sandwich stuffed with chicken cutlets goes back further than its origins in Philadelphia and is in and of itself not a particularly clever creation. That said, it seems safe to say that the idea of putting a breaded chicken (or, less commonly but still authentically, veal or eggplant) cutlet on a long roll with cooked spinach or broccoli rabe and sharp provolone is distinctly Philadelphian.

Though an origin legend like that of the cheesesteak hasn't made its way into the popular lexicon, it is evident that the popularization—and perhaps invention—of this sandwich can be traced back to Shank's & Evelyn's Luncheonette (colloquially "Shank's"), which resided at 932 South 10th Street in South Philly from approximately 1962 to 2009.

While working at a battery and tire garage, the story goes, Italian American Frank Perri (also known as Shank, so nicknamed because he had trouble pronouncing Fs as a boy) began making hot dogs and other food for customers. This gave him the idea to start a restaurant, which he eventually opened in place of the garage, around 1962.[320]

Shank was "a happy-go-lucky, stand-up kind of guy," said his son Frank Jr. "Very sociable, always joking around" but also a workaholic. "The restaurant was his life. It was all he had time for." He would take a nap, his son recalled, and wake up knowing what soup he was going to serve all week. Shank married his childhood sweetheart, Evelyn DeGregorio, in 1958, and "they were side by side all the way" at the restaurant until Shank died in 1994.[321] (Evelyn retired in 2009 and passed away in 2021.)

The interior of Shank's & Evelyn's was tiny, with approximately twenty seats at six small tables so close together that customers seated nearby would have to adjust their position whenever someone attempted to sit at the rare unoccupied table. (There were also several stools available at the counter.) Even as the century turned, according to Zagat, Shank's remained a classic hole-in-the-wall Italian luncheonette, a "true South Philly experience," brimming with attitude, surly waitresses and colorful characters. And while this attitude meant customers would endure being yelled at or having their plates slammed down in front of them, the ensuing reward was, of course, the "best sandwiches in the world."[322]

Eating at Shank's was "like eating in my mother's kitchen," recalled Bob Santoro, a frequent patron, upon Frank Sr.'s death. "The sauces, the greens, the peppers—it's like what [I] would get at home."[323]

"[He] served street hucksters, politicians, actors, lawyers, doctors, sports personalities and folks from around his neighborhood and around the country," read Frank Sr.'s *Inquirer* obituary. "The luncheonette was continuously crowded with connoisseurs of Italian American breakfast and lunch cuisine."[324]

Evelyn sold the South Philly building in 2009, initially planning to open a Center City location with her daughters. Later that year, however, the family sold the brand to realtor Marcello Ciurlino, who ran Shank's Uptown at 15th and Sansom Streets until 2011. In late 2009, Phil McFillin opened a second location, Shank's Original at Pier 40—the rare Philly sandwich shop with easy parking—which remains operational to this day. For a time, these new owners enlisted Evelyn to make her famous meatballs each week and employed both her daughter Pamela and granddaughter Margoux.[325] In 2022, longtime employee Ed Brennan purchased the Pier 40 location, and while the cooking roster no longer features any Perris, Brennan says they still use the same recipes.[326]

# The Masterpiece

Shank's & Evelyn's was no one-trick pony; it served a variety of homestyle Italian fare, including but not limited to meatballs, eggplant parmesan, roast pork, escarole soup, roasted peppers, etc. Breakfast included not only egg sandwiches but also Evelyn's famous *giambotta*, a huge, kitchen sink–style omelet packed with a variety of meats, vegetables and cheeses. Additionally, the iconic RC Cola sign that hung above the restaurant heralded yet another specialty that mostly fails to gain traction in today's crowded sandwich marketplace: roast beef. (See chapter 6.)

All that said, Shank's true opus, its enduring contribution to the canon of great Philadelphia sandwiches, was the chicken cutlet Italiano, a stroke of genius that spawned countless imitations, modifications and wildly creative takes. Like the other sandwiches previously discussed, it, too, is a relatively simple combination of humble ingredients that somehow, when combined, become far greater.

To prepare the star of this creation, the luncheonette would dip fresh—never frozen—chicken cutlets in egg wash, coat them with an impossibly delicate layer of breadcrumbs (seasoned with a mixture of Italian herbs, salt and pepper) and then pan fry them in a cast-iron skillet. Of this now-famous recipe, Shank and Evelyn's daughter Pamela Perri said, "There's no

The chicken cutlet Italiano with spinach from Shank's Original, the last bastion of Shank's & Evelyn's in Philadelphia. *Author photograph.*

secret....They're simple. I enjoy them and we've got lots of customers that love 'em too."[327]

Despite Pam's modesty, pan frying may have indeed been the secret; she certainly was adamant that her cutlets were "never deep fried!"[328] And at Tony Luke's—the shop that assumed the mantle of Philly's most famous cutlet spot when Shank's eventually closed—Luke Jr. also emphasized the frying method's importance. "When we first opened," he said, "we fried every chicken cutlet in a pan. I have never put a chicken cutlet in a deep fryer—ever! We stopped using the frying pan when we got the clamshell oven because it gave us the same effect, but we would never put a cutlet in a frialator because that's not how we would make it at home. Deep frying changes the texture and the flavor of the cutlet."[329]

At Shank's, Pam would spend the morning pan frying, on a good day, twenty-five to thirty pounds of chicken cutlets, plus veal cutlets and long strips of eggplant. By lunchtime, piles of each would mount behind the counter, ready for sandwiches.[330] (The current incarnation on Pier 40 does deep fry cutlets to order, Brennan said, for food safety reasons.)[331]

Alongside the chicken came the greens—spinach or broccoli rabe— quickly blanched and then sautéed with olive oil and plenty of garlic, salt and pepper. (See chapter 4 for more on these greens.) Though the quintessential Philadelphia choice has become the pungently bitter broccoli rabe—a vegetable that matches the city's soul, perhaps—it wasn't *always* available at the original Shank's & Evelyn's. "Broccoli rabe can be expensive and my customers don't like it when I raise the prices. So I only use it when I can get it cheap,"[332] said Evelyn in 1999.

To bring everything together, a freshly baked roll would be layered with shards of wonderfully aggressive sharp provolone, followed by the meat and vegetables. A "small" sandwich at Shank's, the *Inquirer*'s Mystery Muncher once wrote, meant that it fed "only three people."[333]

Although Shank's cutlets surely started to build a following in the 1960s, more recent depictions suggest they continued to dazzle in later years. In the mid-1990s, for example, *Inquirer* food writer Michael Klein introduced the sandwich to his young daughter. Even as an adult, according to Klein, she remembered "her first Shank's chicken cutlet, at age 7, as a religious experience."[334]

In 2008, *Esquire* included Shank's cutlet in its "Best Sandwiches in America" article, proclaiming it the top "morning-after sandwich in the world," adding that while one doesn't "need a hangover to appreciate [it]," this situation can be arranged with "a little planning."[335]

Even after Shank's had changed hands—the Perri family was still involved with some of the cooking at the time—Philly Sports Radio station WIP and host Glen Macnow still bestowed the best hot sandwich honor on the chicken cutlet Italiano (with rabe) in 2010. It also won the Listeners' Choice Award.[336] During the judging, iconic Philly chef Georges Perrier (of Le Bec Fin fame) gave the sandwich a perfect score.[337]

## CREATIVE CONSTRUCTS

Cutlets are undergoing a renaissance today, with new sandwich shops devoting more attention to and—perhaps more importantly—innovating with the humble cutlet. "When we first started making them [in 2014]," said DiGiampietro of Angelo's, "there weren't many options for cutlets. Tony Luke's of course, but beyond that, there weren't many people doing it.…Or if they were, there was no love in it."

"Now," he continued, "they're everywhere…with all kinds of variations.… Take your pick of where you want to go."[338]

One of the most exciting aspects of this cutlet revolution is the seemingly unlimited creativity that some local chefs have showcased. It makes sense, with steaks or pork, that those meats can speak for themselves and don't need a lot of adornment to shine. Chicken, on the other hand, is less assertive, so it often perks up with inventive sauces, condiments and other toppings, acting, perhaps, as a blank canvas for culinary invention.

Italian style remains the default, with the greens and provolone combo being most common and roasted peppers also figuring in regularly. It's become easier, too, to find shops offering cutlets with some combination of ingredients like prosciutto, balsamic vinegar or pesto. "We started messing around and doing the Philly Food Dude (PFD)," said DiGiampietro, "with roasted artichokes and proshoot, fresh mozz that we pulled, arugula pesto and balsamic glaze.…Come on, man!"[339]

Tortorice Sandwich in Center City also got wild with its Italian-style cutlet specials, such as the Uncle Sammy, which topped cutlets with mini cheese ravioli, ciliegine mozzarella, grape tomatoes and creamy basil sauce.

Beyond the Italian styles, Buffalo chicken, topped with hot sauce and blue cheese, is so common it has almost become a default. And at Carmen's Famous in the Reading Terminal Market—formerly known as Rocco's— cheesesteaks are popular with tourists, but those in the know order the

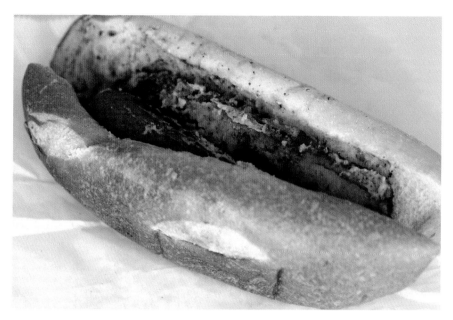

A fish cake/hot dog combo with mustard from Johnny's Hots. *Author photograph.*

A homemade fish cake/hot dog combo with pepper hash. *Author photograph.*

A homemade fish cake sandwich with pepper hash. *Author photograph.*

A Texas wiener from A.P.J. Texas Weiner on North 13th Street. *Author photograph.*

DiCostanza's Italian hoagie with tomato and sweet peppers (the shop does not offer lettuce). *Author photograph.*

The Old Italian from Primo Hoagies. *Author photograph.*

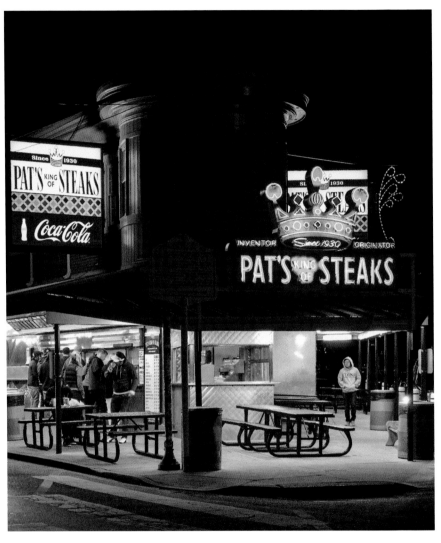

Pat's at night, circa 2015. *Wikimedia Commons/Jason Knauer.*

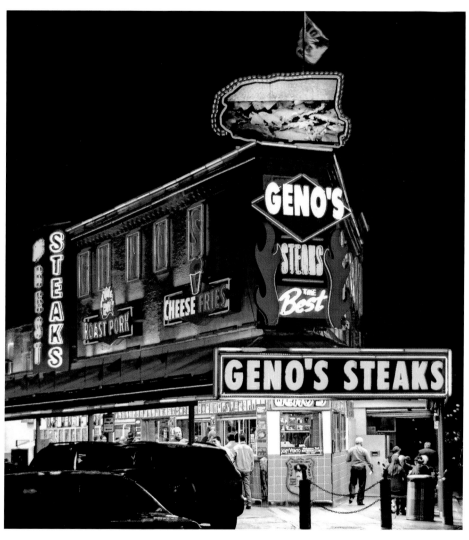

Geno's at night, circa 2009. *Flickr/Kevin W. Burkett.*

Pat's whiz wit in a promo photograph from the restaurant. (It's much sloppier in real life.) *Pat's King of Steaks.*

Angelo's cheesesteak made with Cooper Sharp. *Author photograph.*

Dalessandro's pizza steak. *Author photograph.*

Dolores' version of the original (Milano) pizza steak. *Author photograph.*

A Donkey's cheesesteak served on a poppy-seed kaiser roll. *Author photograph.*

A Schmitter purchased from the stand at Citizens Bank Park. *Unbreaded.*

The famous roast pork from John's Roast Pork. *Author photograph.*

The original roast pork from DiNic's. *Unbreaded.*

DiNic's pulled pork. *Unbreaded.*

A porchetta sandwich with sharp provolone and roasted red peppers from Luigi & Giovanni's. *Author photograph.*

The chicken cutlet Italiano with spinach from Shank's Original at Pier 40. *Author photograph.*

The Chicken Lorenzo from A Cut Above in Newtown Square, featuring cutlets alongside Parma prosciutto, sliced tomato, arugula, shaved Parmigiano Reggiano and balsamic glaze. *Author photograph.*

The Chicken Supremo, cutlets with fresh mozzarella and roasted red peppers, from Primo Hoagies. *Author photograph.*

Roast beef with provolone from Old Original Nick's Roast Beef. (It doesn't look like much, but it packs a ton of flavor.) *Author photograph.*

Angelo's meatball parm. *Author photograph.*

The Antipasto hoagie from A Cut Above in Newtown Square, which pairs Italian tuna with Parma prosciutto, sharp provolone, sweet roasted peppers, Sicilian olives, lettuce and special seasonings. *Author photograph.*

A pork roll, egg and cheese sandwich on a kaiser roll. *Wikimedia Commons/Austin Murphy.*

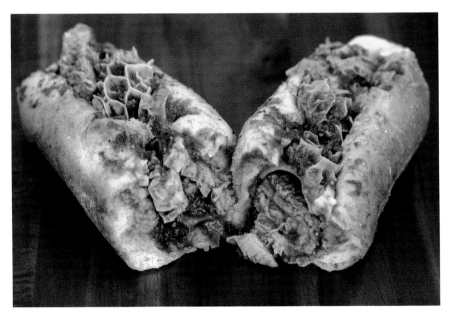

George's tripe sandwich. *Author photograph.*

An extra-lean corned beef special from Murray's in Bala Cynwyd. *Author photograph.*

The Henry, a veggie hoagie from Dolores' 2Street. *Author photograph.*

The original stromboli. *Romano's.*

Huda's Korean chicken with gochujang glaze, kimchi coleslaw and pickled daikon. *Huda.*

The Chicken Lorenzo from A Cut Above in Newtown Square, featuring cutlets alongside Parma prosciutto, sliced tomato, arugula, shaved Parmigiano Reggiano and balsamic glaze. *Author photograph.*

Chicken Rocco, which features a hearty slathering of the family's addictive Dijon mustard sauce.

As with cheesesteaks, regional and international flavors have also been making inroads with this once-Italian bastion. Examples include Mi-Pals Deli's spicy chicken cutlet, with chipotle gouda, imported hot capicola, roasted peppers and jalapeño aioli, and Dolores' Purple Bag Jawn, featuring cutlets encrusted in spicy sweet chili Doritos with sharp cheddar cheese, lettuce, pickled onion, daikon, carrot and sweet and spicy mayo.

At the restaurant Cotoletta on Fitler Square—whose name literally means "cutlet" in Italian—cutlets are the menu's centerpiece, available in a variety of preparations. A fine-dining restaurant, it doesn't serve sandwiches, but the signature Cotoletta Stack riffs off the KFC Double Down concept, in which fried chicken pieces replace the bread. Here, they create a sandwich of sorts (that's best eaten with cutlery) by layering sausage-stuffed long hot peppers, eggplant cutlets and melted provolone in between two thinly pounded, breaded and fried chicken cutlets. "Every single layer was so carefully built and distinct," wrote LaBan of the Stack, "yet forked into one deliciously complex bite."[340] At brunch—which isn't currently being served as of this writing—Cotolctta's Breakfast Stack kept a more traditional flour-based sandwich holder, this time jamming chicken cutlets and sausage-stuffed long hots between two Belgian waffles and then topping it all with a sunny-side-up egg.

With concoctions like these—some of which were limited-time specials—cropping up regularly, it seems the future of cutlet sandwiches in Philadelphia is indeed bright...and delicious.

# OTHER NOTABLE SANDWICHES

Beyond the major players who have earned their own chapters in this book, there are dozens of other sandwich options in the Philadelphia area, with creativity often bolstered by the enhanced local appreciation for sandwich art. This could come in the form of well-known international sandwiches, such as hamburgers (Village Whiskey) and grilled cheeses (Mighty Melt); unique one-offs like Chicken Maroosh (Saad's Halal) and Egg Keema (Little Sicily II); or just about anything in between.

There is, of course, a distinctly Italian thread to many of the *other* sandwiches that proliferate, whether it be meatball (see page 135), sausage and peppers or old favorites like veal scallopini and chicken marsala. Though these combinations may not be unique to Philadelphia, the availability of quality local bread, well-cooked broccoli rabe and roasted peppers or pungent sharp provolone might just put them into their own category when compared to similar concoctions from elsewhere.

All this said, there are a few additional sandwich styles that—while perhaps not warranting consideration at the level of those mentioned previously—deserve at least some exploration as part of this historical sandwich analysis.

## Roast Beef

"No one talks about roast beef in Philadelphia," wrote LaBan in 2018, "but it shares a local lineage with roast pork as a staple of old-time Italian

Anthony (*left*) and Dominic Nicolosi pose in front of their sandwich shop in the mid-1970s. *Tommy DiNic's.*

American banquets."[341] This is further evidenced by the sandwich's legacy at John's, Nicolosi/DiNic's and Shank's.

"For the history of DiNic's, certainly my entire life," said Joe Nicolosi, "it was always pork heavy, minimum double pork to beef." So why, then, did both Nicolosi's and the early DiNic's list beef before pork on their signs? (Today, it's "DiNic's Roast *Pork and Beef*.") "I don't know how much thought they necessarily put into that," Joe said. "It might have been some arbitrary reason; I don't think it was a grand plan."[342] It's a convenient explanation to fit the roast pork legacy. Then again, Shank's & Evelyn's also had the opportunity to list just one of its many specialties on the iconic RC Cola sign that hung from its building, and it chose roast beef. But ask an old-timer why they remember Shank's, and they probably won't mention beef first. It's perplexing.

Regardless, the venerable roast beef sandwich persists, still lingering on the menu at places like DiNic's and John's, Cosmi's and George's. (Shank's Original no longer sells them.) "It would be overstating things to suggest that the hand-carved roast beef sandwich is without honor in this city," wrote Nichols.[343] It nonetheless takes a persistent backseat to the cheesesteak (for beef cravers) or roast pork (for slow-cooked meat cravers), among others.

Perhaps part of the issue is that the concept of a hot, freshly carved roast beef sandwich, served with juicy gravy and maybe some melted cheese or horseradish, is not unique to Philadelphia. There are plenty of similarities here to Buffalo's beef on weck, LA's French dip or just about any other roast beef au jus in any city in America.

In addition, Luke Jr. said, "It's tough to do right. You've got to use a steamship round and cut it by hand. It needs to be sitting under a heat lamp and cut to order. It's an art and not something where a place can make thousands of sandwiches an hour."[344]

Maybe Domenico Bucci was the first to sell an Italian-style roast beef sandwich from his catering business that would eventually become John's Roast Pork, or perhaps the dish was here long before then. Either way, the enduring Philly icon in this category is undoubtedly Nick's Roast Beef, founded in 1938 by Nicholas DiSipio—with a recipe from his mother, Elsa—and still located at 20th and Jackson Streets.

To clarify, this is "Old Original" Nick's, not to be confused with several other roast beef joints called some version of "Nick's" that are scattered throughout the region. In the late 1960s, DiSipio's Nick's did flirt with franchising but eventually pulled the plug on that experiment. Because the family had failed to trademark the name, however, several pretenders also began to utilize it. "Unless it's 'Old Original,'" said DiSipio's granddaughter Megan Rose, "it's fake. Don't buy it."[345] (Old Original does currently have two outposts, in Springfield Delco and West Chester.)

"The sandwiches sliced to order from a giant side of beef behind the bar at this 80-year-old tavern in South Philly are as good as any I've had anywhere," wrote LaBan of the authentic Nick's. "Order with provolone, long hots, and extra trimmings from the roast's flavorful outer edge plus a spoonful of extra juice—the 'combo overboard on the outs'—and you'll be in a race to devour it before it dissolves."[346]

Nichols offered similar praise, calling it "a serious-minded sandwich, the beef well-done, toothsome, but tender," colorfully adding that the gravy helps create "a beefy mess."[347]

A QUICK GUIDE TO NICK'S ORDERING SLANG:

combo: add sharp provolone
toppers: add broccoli rabe
on the out(s): extra beef crust
operation: scoop out the insides of the roll
overboard: extra gravy
wet: normal gravy
wet meat: light gravy, on the meat but not the roll
dry: no gravy

To produce this underrated specialty, Nick's meat supplier Kissin Fresh starts with a ninety-pound USDA Prime steamship round (which includes both the top and bottom round), then debones it, cuts out the nerves and leaves a thin layer of fat cap, the final cut weighing about fifty pounds. These enormous roasts are then hand tied and slow cooked for eight hours in old ovens in Nick's basement. "They're about sixty years old now," said Rose of the ovens, which have no doubt have built up wonderful layers of seasoning with decades of use. "We're terrified of the day something bad happens to them."[348]

"We are strictly USDA prime, which you're not going to find at other places," continued Rose. "We have an exclusive contract with our vendor; they can't sell the same type of rounds to other locations in the area, so the beef quality is a huge part of our draw." Carvers, who go through up to forty knives a week, slice the beef by hand, thinly and to order, following the grain. "It takes at least a month to get new cutters up to speed," Rose added. "To where the slices are thin and proper. It's an art."[349]

The seasoned crust, nicknamed "the outs," is set aside for those who request it while it's available. Though Nick's originally offered rolls from the now-defunct Tally-Ann Baking Co., it now uses oversized Amoroso kaiser rolls, which are baked longer to withstand an abundance of juicy gravy.

While still cranking out delicious sandwiches, the original Nick's location at 20th and Jackson Streets is no longer as busy as it once was. Back at the height of the Navy Yard days, Nichols suggested, it was "maybe the biggest beer drop in the city, measured by keg count," and went through as many as 150 beef roasts per week.[350]

"People would come from miles away to eat [our roast beef sandwich]," said Gene DiSipio, Nick's son. "Some of the biggest celebrities would be there; movie stars, admirals from the Navy Yard, sports figures....Also some of the biggest bums in the world. It didn't matter to us who they were, just so long as they had the price of a sandwich and a beer."[351]

"It was a rocking business," added Rose. "People would line up, and sandwiches cost only a nickel....But times were different. The men wore suits...and women weren't even allowed in the bar; they had their own private entrance."[352]

Today, Old Original Nick's soldiers on, still looking the part of the prototypical corner tappie, wrote Nichols, "dark-paneled, a Yuengling clock marking time...its red-and-green neon muted with age, its bay window upstairs evoking a cinematic Little Italy."[353] (By contrast, the *Daily News* described it as "a modest, almost crummy spot" in 1971.)[354]

At the height of Nick's popularity, continued Nichols, "the roll bakers got bombed at the bar," and "hoods sat two stools down from detectives. Nick's sandwiches were legal tender; locals paid their barber with them. Now and then, a limo pulled in from Atlantic City, sent to South Philly to scratch an itch.

"Those were the days."[355]

# Meatball Parm

Like roast beef, meatballs—and, eventually, meatball sandwiches—have deep roots in the cuisine of Italian American banquets. Brought over with the wave of immigrants, it's difficult to pinpoint exactly where or when dishes featuring meatballs made their way into Italian American cuisine. Most likely, they emerged, in parallel, in the early 1900s within enclaves across the Northeast, as well as in places like Chicago and New Orleans, their popularity accelerated by the Great Depression, when inexpensive but filling foods were important for survival.

In Philadelphia, Domenico Bucci comes to mind again, with his early catering business that specialized in roast pork and meatballs. Whether he was the first to package and sell a meatball sandwich is difficult to know, though it's probable the sandwich's commercial origins in South Philly date to around the same time he was starting up (and just as likely that home cooks made similar dishes even before that).

"In my Italian household, on Sunday morning," recalled Danny DiGiampietro, "I remember when my mother was getting ready to put the meatballs in the gravy, we'd steal them—the meatballs that were fried and ready to go—and smash 'em into a fresh roll with some sharp Provolone.… Man, it don't get no better than that!"[356] (Angelo's Sunday Morning, a rotating special sandwich, pays homage to that creation.)

More common, of course, is the meatball parm, or meatballs in tomato sauce with mozzarella and Parmesan cheeses. And while this throwback is rarely given much attention in the grand scheme of Philly's modern food culture, it remains a South Philadelphia classic that is still lovingly served at classic Italian sandwich shops like John's Roast Pork, George's, Cosmi's and even Geno's Steaks—not to mention just about every pizza place in the area.

## Italian Tuna

As with meatballs, the idea of a tuna sub is clearly not unique to Philadelphia, though it is worth briefly covering the idea of "Italian tuna," a modification typically found almost exclusively—at least in the pre-internet days—in urban Italian American neighborhoods. Most delis nationwide, whether a big chain like Jersey Mike's or a small mom-and-pop shop, offer a tuna option, water-packed fish mixed with mayo and maybe some celery chunks. That can be found in Philadelphia, too, but this other tuna is packed in extra virgin olive oil, without any mayo to be found. *The Italian way.*

This allows for more interesting creations, too, that go beyond just the standard tuna salad sandwich or tuna melt. Consider the Antipasto from A Cut Above in Newtown Square, for example, which combines Italian tuna with Parma prosciutto, sharp provolone, sweet roasted peppers, Sicilian olives, lettuce and special seasonings; Antonio's Don Tuna, Italian tuna with artichokes, prosciutto and balsamic vinegar; or Paesano's Tuna Italiano, Italian tuna with green olives, onions, herb cheddar spread, hard-boiled eggs, roasted tomato, pepperoncini, arugula and rippled potato chips.

## Egg

Speaking of eggs, like in many Northeast U.S. cities, there's also a strong culture of egg-based breakfast sandwiches in Philadelphia, aided by high-quality bread choices with which to make them. Beyond the obvious meats like bacon or sausage, regional concoctions often feature two other local-ish specialties: scrapple, from the Pennsylvania Dutch tradition, and pork roll (also known as Taylor ham), a central New Jersey delicacy.

Being made with offal and other meat trimmings, scrapple often gets a bad rap compared to other breakfast sausages, which makes little sense considering the production process is similar. If anything, the fact that scrapple is often cut heavily with cornmeal and/or buckwheat flour means its ratio of mystery meat to other ingredients is lower than in most sausages. Regardless, when fried up thin and crispy, it's a wonderful addition to any already delicious egg and cheese sandwich.

Pork roll is another egg sandwich–friendly product from the broader region, invented in 1856 by John Taylor in Trenton, New Jersey. While describing it as "a lightly smoked and cured pork product, with spices, salt, and preservatives," food writer Peter Genovese added that "its makers have never been forthright into what exactly goes into the stuff."[357]

Originally dubbed "Taylor's Prepared Ham," the name became "pork roll" after the 1906 Pure Food and Drug Act determined the meat didn't meet the legal definition of *ham*. That said, there remains fierce debate between North and South Jersey about what to call this product, the former clinging desperately to the illicit "Taylor Ham," even for other brands' pork roll.

At one point, Taylor tried to sue competitors who promoted products with similar monikers, such as "rolled pork" and "Trenton-style pork roll," but in 1910, after establishing its definition as "a food article made of pork, packed in a cylindrical cotton sack or bag in such form that it could be quickly prepared for cooking by slicing without removal from the bag," a court declared that the words "pork roll" could not be trademarked.[358]

Jumping back to egg sandwiches, the Italian tradition of mixing eggs and fried bell pepper strips is another common one, especially in South Philly. "The pizza joint is for pepper & egg," sang local rockers Marah in their song "Christian Street," a vignette of life in the Italian Market neighborhood, aptly and succinctly summing up Philly attitude toward the classic sandwich.[359] Despite being egg-based, this creation is certainly delicious any time of day.

# TRIPE AND TONGUE

If anything, this book has hopefully illustrated the abundance of sandwich options throughout the city, particularly favorites like steaks and roast pork.

But what about tripe and veal tongue? These curious creations are also available, though perhaps only—in sandwich form, at least—at George's Sandwich Shop, located in the 9th Street Italian Market since the 1930s.

Born in 1885 in Terpitsa, a mountain town in the Evrytania region of Greece, George Vellios immigrated to the United States in 1908. He soon started a food cart on 9th Street in the Italian Market area, and in 1936, he began renting out a portion of the same building where George's Sandwich Shop still operates. At first, said George's great-grandson and current owner Jon Vellios, "it would have been pretty basic: hamburgers, hot dogs, roast beef, roast pork and tongue. I don't think he sold tripe back then…and, of course, the cheesesteak. We were only two blocks from Pat's, so could he have copied it right after the steak was invented? Probably."[360]

Though George's sells plenty of mainstream sandwiches today—it's located on a busy stretch of the popular Italian Market—its specialties barbecue veal, tripe and ground veal stand out as unique, possibly intimidating creations not often found in other shops in the area.

The barbecue veal, oddly, has no relation to what any American would consider barbecue. "It's a veal tongue sandwich," said Vellios. "The story told to me was that no one knew how to say those words, so they just called it barbecue."[361] Odd name aside, this sandwich is a special one. "That's definitely my favorite sandwich," continued Vellios. "Tongue is so tender; it tastes like filet mignon. If you close your eyes and just taste it, it falls apart in your mouth, and it's so flavorful."[362]

It can, however, be tedious to prepare. "We get this big box of tongues," Vellios added. "And we have to take them apart, to peel them."[363] Once broken down, the meat is stewed in a mixture of George's tripe sauce, tomato sauce, vinegar and roasted peppers. It's not overly saucy—at least compared to some of George's other sandwiches—which is perhaps why Vellios also suggests adding some of the old-style bran mustard the shop carries.

"It's delicious," said Andrew Zimmern of the tongue when he visited George's with his Travel Channel show *Bizarre Foods*. "You would never know what it is. Everybody thinks when you're eating tongue that it's going to taste weird.…[But it's] one of the best cuts of meat on the cow."[364]

It's unlikely many people (except maybe Zimmern) would say something similar about tripe, the much maligned and, frankly, extra-chewy lining of the cow's stomach, yet this has remained a big draw for George's. "Tripe is one of the most famous things we sell," said Vellios. "We're probably one of the last people to make it, which is both good and bad because it is a time-consuming art, loosening up that intestine."[365] He estimates that tripe made its way onto the George's menu in the 1970s, based on local interest when the area was still predominantly Italian.

"There's a guy who comes in, 'Gigs,'" Vellios said of longtime patron John Gigliotti, "who I've known for over twenty years."

> *He is probably in his nineties. In Wildwood, he's a legend, because he used to operate the Wildwood tram. And he comes in, and he'll get his tripe, sit there for an hour, pay for a girl's sandwich, that kind of stuff. When we reopened, he gave me a signed picture of himself. So, there's still that kind of guy, but it is a mixed neighborhood now, and we've always respected that, not being 100 percent Italian ourselves. The Mexican population, lots of restaurant workers, eat tripe. A lot of Asians in this area also like to eat it.*

If George's didn't introduce the idea of a tripe sandwich, it may have instead come from a nearby competitor like Willie's Sandwich Shop or Shank's & Evelyn's. "George's and Willie's [which were both in the Italian Market] used to be the Pat's and Geno's version of the veal and tripe rivalry, back in the '80s and '90s," recalled Vellios. "A guy named Duke [Capocci] ran it; his son still comes to my store every day….We were definitely similar, had the same vibe. We were both great sandwich places that people loved, luncheonettes where customers stood at the window. We both sold the same stuff: veal, tripe and pork."

Though this was once a spirited rivalry, Willie's has been closed for more than a decade, so those feelings have faded for George's. "People still call us Willie's all the time," said Vellios. "We don't even correct them because [Willie's was] part of the market experience. They probably came here forty years ago, and they're trying to remember, so we don't mind."[366] (For Willie's tripe recipe, see appendix.)

Tripe is, of course, not for everyone, primarily known for its chewy texture and unique flavor. "But that's good," said Zimmern while chomping on George's version. "You know you're eating real food….Breathe through your nose; you get a little bit of the barnyard."[367]

"It used to come with little hairs in it," remembered Vellios. "Now, everything's done more commercially in the world of meat, so when we get it, it has already been cleaned."[368] Yet cooking tripe is still a timely process, especially in the fast-paced world of sandwich shops, requiring, like the tongue, several hours of stewing time. So, why does George's continue selling the stuff? "People keep coming," Vellios replied, simply. "These meats are nourishing, very good for you, and that's probably why—besides the fact they were cheaper—people used to eat them, because of all the nutrients."[369]

Funnily enough, many regulars don't even know what tripe is. "There are people that have been eating here for decades—maybe their grandmother brought them—and we don't tell them what's in it," Vellios said. "I remember how disgusted one customer looked when she found out. She said, 'I've been eating this every week for fifty years, and I never thought to ask.'" Still other patrons confuse the name with a similar-sounding fish. "That never ceases to amaze me," Vellios continued. "They say, 'Can I get a trout sandwich?'"[370] (They get a tripe sandwich.)

As a kid, Vellios himself was scared to try the crazy-looking food his family made, staunchly avoiding it for many years. Now, however, he said, "It's my favorite thing….Anyone who works at the shop, we all get tired of pork sandwiches or cheesesteaks. If we're going to take a sandwich home, it's going to be the tongue or the tripe."[371]

If these organ meats are too much to swallow, George's also offers a unique ground veal sandwich. "Imagine regular ground meat but more tender and flavorful." described Vellios. "We try to do as little to it as possible. We don't even use much salt or seasoning, so you can actually taste the meat." When the meat is raw, its rich, tender texture is evident, he added. "If you imagine a slab of ground meat from a grocery store, it's all red with a little bit of white. This is almost all white, with a little bit of tan meat. There's lots of fat, and it is very tender, almost like Kobe-style ground meat."[372]

The name of George's Roma sandwich, which mixes ground veal with ground pork, is not a reference to the Italian capital but instead a tribute to the Romani people who have adopted George's as their own. "They travel a lot, and they spend a lot of their money on food." explained Vellios. "And some places look down on them or spit at them, I guess, but we've always taken care of them. We'll get fifty of them in sometimes, and we'll close the store because it's a wedding or a funeral or someone's in from out of town. They bring us a ton of people."[373]

# Veggie

On perhaps the opposite end of the spectrum from tripe and tongue is the vegetarian hoagie, of which options have steadily increased in recent years. The most famous sandwich in this category thus far, however, undoubtedly

Dolores' vegetarian hoagie, The Henry. *Author photograph.*

came from "veggie-hoagie mecca" Chickie's Italian Deli, which thrived at 1014 Federal Street from 1993 to 2015.[374] This oft-awarded and highly revered sandwich, wrote Michael Klein, featured "a luscious layering of baked eggplant, sautéed broccoli rabe, house-roasted peppers and sharp provolone cheese inside a Sarcone's roll."[375]

When Chickie's closed after a divorce between the owners, Antonio Sawan rebooted the location as Antonio's Deli. Thankfully for the former spot's devoted fans, the new proprietor not only brought back several employees from the Chickie's days but also kept the veggie hoagie on the menu.

While this sandwich has, by now, spawned many imitations and spin-offs, its spiritual successor may just be The Henry from Dolores' 2Street, named for the late Henry George, who created Chickie's version. Similar to but not an exact replica of the original, it features hefty portions of shaved sharp provolone, fried zucchini, grilled eggplant, roasted peppers and broccoli rabe.

The idea that anyone *invented* the vegetarian sandwich, of course, would be somewhat dubious. At DiNic's, for example, they've long sold—especially during Lent—"the only vegetarian dish…with the true heft and authority of Philly street food," wrote Jim Quinn, a "drippy sandwich…crammed with nothing but garlicky spicy-hot roasted peppers and provolone."[376] And from the beginning of Tony Luke's, the Lucidono family proudly featured the

Uncle Mike, a sandwich stuffed to the brim with sweet and hot peppers, red gravy, fried onions, spinach and broccoli rabe.

The recent proliferation of both creative vegetarian fare as well as "Impossible" meat alternative products has obviously changed the game in terms of plant-based sandwich filling options, opening the door for an endless variety of vegan and vegetarian cheesesteaks and other innovative creations. Of all the sandwich categories to consider going forward, then, this one may be the most interesting to watch.

# BÁNH MÌ

The Vietnamese sandwich bánh mì—a byproduct of failed French colonialism that originated in Saigon in the 1950s—is now eaten worldwide, so it would be disingenuous to suggest Philly has any unique claim to it. That said, Philadelphia is a sandwich city, and as LaBan once wrote, it is certainly "no surprise our hoagie spirit has embraced the lighter, crispier notes of the Vietnamese bánh mì."[377]

"In their first South Philadelphia sightings (by non-Asians) in the Vietnamese enclaves that sprang up after the [Vietnam] war, they were a paradigm shift: more salad than meat," wrote Nichols. "More shapes—airy shreds and spears and spreads to lighten the density. More contrasts—vinegars and fish sauce, sweet mayos and garlicky meats—than the sandwich they were first compared to."[378]

Reportedly the first to serve what she called a "Vietnamese hoagie," Elizabeth-Ha Levan opened Elysees Cafe in the mid-1980s in South Philly. It was, wrote Quinn at the time, "the newest addition to the growing number of Southeast Asian specialty stores and restaurants on the fringes of Philadelphia's Italian Market."[379]

Initially labeling them "dainty and elegant," Quinn described these early Philly-style bánh mì as "a combination of excellent Sarcone's sandwich rolls, crisped in the oven, filled with either Elizabeth-Ha's homemade roast pork or her homemade liver pâte (or a combination of the two), with scallion, sweet and sour carrot, cucumber and coriander sprigs, sprinkled with a little Vietnamese fish sauce—an East meets South Philly masterpiece."[380]

"The first time I saw a sign in the Italian Market for Vietnamese hoagies, I didn't give it much thought," added *Daily News* restaurant critic Maria Gallagher in 1990. "I envisioned a regular hoagie with nuoc mam—

Vietnamese fish sauce—instead of oil or mayo. I've since discovered the Vietnamese hoagie is something with a personality all its own." Of the sandwiches at Viet Huong Cafe, which opened at 16th Street and Washington Avenue in 1990, Gallagher noted that the "excellent hoagie ($1.50) comes on fresh Italian bread that's been warmed to crisp the crust. Inside are slices of chicken roll and a pork-based lunch meat, crinkle-cut carrots, green pepper and scallion strips, a handful of fresh coriander and a cloud of pungent ground pepper....No tomato, no lettuce, no cheese, no oil, no mayo. It's not overstuffed like the typical hoagie is, but it's a satisfying sandwich for the price."[381]

"Bánh mì culture here has thrived in ways that are probably greater than in other cities because of our rolls, the bread culture," mused LaBan. "Many even use Sarcone's rolls, which is interesting, and adds some synergy."[382]

Over time, these Vietnamese-style sandwiches have picked up fans all over the city, notably spreading to Chinatown (e.g., QT Vietnamese Sandwich) and to fine dining in Center City (e.g., Sampan). Today, this style has become arguably as integral to the sandwich scene, from a local perspective, at least, as any other.

# Corned Beef Special

Though Philadelphia's sandwich culture is obviously superior to New York City's, the former would not attempt to also claim Jewish delis as their own. That said, in the 1800s, Philadelphia also saw a significant influx of Jewish immigrants, mostly from Germany and Poland, who, of course, brought with them unique culinary traditions that eventually manifested into restaurants and delis in and around the vibrant Jewish communities of the city.

By the 1950s, wrote Stacia Friedman, "Jewish delis were as omnipresent as Starbucks coffee shops are today. Popular delis in Center City included Bain's, the Corned Beef Academy, Robert's, the R&W, and Day's." In the 1960s, however, as urban blight overcame the former Jewish Quarter (today, Queen Village), much of the city's Jewish population "began to migrate out of the city for the western suburbs, Cherry Hill, and the far Northeast," Friedman continued. "They didn't want the next generation to slice pastrami. They wanted them to go to law school."[383]

Today, only a few shrines to the old Jewish deli remain, such as Famous 4th Street, Schlesinger's, Herschel's and the Pat's/Geno's–style codependence

A History of Philadelphia Sandwiches

of Murray's and Hymie's in Bala Cynwyd (just outside the city). Beyond that, however, one creation unique to Philadelphia perseveres: the corned beef special.

Unlike the Reuben, the corned beef special is always served cold. Its lean beef must be sliced impossibly thin, and then the oversized portion, which should be piled on rye, is topped with coleslaw and Russian dressing. These ingredients have obviously been served together—or at least alongside each other—at many places, most notably in the triple-decker combos of New York City spots like 2nd Ave or Carnegie Deli, which contain multiple meats—but this specific sandwich seems to only go by the 'special' moniker in the Philadelphia area.

According to the late Allen Meyers, a fellow author with The History Press who penned *The Jewish Community of West Philadelphia*, among other titles, Morris Blank created the sandwich in 1905 at his eponymous deli, located at 7th Street and Snyder Avenue in South Philly. Though Blank's Delicatessen is long gone, Blank was also uncle to Murray Chudhoff, who ran the famous Murray's Delicatessen on 60th Street and, later, 54th Street, and his brother Herman Chudhoff, who opened the Murray's outpost in Bala that still thrives.[384]

Over time, hot corned beef has become more prominent. "I like a corned beef special," said LaBan, "but the New York style of corned beef, thankfully, has taken over. The guy who owns Famous 4th Street is a Brooklyn deli guy, and he's really dominated local deli for a while, because he's a lot better than everybody else.…So, increasingly, I do see hot corned beef sandwiches."[385]

That said, the Philly-style corned beef special is still available around the region and offers a glimpse at a bygone era of Jewish delis that's truly unique to this city. (A turkey special, by the way—as long as it's the good stuff, hand-carved—is also excellent.)

# Zep

In Norristown—a small city in the western Philadelphia suburbs—and its environs, the curiously named zep reigns supreme within a strong Italian American sandwich tradition. "A zep is like a hoagie, but it's not," wrote LaBan. "And there are rules that define it. It comes on a roll that's wider than a typical hoagie roll, and, yes, its shape evokes a zeppelin. You don't

144

mix meats. The onion and tomato are cut extra-thick. There's a nice zesty smear of hot pepper relish. And there's absolutely never, ever any lettuce."[386]

A proper zep starts with—what else—the bread, always "Conshy" rolls from the nearby Conshohocken Italian Bakery. (In contrast to the hoagie, zep makers employ both round rolls and long rolls to offer a choice of sandwich size.) "It is a niche; not that many people make the zep," said Michael Gambone, assistant vice-president at the bakery, which produces three hundred or so zep rolls a day, compared to thousands of slimmer, shorter hoagie rolls.[387]

The default meat for a zep is cooked Hatfield salami, though nowadays there are a variety of options available—everything from the obvious (ham, turkey) to the less so (cheesesteak, hamburger or tuna salad, the latter of which LaBan called a "sleeper hit")—with the caveat that a true zep can only ever contain one kind of meat.[388] Provolone, oregano, salt, pepper and olive oil are also staples, as is the optional hot pepper relish. The secret to a zep's unique flavor, however, is the raw onion and tomato, hand-sliced extra-thick to order. "You want all the vegetables' juices to go straight into that sandwich," explained Josephine Wieber, the longtime master zep maker at Eve's Lunch.[389]

Zeps, just after completion, at Lou's in Norristown. *Lou's Sandwich Shop.*

Aside from single meat stubbornness, another peculiarity here is the staunch aversion to lettuce. "Not allowed on the premises," said Anthony Mashett, the current owner of Eve's Lunch, "because then you're getting into hoagie territory."[390]

Like so many of these sandwiches, the zep's origins are shrouded in legend and mystery. Marge Alba, whose father, Lou Bondi, founded zep mainstay Lou's in 1941, told the *Inquirer*'s Derek Nunnaly that a local Greek man invented the sandwich in 1938, naming it after the zeppelin shapes its thick rolls evoked. At Eve's, Mashett—whose parents bought the shop from early zep adopter Joseph Linfante—said he'd heard the inventor was Italian, possibly with a name that started with "Z-e-p."

"Norristown's city directory for 1938 lists James and Anna Pascuzzi as owners of a restaurant on Main Street, a block from Linfante's," reported Nunnally. "Both Pascuzzis are long dead, but Anna's niece Barbara Stankus said the sandwich was indeed born in her uncle's small, crowded shop."[391]

"When the [*Hindenburg*] zeppelin crashed in New Jersey, it was around the time that he had this brilliant idea for a sandwich," said Stankus. "He used Italian hard-crusted rolls that were shaped like a zeppelin, so he named it the zep."[392]

"He may have been a better sandwich-maker than businessman," continued Nunnally, noting that the store disappeared from local directories by the end of the 1940s.[393] Another place called Jim's Original Zep Shop—as in Jim Pazcuzzi, maybe—appeared briefly in the '50s but also disappeared somewhat quickly.

While zeps are inextricably associated with Norristown, the concept did spread to nearby blue-collar towns, such as Pottstown, Conshohocken, Phoenixville and Royersford, where the term is still occasionally used, typically to indicate a special type of hoagie. That said, the zep's epicenter remains the Pat's/Geno's–style rivalry of Norristown mainstays Lou's and Eve's—the former "a vintage-1941 lunch counter a couple doors down from a funeral parlor" and the latter "a bare-bones, tile-floored sandwich shop" that originated as Linfante's on Main Street, a block from Lou's.[394] (Today, the shops are located about two miles from each other.)

As for whether the zep is truly a unique sandwich style, those opinions tend to vary based on one's vicinity to Norristown. "It's a localism," said etymology specialist Howard Robboy. "It's just a variation of the same sandwich."[395] Lou Bondi, who passed away in 1988, would've staunchly disagreed. He used to say, according to his grandson, "You want a hoagie? Go to a hoagie shop. This is a zep shop."[396]

# STROMBOLI

A first thought when encountering a section about stromboli in a sandwich book might naturally be to question whether this is even a sandwich. Isn't that an offshoot of pizza? Nope. Well, sometimes—and perhaps more often than not. The original incarnation, however—invented in the Philly suburb Essington in 1949—distinguishes itself from pizza-adjacent variations by the type of dough that's used, which creates a crispy, bread-like exterior, in contrast to the much softer pizza dough. (Does the dough type change the definition? That may be a question better left to social media.)

Nazzereno "Nat" Romano, undated photograph. *Romano's.*

"I've always considered it a sandwich," said Peter Romano, the current owner of Romano's Pizzeria & Italian Restaurant and grandson of creator Nazzereno "Nat" Romano. "And my grandfather called it 'the prefabricated sandwich.'"[397]

When Nat created the dish in late 1949, he used an Italian bread dough, which requires a more complicated production method than pizza dough. "A bakery is different from a pizza shop," said Peter. "When we're making baked goods like stromboli, it's a seven- or eight-hour process; the dough is worked four or five times and raised four times. And then we do a final proof for almost an hour in a proofing box…as if we're making an Italian bread roll."[398]

As Romano's stromboli started to gain notoriety in the 1960s and early '70s, other area pizza shops tried to replicate it. But, instead of using a bread crust like Romano's, they'd flop over or roll their pizza dough after putting toppings inside. "Pizza dough is very soft," Peter continued, "it doesn't have the same texture as bread… It's much easier, so I don't blame them… but it's not the same."[399]

Nat Romano came to the United States in 1923 from L'Aquila in Central Italy. His is not the typical Italian immigrant story of a peasant looking for a better life; rather, his is the story of a man active in the resistance against Benito Mussolini. When it became evident that Il Duce's rise to power was inevitable, Nat's family encouraged him to get out of dodge. "I don't know what exactly he was doing," said Peter. "But my grandfather's family in Italy told him, 'You better leave the country; it's not going to be good for you.'"[400]

Nat Romano's original storefront, opened in 1944. (Note: the lettering on the window appears to have been digitally enhanced.) *Romano's.*

A stonemason by trade, Nat worked on several projects in the area, including ones at Villanova University and St. Charles Seminary, but when the Depression came and work was scarce, he started selling pizza (tomato pies, really) along Washington Avenue in South Philly. In 1944, when an opportunity arose to move to the nearby suburb of Essington and open his pizza business in a storefront, he took it. The new spot was located two doors down from the corner of Route 420 and the Industrial Highway (Route 291), which, during the war, was situated along the popular trolley line from Chester to the Navy Yard in Philadelphia, meaning many hungry men would pass by every day.

What's also interesting about this move is that, at the time, pizza was virtually unknown outside the Italian enclaves of big cities. "In that area, there were a lot of people with Swedish, Irish and Dutch backgrounds, and they thought his last name was Pizzeria," said Peter. "Because that's what it said on the window. Until the day he died, some people in town still called him Mr. Pizzeria."[401]

In late 1949, while experimenting with his bread dough—not the pizza dough, Peter was quick to reiterate—Nat created the first incarnation of what would become the stromboli. He was already familiar with a similar Italian dish, *pane imbottito* (literally "stuffed bread"), and he was regularly making hoagies at his shop, both of which provided inspiration for this new creation. At first, he offered three options: sweet, hot and pepperoni. Like his Italian hoagie, all of them contained boiled ham, cotechino, capicola and cheese, but roasted bell peppers, which Nat believed would better endure the baking process, replaced the standard lettuce and tomato. In the hot stromboli, he also added spicy banana peppers, and in the pepperoni, he removed the vegetables altogether, instead adding more tasty, spicy meat.

"Grandpop had been selling these for a month or so with no name," said Peter.

*There was a gentleman named William Schofield—he eventually married my aunt Celia and became my uncle Bill—who lived right across the street. He was in the shop one day, probably in January 1950, and saw the sandwich sitting on the counter. He inquired as to what it was, to which Grandpop said it was just something he made up and that Bill should try it. There was a conversation, and Bill kept insisting it needed a name. So, my grandfather invited him to put a tag on it. Of the top of his head, Bill said, "Call it stromboli!"[402]*

At that moment, it turns out, the movie *Stromboli*, which took place on the impossibly beautiful Aeolian island of the same name, had captured the world's attention. Back then, it was still shocking for a Hollywood star (Ingrid Bergman) to leave her husband and child for a film director (Roberto Rossellini), and this shock was further amplified by Bergman's out-of-wedlock pregnancy. The movie's title stuck as the sandwich's name. (A vintage poster still hangs in the restaurant.)

In the mid-1960s, while Nat was plugging away, pizza shops began to proliferate in the area. "Before that," Peter said, "we were virtually the only one in Delaware County. There were a few others—Pinocchio's, Marra's—but not many." Once these shops were everywhere, the addition of stromboli to their menus was a natural evolution. "A new shop would open in, say,

Bryn Mawr, and people familiar with Romano's would go in there and say, 'Where's your stromboli?' The owner, of course, would have no idea what they were talking about. But the customer would describe it, and sure enough, the next time they went in, a stromboli would be on the menu. It might not be what we were doing—in most cases, probably not—but that's what would happen, and that's how stromboli eventually became different things in different parts of the country."[403]

Even after pizza dough floppers took over the public's understanding of stromboli, Romano's has staunchly held firm with Nat's bread-based recipe. "Sometimes, I wish I could have changed," said Peter, "because it's so much easier to do pizza dough stromboli than to be a bakery. But I have my father, at ninety-one, living in his house connected to the restaurant, keeping an eye on things. In that sense, I'm more of a caretaker; I must do everything the way it's been done since Grandpop was alive. And it's a lot of work…but it's still made the same way he made it in 1950."[404]

Nat Romano originally described his stromboli as "the prefabricated sandwich," which illustrates another differentiator for the restaurant that's not always appreciated by customers. "We make them in batches, just like a bakery," said Peter. "You can't go to a bakery and say, 'I want a loaf of bread, but I want pickles and onions in it,' but at most pizza shops, you can order a stromboli any way you want because they're assembling it to order. That isn't done at Romano's. Ours are all prefabricated; to get the bread right, they have to be. So, we have about fourteen different types, but you can't come to the counter and order your own because stromboli this way cannot be made in twenty minutes while you wait."

"Sometimes, it gets me in trouble," he continued. "Because I'm one place, and there are thousands of others selling something they're calling stromboli. It's this flopped-over pizza version that you can get any way you want. But I can't do that and get that bread correct. Some people don't understand that…but fortunately, enough people do that it's kept us going all this time."[405]

After assembly, the stromboli go into the oven for thirty-five to forty minutes, which par-bakes them until almost complete. This is a notably longer cook that allows the bread to develop its distinctive crispy exterior, a texture that's nearly impossible to recreate with pizza dough. Once that step is complete, the stromboli are frozen, and they'll wait to be eventually finished to order in the oven. (Peter is, at the time of this writing, working on a production change that should allow for most of the stromboli ordered at the restaurant in a day to be ones made that morning.)

## May We Suggest You Take Home Any Item on the Menu

### PIZZA – TOMATO PIE

| | | |
|---|---|---|
| 1. With Mozzarello Cheese | .90 | 1.30 |
| 2. With Provolone Cheese | 1.00 | 1.50 |
| 3. With Grated Cheese | 1.10 | 1.60 |
| 4. With American Cheese | .90 | 1.30 |

#### EXTRA

| | | | | |
|---|---|---|---|---|
| Onion | .15 | .25 | Salami | .30 .50 |
| Mushrooms | .30 | .50 | Pepperoni | .25 .45 |
| Anchovies | .30 | .50 | Fried Sweet Pepper | .30 .50 |
| Sausage | .30 | .50 | Ground Beef | .40 .65 |

#### ROMANO'S SPECIAL
FRIDAY, SATURDAY, SUNDAY ONLY

Strambolli .......................... .85
The Prefabricated Sandwich

### SANDWICHES ON ITALIAN ROLL

1. Hoagies .............................. .45 .90 /30
2. Special Hoagies, All Ham and Cheese ...... .55 1.00 150
3. Special Hoagies with Italian Salami, Cheese, and Capacoli ........... .90 1.20 170
   Hoagie Sandwich Includes Oil, Tomato, Lettuce, Onion, Pickle and Hot or Sweet Pepper
4. Steak Sandwiches ...................... .50 .90 130
5. Grilled Ham Sandwiches ............... .55 1.00 140
6. Grilled Italian Sausage Sandwiches ...... .50 .90 140

#### EXTRA

| | | |
|---|---|---|
| With Cheese | .10 | .15 |
| With Mushroom | .15 | .35 30 |
| With Fried Sweet Pepper | .10 | .20 |

7. Veal Scaloppine Sandwiches ........... .50 .90 140
8. Meat Ball Sandwiches ................. .40 .70 120

### SANDWICHES ON SLICED BREAD

| | | |
|---|---|---|
| Lettuce and Tomato | 3.5 | .25 |
| Ham, Lettuce and Tomato | 6.5 | .45 |
| Ham, Cheese, Lettuce and Tomato | 7.5 | .55 |
| Bacon, Lettuce and Tomato | 7.5 | .55 |
| Hamburger on Roll | 5.0 | .30 |

### FOUNTAIN MENU

Delicious Ice Cream Sodas .... .35
Made with Two Dips of Ice Cream, Syrup, Whipped Cream and Cherry

| | |
|---|---|
| Vanilla | Cherry |
| Chocolate | Lemon |
| Strawberry | |

Without Whipped Cream and Cherry .......................... .30

Double Rich Milk Shake ...... .40
Any Flavor

Double Rich Milk Shake with Egg .......................... .50

Sundaes .......................... .45

Chocolate Nut
Pineapple
Crushed Cherry
Strawberry

Ice Cream

| | |
|---|---|
| Small .15 | Large .25 |

### BEVERAGES

| | |
|---|---|
| Soda | .15 .25-35 |
| Iced Tea | .15 |
| Hot Tea | .10 |
| Coffee | .10 |
| Milk | .10 .15-25 |

An early Romano's menu including the "prefabricated sandwich," creatively spelled "Strambolli." *Romano's.*

This construction method also makes Romano's stromboli ideal for shipping, a business that has grown considerably in recent years. "I can't tell you how different it's been since *Delicious Destinations* aired on the Travel Channel in 2016," said Peter. "My Yelp hits went from seventy to seven thousand in one month. There was a lot of exposure from that."[406] (The

Travel Channel segment also suggested getting a side of marinara with Romano's stromboli, which became so popular that they now offer it by default for every eat-in and takeout order.)

"One of the great things about shipping them around the country," Peter continued, "is that they're sealed. If you want a Philly cheesesteak [one of the fourteen available flavors] and you're in Las Vegas, why get a sandwich kit that you need to put together when you can get a sandwich that's already constructed? You just pop it in the oven, and then away you go."[407]

Despite Romano's successes, Peter laments what he perceives as missed opportunities to expand the business. "I wish I could have done more with it than what I have," he said, while reflecting on an opportunity to sell at the Sixers and Flyers arena in South Philadelphia that never materialized. "I've talked to people about mass-producing, copacking, etc., to see if I could do branding on a large scale, but I've never been able to make that move. That's just not what I am; I'm a little, family-owned, corner Italian restaurant."

"The older I get, the more I think about my grandfather and how he came to this country with nothing," he continued. "I've tried to stay true and loyal to what he created. I often wonder what he would think if he could see us today, a business that he started seventy-nine years ago, still here. That doesn't happen too often."[408]

# 7

# BREAD

W hile so far, this book has mainly focused on sandwich *fillings*, Peter Romano would likely agree that this approach omits perhaps the most important part of any sandwich: the bread. In other words, a sandwich is only as good as the bread it is served on, and great bread is arguably what truly makes Philly sandwiches superior.

A common refrain from locals who have left the area is that even the good Philly-style sandwiches made in Florida, California or elsewhere are *decent enough*—but the bread's just not the same. There's less agreement, however, on what specifically makes the rolls better in Philly. Is it consistency, freshness or something in the water? The answer is more complex than it might originally seem.

Although Philly-style bread is often considered a monolith, in reality, there is a reasonable amount of diversity among area shops. The Amoroso-style roll, popularized at Wawa, is likely the most common, with its thin-but-crispy crust and soft interior, but many afficionados prefer mouth-destroyers, which are firmer on the outside and often coated liberally with sesame seeds. There's certainly room for both styles and anything in between, and perhaps a cheesesteak is better with one style (the former) and a hoagie another (the latter).

When asked to describe the perfect cheesesteak roll, Frank Olivieri Jr. of Pat's Steaks said it should have the "consistency inside of soft Italian bread. And the crust has—I would not say baguette-like—but, depending on the weather or humidity…it could have a crunchy appearance on the outside or it could be like [soft] pretzel skin."[409]

"I'm looking for cooked bread, not pale and soft," said Danny DiGiampietro. "I like a crispy crust and a soft interior. It should be easy to eat but still give that crackle of crispiness....And I'm looking for a star. The bread should be as big a star as the protein."[410]

In addition, said Ken Silver of Jim's, "a good roll must hold up to the actual sandwich. The biggest problem with a lot of rolls—the reason we don't sell gluten-free rolls, for instance—is because they just fall apart.... You don't want to not be able to bite through, or bite through too easily. Consistency is important. That whole mouthfeel thing is the thing."[411]

If a hot sandwich is eaten just after it is made, the roll is more likely to be crispy. If it is wrapped and taken away, however, the outside is naturally going to soften, though a pleasant chewiness should persist. With a cold hoagie, on the other hand, a natural outer crispiness should be retained.

Freshness also plays a key part. Enough sandwiches are consumed every day in the city that the rolls don't have time to sit around and get stale or lose flavor. At high-volume places like Pat's and Jim's, bakeries need to produce and deliver rolls throughout the day to keep up with demand. And no self-respecting shop would serve a roll from the previous day or one that had been frozen. (Amusingly, at Shank's Original on Pier 40, birds begin to gather in the water each day around 3:00 p.m., knowing any leftover bread is about to become a tasty snack for them when the shop closes.)

Bread preference can produce fierce loyalty and even fiercer arguments. "Living in South Philly is a lot like living in the border states during the Civil War," wrote the *South Philly Review*. "Brother was pitted against brother, fathers against sons, based on whether they were loyal to the Union. In South Philly, the bread war divides families based upon loyalties to bakeries."[412]

Perhaps comparing these disagreements to war takes it too far. "They're cousins," Frank Jr. quipped, referencing the tendency for different local bakery companies to share actual relatives (or, at least, come from the same neighborhood). "They all make the same exact bread. Anybody who's making a decent sandwich in Philadelphia is using this [style of] bread."[413]

# City of Bread...erly Love

From the beginning of European settlement, baking was an important industry in Philadelphia. One of the first prominent local bakers was Welshman Evan Thomas, a Quaker miller who, in 1735, built a large bake oven on a tract of land along the Delaware River, near the northern edge of Philadelphia County. The Bake House, as it was known, was a major operation that supplied bread and biscuits to ships that plied the river.[414] Reportedly, Thomas's property featured an oven "large enough to hold three or four hundred weight of bread at one time" and "facilities for loading and unloading vessels…so good that many ships had all their baking done at the place."[415]

When Benjamin Franklin came to Philly in 1723—at the age of seventeen, with barely any cash—one of the first things he did was buy some bread. "I was fatigued with travelling, rowing, and want of rest, I was very hungry; and my whole stock of cash consisted of a Dutch dollar, and about a shilling in copper," wrote Franklin. "[Then] I met a boy with bread.…I went immediately to the baker's he directed me to, in Secondstreet, and ask'd for bisket, intending such as we had in Boston; but they, it seems, were not made in Philadelphia.…I made him give me three-penny worth of any sort. He gave me, accordingly, three great puffy rolls. I was surpriz'd at the quantity, but took it, and, having no room in my pockets, walk'd off with a roll under each arm, and eating the other.[416]

The large migration of German immigrants to southeastern Pennsylvania—during both the colonial period and the early 1800s—allowed them to establish an initial stronghold on this budding industry. Christopher Ludwick (also spelled Ludwig) was one example, appointed in 1777 by the Continental Congress as the superintendent of bakers for the Continental army.[417] Another was Godfrey Keebler, who started an eponymous bakery in 1862 that would go on to have reasonable success as a manufacturer of cookies. Other key players included Freihofer and Pyle-Knadler.

One of the popular curiosities of the 1876 Centennial Exhibition in Philadelphia was the Vienna Model Bakery, where the Fleishmann brothers—Austrian immigrants who lived in Cincinnati, Ohio, at the time—showed off the packaged compressed yeast cake they had invented and how it affected the bread-making process. At the end of the exhibition, they moved their Model Bakery to Broad Street, where they would expand to become a nationwide baking company. "The Fleishmanns' process greatly improved the commercial production of bread," wrote historian Jack McCarthy, "[and] became widely used in commercial baking, ushering in the era of mass-produced, store-bought bread."[418]

An 1882 census of Philadelphia bakers reported that the city was home to 934 baking establishments, employing a total of 3,240 workers. Interestingly however, only 10 of these establishments—a mere 1 percent—were "steam"

A trade card for Fleishmann's Vienna Model Bakery at the 1876 Centennial Exhibition. *Free Library of Philadelphia.*

bakeries. "At a time when most industries were powered by steam engines and many manufacturing processes were automated," McCarthy wrote, "baking in Philadelphia was still done primarily by hand."[419] (Despite a few larger bakeries, at this time, the industry generally consisted of small, neighborhood stores.)

Bread was, of course, a staple in Italian immigrant homes from the time they began to arrive in Philadelphia in the late 1800s, and while much of it was surely homemade, small shops or grocers in the Italian enclave of South Philly also began to carry it. An entry in the 1880 U.S. census lists a Joseph Sassa, for example, as a baker on Christian Street.[420] It would take some time, however, for the Italians to eclipse the Germans as the city's preferred style of bakery. (A concept soft pretzel lovers might still dispute.)

Around the turn of the twentieth century, two Italian bakeries that would become particularly important—especially when it comes to sandwiches—began operations. Luigi Vilotti came to Philadelphia in 1884 from Calabria, and by the following year, he had established a bakery at 726 Carpenter Street. After briefly relocating to 770 South 7th Street, he settled at 633 Fitzwater Street, near Marshall Street. Around the corner, in 1898, Nicolangelo Marinelli, who arrived in Philadelphia from Molise (then Abruzzi) in 1881, purchased an existing bakery business at 1020 South 8th Street from Charles H. Kiesel.[421] Early on, these locations were "convenient for the day workers who had to leave early in the morning to be tracked off for road work locally or to New Jersey to work in the farms," wrote Morello, and "mothers with large families [who] could rely on bakers to do what time would not allow, if they could afford it.[422]

During the first half of the twentieth century, Vilotti and Marinelli would become Philadelphia's most prominent Italian bakeries and cash in on the first wave of sandwich fever that hit the city between world wars. (Marinelli also created and produced the famous Bookbinder's dinner roll.[423])

In the late 1950s—in the first of many Philadelphia bread family mergers—Nicola's daughter Mary Marinelli married Luigi's son Charles Vilotti. Though Nicola's son Joseph continued to run Marinelli Bakery independently until the mid-1960s, the Vilotti bakery changed its name to Vilotti-Marinelli and prepared for hoagie roll dominance. (The company changed its name once again in the 1990s to Vilotti-Pisanelli, referencing a third family that had helped run the bakery's operations for several generations.)

"The Vilotti-Pisanelli bakery's bread is, unknowingly, very well-known, well-eaten and well-digested," wrote Morello in 1999, alluding to the fact that, while today, the bakeries themselves can be as famous as the sandwiches they are made on, that was not always the case. "It's at Pat's Steaks and Geno's Steaks," continued Morello, "eaten by the thousands, maybe over 25,000 people in some weeks. Almost everyone has eaten this bread, without realizing its name. U.S. presidents ate Vilotti-Pisanelli, as did Oprah, prizefighters, major (and minor) celebrities, sports figures and regular people."[424]

The evolution of bread options during the early days of Pat's Steaks is, unfortunately, somewhat unclear. "Pat wasn't doing thousands of sandwiches," said Frank Olivieri Jr., "so he probably just got it from a small, local bakery."[425] Was it Vilotti? Marinelli? Someone else? Frank Jr. did add, however, that his father—who was in his eighties in 2023—assured him they had been using Vilotti-Marinelli as far back as he could remember, which aligns to the period of the merger. It's likely, too, that Geno's used Vilotti-Marinelli from the time it opened in the '60s, as it often promoted the bread in its advertisements.

"The bread was always perfect back then," said Nick Miglino. "Everybody had good bread. It was a long, lanky roll, not exactly like a baguette, but thin, not wide, maybe ten to twelve inches long and always light and crispy, well cooked on the outside, not doughy or heavy.…Most places back then used Vilotti-Marinelli.…Yeah, that was the bread."[426]

**PANETTERIA ITALIANA**

NICOLA MARINELLI

1020 So. 8th St.     Phila., Pa.

Special Italian Style
FRENCH BREAD
Served at the Hof Brau
*Supplied Fresh Daily by*
CHARLES VILOTTI
BAKERY
Marshall and Fitzwater Sts.
Phila.     Both Phones

VILOTTI & MARINELLI BAKING CO INC

**CENTER CITY**

EST - 1900
**VILOTTI**
City Wide Delivery

For Prompt Courteous Service
**Famous For**
**ITALIAN & FRENCH BREAD**
STEAK & HOAGIE ROLLS
HOAGIE BREAD
CATERING TO
RESTAURANTS - LUNCHEONETTES
STEAK & HOAGIE SHOPS
**MArket 7-5038**
Marshall & Fitzwater . . . . . . . MArkt 7-5038

*Above*: An advertisement for Nicola Marinelli's bakery from the Italian-language newspaper *La Libera Parola*, 1922, and one for Charles Vilotti's from the *Morning Post* (Camden, NJ), 1939. *Newspapers.com.*

*Left*: Vilotti's bakery became Vilotti-Marinelli in the late 1950s, illustrated here in a 1959 Yellow Pages advertisement. *Library of Congress.*

Around the turn of the twenty-first century, Vilotti-Pisanelli began to suffer from consistency problems, and Pat's decided to look elsewhere. "It's *this* close to the original recipe," said Frank Jr. of his new bread supplier, South Jersey-based Aversa's Italian Bakery. "It looks, smells and tastes similar. It's almost the same."[427]

In 2006, Vilotti-Pisanelli sold out to D'Ambrosio Bakery—originally founded as a family bakery in 1939 at 9th and Wharton Streets—which itself had been acquired by leveraged-buyout specialist Gatehouse Ventures a year before. D'Ambrosio closed for good in 2013.[428]

This consolidation and elimination opened the door for Liscio's Bakery, founded in South Jersey in 1994, to rapidly expand and become one of the largest and most well-known suppliers of fresh bread to sandwich shops in the area. In the relatively small world of Philadelphia bakers, it is perhaps not surprising that Liscio's is co-owned by Chad Vilotti, Luigi's great-grandson.

# THE ICON

The most recognizable Philadelphia-area sandwich roll today is that of Amoroso's Baking Company. It's the brand every denizen is raised to know and the one most likely to be cited colloquially as a requirement for any *authentic* hoagie or cheesesteak. Locally, however, as trends have swung toward both artisanal house-made bread (e.g., Angelo's) or bread from smaller bakeries like Sarcone's (see the following section), it may seem like Amoroso's has become less cool. Nonetheless, the bakery's reach across a huge variety of Delaware Valley steak houses, pizza joints, delis, etc., remains both broad and strong. Beyond that, Amoroso's retail, frozen and par-baked programs have helped establish it as *the* Philly sandwich bread brand outside the immediate area.

Founded by Italian immigrant Vincenzo Amoroso and his two sons in Camden, New Jersey, in 1904, the company moved to West Philly in 1914, where it remained for almost ninety years. (It is now based in South Jersey.) Amoroso's first major impact on local sandwiches came from a partnership with its neighbors and friends at Jim's & Millie's Steaks. "They were using hot dog rolls, [which] couldn't contain the onions and the peppers and the toppings that would go on the steak," said Leonard Amoroso, the current CEO. "The rolls would just kind of melt and fall apart. We provided them a roll [that] held up….It was able to hold the onions, the cheese, the peppers, mushrooms, whatever people ultimately put on the steak sandwich."[429]

Though originally a small family bakery built up through twice-a-day home delivery, today, Amoroso's is a success story of expansion through innovative, large-scale distribution. The company's first major business shift came in the early 1950s, when it began selling its bread to the A&P supermarket in Overbrook Park. Jesse Amoroso, the bakery's COO and executive vice-president, told an eye-opening story about how this first went down. "My Italian grandfather went to talk to an Irish buyer at the

Long after moving away, Vincenzo Amoroso poses with his original Camden, New Jersey oven, circa 1960. *Amoroso's Baking Company.*

A&P right near City Line Avenue, and the buyer said to him, 'Who do you think's gonna buy that *dego* bread in this store?'"[430]

Despite the buyer's usage of a slur that would provoke the most docile of men, Vincenzo remained cool. "Listen," he said, "give me a couple of days to sell the product here. If it doesn't sell, call me, I'll come back and take it, and you'll never hear from me again. If it sells, we'll talk."[431]

"Well," said Jesse, "the rest is history."[432] He admitted to not being sure how precisely accurate this exchange is but said that it has become a popular family fable. Regardless, this retail opportunity had perfect timing, coinciding with the suburban expansion of the 1950s and '60s. Soon, more grocery stores signed on, and by 1960, Amoroso's had moved into a larger facility at 845 South 55th Street and expanded delivery reach to New Jersey and Delaware.

One day in the early 1970s, Amoroso's fate would shift again. A man came into the office, recalled Leonard, and said, "I want to open a steak shop in California, and I need your rolls. Can you do it?"[433]

*Left*: An Amoroso advertisement from the 1959 Yellow Pages. *Library of Congress.*

*Below*: An undated photograph of the famous Amoroso's truck. *Amoroso's Baking Company.*

"Sure," Leonard thought, "we can send them out frozen," and just like that, a new business line was born.[434] (As of this writing, The Cheese Steak Shop franchise, whose now-retired founder, Keith Layton, was the aforementioned office visitor, has more than twenty-five stores in Northern California.)[435]

Today, Amoroso's frozen business is crucial to the brand's success and perhaps what most distinguishes it from other Philly-area bakeries. The New Jersey facility now produces more than 60,000 rolls a day, working with 250 distributors in 42 states, plus Puerto Rico and Guam. For the frozen bread, said Leonard, the product is frozen solid five to seven minutes after it comes out of the oven, "so all of that freshness is locked in."[436]

Amoroso's other claim to fame is that it has been the main bread supplier for beloved convenience store Wawa since around 1970, when the chain started selling sandwiches. (Wawa now sells more than eighty million hoagies in a year.)[437] Originally, Amoroso would deliver fresh rolls each morning in their bakery trucks—just like they do for countless other sandwich shops—but as Wawa began to expand beyond the local area, the need to keep up with demand would lead to production and distribution changes.

Experimentation at new facilities in New Jersey began in the mid-1990s. "We went to the city years ago," said Leonard Amoroso about why they chose not to expand in Southwest Philly. "But we were landlocked. And Vineland [New Jersey] was an attractive area because it had a good development program."[438] By 2008, all of Wawa's rolls were being produced at the Omni Baking Co. facility (a partnership between the Amoroso family and Atlantic City's Ginsburg Bakery) in New Jersey.[439]

In 2012, as Wawa began to expand into Florida, the chain partnered with Amoroso's to pilot a par-baking program, where rolls would be cooked most of the way at the bakery and then finished at individual stores. "Fresh baked rolls," pledged Wawa CEO Chris Gheysens at the time. "By the end of [2013] you will have an oven in every Wawa."[440] It's unclear, however, what the current state of this program is, and Jesse declined to provide any further details, other than to say par-baking isn't an important part of Amoroso's current business.[441]

It is, of course, an ongoing challenge to manage such a massive production while maintaining quality across all aspects of the business. "As we've grown in other areas," Jesse said, "that are not the up and down the street, mom and pop shops, people have perceived that we're not the local corner bakery anymore. We're much larger than that, I'm proud to say, but the ability for us to grow our retail and our merchandising presence is made possible because

An Amoroso hoagie roll, purchased at the local supermarket Wegmans. *Author photograph.*

of the insistence we keep on our core business....We consider that to be as critical to what we do as we always have."

"The testament," he continued, "is how many places in the inner city—corner stores, bodegas and mini marts, for instance—are using our products, that aren't the namesake places. This speaks to the fact that we are part of the fabric and the quilt of the institution of the Philly sandwich."[442]

What is also interesting about Amoroso's is how the alternative business lines have cemented it as the brand name synonymous with Philadelphia bread all around the world. The frozen program, for example, allows countless businesses that want to serve *authentic* steaks and hoagies elsewhere to do so. And the bakery's diffuse grocery store circulation, of course, lets all those hungry expats get a taste of home from the convenience of their new one. Though critics might argue that the quality coming out of such a large production can't match a freshly baked roll from a smaller bakery, it's inarguable that Amoroso's has become a de facto Philadelphia ambassador, spreading brotherly love far and wide.

# THE ARTISAN

The antithesis of Amoroso's vast expansion and innovation might just be Sarcone's Bakery, a 9th Street mainstay since 1918. Despite the challenges of depressions, recessions, automation, industrialization, changing eating habits and the never-ending progress of modern society, Sarcone's has remained true to its roots as a bakery made for daily neighborhood shopping. (And, crucially, making some of the city's best sandwich rolls.)

"The only thing that has changed since [1918] is the people making it.... The ingredients are the same, just the hands are different," said current owner Louis Sarcone Jr.[443] This isn't *precisely true*; Sarcone's has evolved minimally. Lou's great-grandfather Luigi did start in the current building's basement in 1918, but in the late 1920s, the bakery expanded upstairs, adding brick ovens on the second floor. Then after World War II, it added two more ovens and expanded into a second building. It's also adapted with small concessions to modern machinery and techniques to promote consistency. But much of what the bakery does remains the same, as does its family-based culture.

"If you don't listen to the generation before you, something gets lost," said Lou Jr. "You have to pay attention, and that's the hardest thing for generational businesses, listening to the one before you. Even if you disagree with that person, you can really screw up a family business if you don't listen."[444]

"For my grandfather [who passed in 2018]," added fifth-generation baker Louis Sarcone III, "I want to make sure that I can keep the product the same.... [So,] when people hear 'Sarcone' they think 'the best bread in the world.'"[445]

One of the most important secrets to Sarcone's success is incredibly simple but costly: time. Starting around midnight, baking a Sarcone's roll takes six hours from start to finish, with plenty of resting to develop flavor. (A commercial bakery, by contrast, might do this in an hour.) After being initially mixed, the dough sits for two hours. At 2:00 a.m., the bakers start separating it into rolls and loaves, which takes another two hours. After that, it's into the proof boxes for another rise, then finally into the oven. By 6:00 a.m., this beautiful bread is ready for the line of patrons that has surely already formed outside. "No commercial bakery shop is going to wait six hours; they're going to put in preservatives and meet the demand," Lou Jr. said.[446]

Another Sarcone's secret is cooking the bread right on the brick oven floor. "The alternative is metal, an oven that revolves," said Lou Jr. "The

Sarcone's original
basement oven.
*Sarcone's Bakery.*

only thing that revolves in a brick oven is our bakers. We go in with
fifteen-foot sticks and move the bread around ourselves, to the hot spots
in the oven."

"Ever see trucks that say 'hearth-baked bread'?" he continued. "That's
baloney, because nobody uses brick, especially in a commercial bakery.
Ours is hearth-baked; there's no metal in between the bread, the dough,
and the hearth."[447]

Sarcone's ovens are almost one hundred years old, so new ones can't just
be picked up at the nearest restaurant supply store. Like a good cast-iron
pan, those hearths hold nearly a century of seasoning, creating a unique
environment that can't be replicated with mere materials.

"It's an art," said Lou Jr. "There's no timer, no thermostat on the oven…
so it's all knowing the dough, how loose it was or how cold it was or how
warm it is out, how long it's gonna take. And the sound; you pull a loaf
of bread out and tap the bottom, you hear a certain sound, you know
it's done."[448]

Not surprisingly, baking bread in this fashion can't be learned overnight.
"Bakers have been here at least ten years or more," he continued. "They like

Sarcone's seeded loaves, ready for the oven. *Sarcone's Bakery.*

what they're doing, so they stay. I treat everybody like we're family. Morale is good here, considering people are getting up at 2:00 in the morning."[449]

The result is something otherworldly, an impossibly crisp exterior that envelopes a fluffy-yet-deeply-flavorful interior. "Nowhere have I eaten such remarkable bread," wrote Rick Nichols, "delicately crisp in its eggshell-thin crust; light, moist and stretchy (but not squishy) in the crumb; a slight tang of salt giving it, for want of a better word, presence."[450]

In more recent times, the bakery's popularity among sandwich artisans has generated pressure to expand beyond the humble single bakery, which produces just two thousand loaves per day. "I could double my business in a minute," said Louis Sr. in 2001. "But I'd be the same as Amoroso. I want to be different."[451]

"A lot of younger generations think," added Lou Jr., "'We've got to go wholesale. We've got to go hit all the restaurants and expand.' Once you do that, you lose something. You become a commercial business, and my grandfather always told me that it's more important for your walk-in store to be your business. You have to have the perfect balance. Some wholesale, some retail. I always paid attention."

Louis Sr. and Jr. pose outside Sarcone's Bakery in the early 1990s. *Sarcone's Bakery.*

"I just remember him telling me," he continued, "'Don't put too much food in your mouth, you can't chew.' What he meant by that was keep things simple. If you try to do too much, you'll overextend yourself, and you're going to lose something."[452]

Despite all that talk, Sarcone's has experimented with expansion, opening a sandwich shop next to the bakery and eventually five franchises. (All of which have since closed.) This, of course, created different business problems, notably consistency and keeping non–family members in line with the Sarcone ethos. "We use Di Bruno cheese. They might go to the supermarket and get it a dollar cheaper," said Lou Jr. "Stuff like that happens. You don't want it to happen, but it could happen."[453]

"We had five delis, not including our own," he continued. "My father had gotten sick at the bakery, and my cousin had a heart attack and was out for a year and a half. I couldn't do day-to-day operations for two businesses. We put too much food in our mouth."[454]

In October 2000, part of Sarcone's Bakery burned down after someone threw a Molotov cocktail through the window. No motive or culprit was ever

## Bread Is Thicker Than Water

Just weeks after having its roast pork crowned the "Best Sandwich in America," DiNic's made a surprising change: they switched their rolls from Carangi to Sarcone's. "People were blown away by it," said Lou Sarcone Jr. "You just won best sandwich in America. Not Philly, America! His answer was, we want to stay the best. How do you improve our sandwich? We improved our bread."*

*Inquirer* food writer Michael Klein suggested pros and cons to each: "A Carangi roll typically comes out soft and dense—the better to sop up gravy—and features an artisan knot at one end," he wrote. At Sarcone's, "where the rolls are baked in a brick oven, they are airy and have a crust that's crunchy yet delicate."†

That said, it's not entirely clear that improving was the reason for the change. When Adam Richman first showed up at DiNic's in 2009, the restaurant was using bread from DiGiampietro Bakery, owned by family friend (and future Angelo's owner) Danny DiGiampietro. When that bakery closed in early 2012, DiNic's switched to Carangi, and DiGiampietro returned to his role as a bread delivery man. He also married a Sarcone, and then, unsurprisingly, connected his new family with his old friends at DiNic's. They made this switch later the same year.

"Blood is thicker than water," Lou Carangi said, seemingly taking it all in stride. "It's not the end of the world." Still, he added, "How do you go from winning the best sandwich in America to wanting to make a change?"‡

---

* Smith, "All About the Bread."
† Michael Klein, "Philly's Star Sandwich Takes on a New Roll," *Philadelphia Inquirer*, October 1, 2012, https://www.inquirer.com/philly/food/20121001_Philly_s_star_sandwich_takes_on_a_new_roll.html.
‡ Klein, "Philly's Star Sandwich."

discovered, but the neighborhood immediately rallied to the cause. "The fire department, the city council, the mayor, they came here to help us get open because they didn't want to see us leave," said Lou Jr. "Contractors, electricians, inspectors, zoning people, they were all here the next day. We didn't have to wait. They were waiting for us."

*We were open a week* [later] *next door. We moved our storefront into the packing area. It wasn't pretty, but people actually liked that better. They saw men work, they saw the flour, they saw everything. We spent thousands to replace the store; they wanted the old way!*

*That was something I'll never forget, the way the neighbors and the city came together to help us.*[455]

Two decades later, the little bakery is still going strong, cranking out two thousand loaves per day the same way they always have. Popular shops that utilize Sarcone's rolls include Molly Malloy's & Tommy DiNic's in the Reading Terminal Market, Dolores' 2Street, Antonio's Deli, Poe's Sandwich Joint and Cosmi's, among others. Bread suppliers do change though, and even if they don't, delis quickly run out of the best bread and sometimes must substitute inferior stuff to meet demand. As such, the best bet is to get to Sarcone's storefront early and grab some good stuff straight from the source.

# SOWING SEEDS

The addition of sesame seeds to the outside of sandwich rolls—a more recent development in Philadelphia gastronomic history—can also be traced to Sarcone's. Sometime in the 1980s, a guy named Bobby Toner first used the bakery's seeded loaf for hoagies at his now-defunct store JR's Deli. "I give him all the credit in the world," said Lou Jr.[456]

By the mid-1990s, seeds were in high demand. "Everybody wanted Sarcone's bread to make a hoagie," Lou Jr. continued. "They all started getting rid of the flat steak bread, the plain hoagie roll. Then all these big commercial bakery shops [started] making bread with seeds on it. You could have called up any bakery and said, 'How much is your *Sarcone* bread?' I had to go out and register the name."[457]

Now-chain Primo Hoagies started out serving Sarcone's seeded bread in the '90s but eventually expanded beyond the bakery's capacity. "Once they establish their name, they leave me," Lou Jr. joked.[458] Today, Primo gets its seeded bread from Liscio's, which uses more than 2,500 pounds of sesame seeds *per week* to keep up with demand.[459] "If I stop making seeded bread, if I only made plain bread," Lou Jr. quipped, "Liscio's would have to change their bread to plain bread. They couldn't fake [being] Sarcone's."[460]

Seeded bread just "tastes better," said former Chickie's Italian Deli co-owner Jean Rizzo George, who used Sarcone's seeded loaves for the entirety of the deli's existence (1993 to 2015). "It just gives it a nice crunch to the roll."[461]

"I wouldn't do anything without seeds," added Anthony Messina, the co-owner of Pastificio Deli, near 15th Street and Packer Avenue, which made its name using bread from the now-defunct Abruzzi Bakery. The meatball sandwich, the chicken cutlet, the roast pork, he continued, "All on seeded rolls."[462]

"Seedless, squishy rolls are for amateurs," concluded Craig LeBan. "For me, seedless is soulless."[463]

## Something in the Water?

There are, of course, other bakeries worth mentioning (and eating), but an entire book would be needed to tell each one's story. The broader question, however, asks about the area as a whole: What is it, exactly, that makes bread in this area so great—and so much better than bread from elsewhere?

The most prevalent explanation is that the secret is the water, specifically whether it is *hard* or *soft*. This phenomenon is most associated with New York City bagels, though it sometimes also extends to pizza and bread. But much of Philadelphia's water comes from the same source—the Delaware watershed, via the Catskills—and considering the passion for quality bread in Philly, it's not surprising that a similar belief is held here.

While there is no consensus on this hypothesis, there is at least some scientific backing to the idea that water composition deeply affects the final bread. Firstly, after flour, water is the second most prevalent ingredient by volume in any bread dough, representing around 40 percent of the total mass. So, its makeup is obviously going to have a significant impact.

This is where the idea of hard versus soft water comes in. Hardness, according to *Bakers Journal*, is "attributable almost totally to the presence of calcium and magnesium." Closely related is the acidity, which tends to be higher (lower pH) in soft water. Both the mineral content—even in minor amounts—and acidity of any water used for baking can greatly affect the final bread.

"Excessively hard waters," explained the journal, "are undesirable because they retard fermentation by tightening or toughening the gluten structure too much. The minerals present apparently prevent the proteins from absorbing water." Just the same, the tendency of hard water toward a lower acidity (higher pH) is generally "undesirable because the high content of alkaline salts tends to neutralize the normal acidity developed during yeast fermentation," which, in other words, leads to a lower-quality fermentation.[464]

Contrarily, soft waters can also be problematic "because they lack the gluten-strengthening minerals and tend to yield soft, sticky dough." In addition, higher acidity can have "an accelerating effect on fermentation, requiring some reduction in fermentation time."[465]

As such, a medium water—such as that from New York City or Philly—is ideal, having that *just right* amount of minerals, which help strengthen the dough's gluten without making it overly tough, and a neutral pH that's best for flavor development during fermentation.

All that said, many experts question how important water composition is. "It's all in the process of making your dough and how you bake your bread," suggested Chad Vilotti of Liscio's, as one example.[466] In 2015, as another, America's Test Kitchen concluded that bagels made from New York City water and water from another area were identical.[467]

Well-known baker and author Peter Reinhart argued that the art of baking—specifically, the techniques that have been perfected over decades—makes a larger impact. "The act of breadmaking is all about evoking the full potential of flavor trapped in the grain," he said. "The longer and slower the fermentation process, the more biochemical activity that takes place, and—usually—the better the flavor."[468]

"I think that what makes these things so good," Reinhart continued, speaking of regions renowned for high-quality breads, "is a long tradition of making them there. That comes with a lot of skill and dedication to the craft itself." Even after saying all that, however, Reinhard conceded that "water is always a big part of it."[469]

One might have expected Gary Lane, the vice-president of sales for New York WaterMaker—a company that sells systems that allow bakers and restaurants to mimic New York City water elsewhere—to preach the virtues of good water. And he did, though quite reasonably. "If you overlook the second largest ingredient, just like if you overlook any other ingredient, or try to switch it out with something else," Lane said, "you're going to get a different product."[470]

Yet even Lane agreed that it is not *just* about the water. "There are several factors involved with producing a quality product," he said. "Your ingredients are going to be one, of course, but also your equipment and your technical skill."[471]

There's a concept from French winemaking that seems to also apply here: *terroir*. It refers to all the ecological and climatic forces—everything from the weather to the soil composition to the bugs that live in the vineyard—that affect the outcome of the final wine. Though there is some debate in the wine industry whether this also includes human intervention, if this concept was applied to bread, it would most certainly include recipes and techniques, especially those handed down from generation to generation, like those of the Sarcone family, as well as equipment used in the baking process.

Thinking back to Sarcone's, as a prime example, there's that long fermentation and proofing time, which develops deeper flavors (a technique the best New York City bagel bakers also use). The circa-1920s ovens, with their century of use and seasoning. The freshness of bread baked every morning, always eaten the same day. Even the passion of the local populace, the insistence of longtime customers—and their offspring—on retaining specific styles.

What is the secret then? The only possible conclusion is that it's all of it, every aspect of the process: the ingredients, of course, including water, but also the recipes, the ovens, the passionate bakers, the history, the culture, the love, all combining to form this unique *terroir* of Philadelphia bread.

No wonder it is so hard to duplicate.

8

# BECOMING SANDWICH CITY

Philadelphians have loved sandwiches for almost a century now, the dish first taking hold as a convenience of immigrant life and eventually evolving into an essential part of just about anyone local's formative experience. It's interesting to consider, however, *how* and *when* the city's great sandwiches became intrinsically and irrevocably associated with its broader identity. This goes beyond the idea of why sandwiches appeal so much to Philadelphia-area residents, continuing to why outsiders have come to consider them such an integral part of the city's culture and a must-do aspect of the tourist experience. As with why sandwiches became so important here in the first place, there probably isn't one incident that made this so, but rather a series of trends and events, both local and global—such as changing lifestyles, obsession with celebrity culture and the introduction of cable TV and the internet—that contributed to this transformation.

## GROCERY STORE HOAGIES

When sandwiches came onto the commercial scene in Philadelphia, the way Americans shopped for and consumed food was already in flux. The 1920s saw chains (locally, ACME and A&P) take over the corner grocery store, while supermarkets began to emerge in the 1930s. The latter decade also brought the synthesis of freon, allowing affordable home refrigeration to proliferate, and fast-food chains became relevant around the same time. It surely took longer for the career prospects of married women to expand similarly, but over the course of a century, these gradually increased as well, further evolving home cooking and eating.

As city life evolved, one interesting phenomenon was how several shops that originated as grocers, butchers, etc. transformed into sandwich shops. As the opportunities to run a successful neighborhood food retailer dried up, in other words, these businesses shifted to focus on sandwich production and, in time, became beloved institutions.

Perhaps the oldest such spot still around today is Ricci's Hoagies, founded as a corner Italian grocer in the 1910s. "The earliest I could find evidence of the store was from 1914," said Raymond Ricci, the grandson of Abruzzese founders Raphael "Ralph" and Louise Ricci. The shop started at one corner of 11th and Annin Streets, at 1164 11th Street, then moved to 1166 and finally to 1165. "They moved," quipped Raymond, "but never gave up the corner."[472]

"It began as a kind of a general store," he said, "a grocery primarily, shelf-stable food and then lunch meat, cheese and things like that…back then, every couple blocks there was a corner grocer. The great appeal, what made this kind of store so popular, was that it was a general store. You could get almost anything there. Baby food. Cereal, paper products.… At one time, they sold shoes, I think. Anything they thought was going to help the bottom line."[473]

Raymond couldn't pinpoint exactly when his grandparents started making sandwiches, though he's sure they were popular by the mid-1950s, when he started working there. "It was busy all the time," he recalled. "We started making sandwiches at 10:30 in the morning and wouldn't stop until we ran out of bread at 4:30 or 5:00 p.m."[474]

When brothers Anthony and Salvatore returned home from World War II, they joined their oldest brother, Carlo—who had taken over when Ralph died in 1941—and rechristened the shop Ricci Brothers. Despite the growing success of their sandwiches, however, they remained loyal to the corner store concept. "They only thought of it as a grocery store that happened to make sandwiches at lunchtime," said Raymond. "I remember one of my cousins trying to convince my father to make it a hoagie shop. It was the main business then, and with the reduced inventory, it would've reduced costs and increased profit margins. But all of this was lost on him."[475]

Eventually, the brothers retired, selling the shop to a cousin who finalized the move to sandwiches. "They may have had sodas and potato chips

Ralph and Louise Ricci at their corner grocery store, maybe with a meat slicer on the counter. Undated photograph. *Larry Ricci.*

and that sort of thing in the '90s," Raymond recalled, "but they didn't have groceries."[476] In the early 2000s, Ricci's was sold outside the family, but it nonetheless retains its reputation as one of the best hoagie shops in the city.

When Italian immigrant Cosmi Quattro opened **Cosmi's Market** at 1501 South 8th Street in 1932, as another example, it was strictly a grocery store, with four aisles of pasta, sauce and nonperishable goods, as well as deli and butcher counters. Nothing much changed at Cosmi's until the 1980s, when teenager Mike Seccia had the idea to start selling sandwiches. "My dad thought I was crazy," recalled Seccia, whose father, Leon (Cosmi's nephew), owned the store at that time. "I told him, 'We live in a fast world; people don't always have the time to make their own sandwiches.' [At first,] we were only doing a handful a day, and we were exhausted from doing it. But each week, each month, each year, we seemed to do a little more."[477]

In 1999, Rick Nichols profiled the then-less-heralded spot in the *Inquirer*, describing his Italian hoagie experience at Cosmi's as nearly religious, and sandwich sales quickly tripled.[478] The following year, after a fire in the apartment next door shuttered the store for nearly nine months, Seccia convinced his father to ditch groceries altogether and go all in on prepared food when they reopened. Today, Cosmi's sandwiches are South Philly

Ambrose Campo and his staff at his butcher shop, undated photograph. *Campo's.*

staples, and they've been featured in all kinds of "best of" lists and food TV shows, with Ron Jaworski even once constructing a Cosmi's cheesesteak live on ESPN.

**CAMPO'S**, which today serves the *official* cheesesteak of the Phillies (among other accomplishments), has a similar origin story. In 1905, three Campo brothers—Ferdinando, Francesco and Venerando, who all had learned the butchery trade in their native Sicily—arrived in the United States, with Venerando eventually opening a butcher shop in South Philly and Ferdinando creating a similar place in Atlantic City.[479] The latter's son Ambrose then founded the current incarnation in 1947 as a butcher shop and small grocery in Southwest Philadelphia.

Current owner Mike Campo, the son of Ambrose and Rose, recalls fondly the days of playing with his butcher father's animals. "They became our pets for about six weeks, and then Good Friday would come, and it was time for the lambs to be taken upstairs and put in the showcase so people could buy them." Ambrose would also make sandwiches for workers that came in around lunchtime. "He would cut some lunch meat and put lettuce and tomato and hot peppers on it," said Mike, but this was never the primary source of the butcher shop's income.[480]

In 1975, when Mike took over, he saw how supermarkets were squeezing family butcher shops out of business. "I wasn't the greatest butcher in the neighborhood," he said, "so we changed it a little bit. We continued the grocery store, sold a lot of lunch meats, and started to concentrate more on sandwiches."[481]

For a time, the deli counter kept Campo's popular. "People would get their lunch meat before the week, for the kids going to school," he continued. "A pound of bologna, mayo and mustard, a quart of milk and a loaf of bread....We were also making deli sandwiches like ham and cheese, turkey, Italian sandwiches. Eventually, we tried [steaks], and they started doing well for us."[482]

In 2000, frustrated with the deteriorating safety of their longtime neighborhood, the Campos opened a new spot in Old City (which is now the flagship location). "When we came to Market Street," said Mike, "I didn't have room for a deli case. We were doing well in Southwest Philly with the sandwiches, so we became strictly sandwiches. We eliminated all the groceries and the cans of Campbell's soup and all that."[483]

A historic pedigree of grocery or butchery tradition is not, of course, an absolute requirement for success today. But it is certainly telling that these shops, as a few examples, were able to survive by pivoting to sandwiches, to remain anchor points of their neighborhoods even as the world changed around (and with) them. These stories, in a way, serve as microcosms of the larger city's evolution.

# The Cult of Celebrity

While Pat Olivieri was not the first restaurateur to feature a celebrity wall of fame at his establishment, he was probably the first Philadelphia sandwich guy to utilize the technique (see chapter 3), and his success would have a lasting impact on the industry. In 1980, for example, Frank Olivieri Sr. joked, "Many people come to Pat's just to see if any celebrities show up."[484]

"Indeed, for many actors and entertainers, a sojourn in Philadelphia is incomplete without a trip to Pat's, and the list of celebrity patrons is lengthy," wrote Ray Kirchdoerffer in the *Inquirer*. "When Frank Sinatra's in town, his chauffeur makes regular trips to Pat's....Don Rickles has mentioned Pat's Steaks often on Johnny Carson's *Tonight Show*, and when the movie *Rocky* was being filmed, Sylvester Stallone wanted a location in South Philadelphia that everyone would recognize. Naturally, he picked Pat's (a fact commemorated by a plaque in the sidewalk out front)."[485]

It wasn't just Pat's. "Movie stars, politicians [and] other public figures," wrote the *Public Record*'s Len Lear, "have frequented [Shank's & Evelyn's] for nearly a half-century."[486] Photographs of Mario Lanza, Marlon Brando, Mayor Frank Rizzo, President Bill Clinton and even Mussolini ("a conversation piece," apparently) adorned the walls.[487] And at DePalma's, of course, Lanza was a regular (see chapter 2), but Wilt Chamberlain reportedly also ate his fair share of hoggies.

Where celebrities rule, politicians are sure to follow, which could explain what Carolyn Wyman dubbed the Cheesesteak Test. "From time immemorial," she wrote, "the cheesesteak 'triangle' at 9th at Wharton has been the place for millionaire politicians…to prove they can get down and greasy with the commoners."[488] The most famous visit—of recent years, at least—being John Kerry's misstep order of a steak with Swiss in 2003, which Wyman half-jokingly suggested may have been the breaking point for his campaign. (Amazingly, a similar story emerged after J.D. Vance's campaign visit in 2024.)

Part of the "Wall of Fame" at Jim's on South Street (pre-fire). *Wikimedia Commons/Tony Fischer.*

While this ritual may be focused on cheesesteaks today, it has roots that go far deeper, all the way back to Old Original Levis, where, the *Inquirer* wrote, "presidents make special stops for the famous hot dogs [and] so do children."[489]

Recalling the impact of then–district attorney Arlen Specter's successful photo-op at Levis in 1967, a campaign manager named "Scoop" Solomon memorably advised his aspiring city council candidate, H. Jerome Stassen, to embark on "one spectacular day of gastronomy" by knocking out every must-visit eatery in one fell swoop. "Just take a nibble here and a bite there. I'll carry the Tums," Scoop told Stassen. By the end of this ill-advised excursion, however, the latter had to be rushed to Hahnemann Hospital to have his stomach pumped.[490]

The idea of visiting dignitaries and luminaries frequenting street and fast-food joints is not, of course, unique to Philadelphia. And yet, in this city, the focus on sandwich shops specifically, especially steak joints, has served to further cement these shops as the focal point of the city's lore and personality.

## INCREASED CONNECTIVITY

Celebrities and politicians, of course, also draw media coverage, and media coverage draws customers. It may seem obvious, but it is nonetheless worth considering briefly how the increase in media coverage over the past half a century has played a crucial role in turning the Philadelphia sandwich brand into a behemoth.

Local press's focus on sandwiches was sparse in the early days. Beyond advertisements, major newspaper stories about sandwiches, sandwich shops or the makers behind them were quite rare through the 1960s. DePalma caught a few headlines with his supposed world record–setting subs, and the *Inquirer* briefly profiled both Old Original Levis and Pat's Steaks in the 1950s, but otherwise, most sandwich mentions were made merely in passing, related to other news.

Change came in the early 1970s, when local interest stories about food began to appear more regularly. This development coincided with sociologist Howard Robboy's research on the geographical distribution of "hoagie" and other regional sandwich names, which received ample newspaper coverage in 1971. "You Can't Leave the City Without a Steak Sandwich," noted

**CHEESE STEAKS**

2 egg whites, beaten with 2
tablespoons water, or 2
whole eggs, slightly beaten
8 slices Gouda or Edam
cheese ¼ to ½ inch thick,
rind removed
1 or more cups fine bread
crumbs
3 tablespoons fat, preferably
bacon (although butter may
be used)
Dip the slices of cheese in
the egg white, which is delicate, or the whole eggs, which
are robust, and then in the
crumbs until they are well
covered. Fry the slices in the
bacon fat, or, less traditional-
ly, the butter, until golden on
both sides and soft inside.
Serves 4.

The *Philadelphia Inquirer* actually
published this recipe for "Cheese
Steaks" in 1966. *Newspapers.com.*

Joe Sharkey's *Inquirer* headline that same year, as if this now-obvious sentiment was newsworthy at the time.[491] "Is a Hoagie Still a Hoagie if It's Not Made in Philadelphia?" asked another article, published in the *Inquirer* magazine in 1972.[492]

This newfound interest from the local press roughly corresponded with the rise of Geno's Steaks, setting up nicely for the establishment of the Pat's/Geno's rivalry as a core aspect of the city's sandwich scene. "The rivalry…started as something that the media did," said Frank Olivieri Jr. "Probably as early as 1970, 1973, around there. We started getting publicity. And people would come down here, and it was exciting.…The media would say, 'Well, Pat's is doing this. What's Geno's doing?' You know, trying to start a fire."[493]

"We pretty much all just climbed on their backs," said Ken Silver of Jim's, "and let them become a tourist attraction." Noting an empty retail location across South Street, he continued, "For years, people asked me what I'd like to see there, and I'd always say, 'Another cheesesteak place!' They'd never believe it, but I'd say, 'Rival corners; where else have you seen that work?'"[494]

While this remained primarily a local feud through the 1980s, in the '90s, the growth of cable TV, particularly the Food Network and the Travel Channel, established a new way to expose these previously regional stories to a national audience. "It all began with the Food Network," said Joel Spivak. "They've taken food to a different dimension. When they started promoting places on shows like *Diners, Drive-Ins and Dives*, and they came to Philadelphia to eat a steak sandwich at Geno's, and they talked about Geno's and Pat's, that's what people wanted to do when they visited the city."[495]

"I absolutely believe it was the Food Network, the rise in popularity of food shows that highlighted sandwiches from different cities," added Tony Luke Jr. "The cheesesteak wasn't known all over the world back in the '50s, '60s or '70s because you didn't have the networking of foodies that [first developed] in the '90s.…Nowadays, there's nowhere in the United States that you can't get a cheesesteak. It has become a staple American food, like the hamburger or the hot dog."[496]

After the establishment of cable, the internet boom, of course, came next, which has obviously changed forever how people talk about, learn about and seek out food experiences. And while there are surely pros and cons to social media's takeover of the food conversation—for one, the idea that anything can go *undiscovered* for long anymore is outdated—it does seem that the prevalence of online food discussion has spurred countless examples of innovation, opening the market beyond just those Italian American standards, adding much-needed diversity and creativity to Philadelphia's sandwich culture.

# What's Next?

If anything, these broader market forces have strengthened the sandwich scene, creating the opportunity for countless variations and much hope for the future. "Where we are as a food culture," mused LaBan in 2023, "we're turning away from fine dining. A lot of chefs are creating more casual concepts, and sandwiches are one way to do that. People have been taking them to the next level, where they're making their own rolls for example, or their own meats."

"The skill level of the people making the sandwiches is increasing," he continued. "A lot of chefs these days are tired of working nights, or thinking about getting older, having a family. They want to start a daytime operation driven by quality of life…but they're still applying skills that they've learned in fine dining kitchens to casual concepts like sandwiches."[497]

This idea of making every component from scratch takes the humble, old-school sandwich art—that of stacking Dietz & Watson or Boar's Head meats and cheeses on a roll from the corner bakery—and sets up an entirely new paradigm for what sandwiches can be going forward. Previously covered Angelo's, of course, has taken the city by storm over the past several years with what LaBan called "probably the best hoagie bread" in the city, made on site. LaBan also raved about Heavy Metal Sausage Company, where former fine-dining chef Pat Alfiero started making charcuterie that's "all over the map" during the COVID-19 pandemic and now also bakes artisanal breads. "I mean," said LaBan, "he's making zungenblutwurst!"[498] (This obscure German blood salami is featured on Poppe's Sandwich, alongside cheddar, pepper relish, garlic mayo and lettuce on house-made rye.)

At Mancuso's, a mainstay cheese shop at the bottom of East Passyunk Avenue, where proprietor Phil Mancuso had long been famous for hand-made mozzarella and ricotta, serving great Italian fare is nothing new, but hoagies are. "Entering Mancuso's tightly packed market was like stepping into a time capsule of mid-twentieth-century aromas and sounds," LaBan wrote upon Mancuso's death in 2021. "Little had changed since Phil's father, Lucio Mancuso, opened the store in 1940, from its heady smell of cured meats and open tubs of olives, to the crowded shelves of Calabrian pastas, olive oils, tinned sardines, and stacks of imported cheeses behind the counter where still-warm braids of freshly pulled mozzarella were dipped in a salt water bath to order. Conversations could be heard in Italian against a soundtrack of classic opera."[499]

The shop is now run by former mozzarella-making apprentice Jimmy Cialella, his nephew Jake Santini (a culinary school graduate who makes the sandwiches) and their friend John Denisi. "In an interesting kind of *Back to the Future* twist," LaBan said, "the successors have kept the traditions but also added hoagies, which is kind of like kind of going full circle....Because they have great ingredients, they're making great hoagies."[500]

It's not just Italian-style sandwiches that are in the middle of a revolution. LaBan also called out El Chingon, a Mexican spot where proprietor Carlos Emery—the baker who started notable restaurant Parc's bread program—is crafting cemita rolls from scratch. "He's from Puebla," LaBan said, "and this is a sandwich roll specific to that region. It's a round, sesame-topped, crusty roll that holds a lot of stuff....These rolls are hard to make correctly, so it's a special thing he's doing."[501]

The classic Puebla cemita comes with a choice of meat, avocado, quesillo cheese, onions, chipotles and papalo aioli, but Emery also branches out with clever creations from a variety of influences. "It's like the Philly sandwich history continues," said LaBan, "because it's a traditional Mexican thing, but he's adding a Philly twist to it."[502]

LaBan also praised Huda on 18th Street, where chef-owner Yehuda Sichel builds off his experience working in Jewish delis growing up and in fine dining with the Cook and Solo group, where he was recently executive chef at Abe Fisher. "He's making all the breads and [fillings] for his sandwiches," said LaBan, "which are eclectic...but outstanding."[503]

Huda's bread of choice is the Japanese-inspired milk bun, which, according to the shop, is "meticulously crafted over the course of four days, from mixing to fermentation to rolling out by hand, resulting in a texture unlike any other bread." As opposed to the crispy-crust hoagie roll, Huda describes these buns as "soft and supple…making for an elevated sandwich experience that enables unique fillings," such as short rib grilled cheese, grilled swordfish, maitake mushrooms, spicy Korean chicken and more, all produced in house. [504]

These are, of course, just a few examples of a myriad of innovative developments throughout the city, meant to be illustrative of trends without attempting to encompass every interesting sandwich. They're all important; whether introducing influences from underrepresented cultures or riffing on old favorites, Philly sandwich culture is better for the effort. "People are having fun with it," concluded LaBan. "This is good, because it keeps things interesting."[505]

# Lingering Ghosts

Even with the innovation that's happening in the 2020s, tradition remains a strong part of the city's sandwich culture, and the emotions tied to those memories are important to the industry's continued health. "Yes, it seems like a lot of new places are opening up with this attention to detail, using really good ingredients and being a little creative with them, too," said DiGiampietro. "But at the same time, you put a cheesesteak or a roast pork sandwich in front of me, and that's really all I need."[506]

At Dolores' 2Street, Miglino brings a different kind of innovation in the form of turning back the clock. "I'm on a mission to go back," he says, in reference to his passion for reviving sandwich styles like the original Milano's pizza steak (see chapter 3) or to recreate his mother's roast pork recipe.[507]

For the latter, wrote LaBan, Miglino "tracked down the specific cut of pork his mother and her friends used to cook at home. It's called the cushion, a large softball-shaped hunk of boneless meat cut from a picnic shoulder that he slow roasts with dried herbs, garlic, wine and cherry peppers in vinegar, which lend a distinctively spicy tang.

"Nick hand cuts each piece a little thicker than the paper thin sheets commonly seen elsewhere pulled off an electric slicer. That might seem like a small thing, but it's huge. My teeth sank through the crusty roll into that cushion of meat, and my eyes opened as it conveyed the sublime tenderness and juicy swagger of this family's roast pork sandwich legacy in a way I've never quite experienced."[508]

Miglino has a similar passion when it comes to the quality, grade and cut of beef for steaks (see chapter 3). "The Philly cheesesteak has never been more popular," he said, "but the overall quality is slightly above mediocre….I want to break away from what's been around here too long: steak meat that just sits there on the grill and is so greasy. God only knows where they're buying that meat from. I'm afraid to eat it.…What I'm trying to do—and I wish some more would get into—is to take the steak more seriously, to get a little more creative with it. And that begins with buying the right product."[509]

These recollections, of course, go beyond just using certain ingredients or recreating specific recipes; food nostalgia can affect human emotion in extreme ways. "Food is so much about memory for me," said DiGiampietro. "My father died when I was sixteen. Before he died, we went to a million Sixers, Flyers, Eagles and Phillies games, but I can't tell you the score of any of them, who they played, whether they won or not. What I can tell you is about going to Nick's Roast Beef before the game or going to Tommy DiNic's when he was on Oregon Avenue. Those are the memories that I hold dear in my heart."[510]

"My father loved roast pork," he continued. "That was his thing wherever we went. It didn't matter if we were in a deli in the suburbs or here in South Philly. He was getting roast pork. So, even now, whenever I smell roast pork, my brain goes instantly to my father."[511]

DiGiampietro isn't the only eater who makes this type of connection. "When [Angelo's] first opened here," he said, "I made sausage scallopini one day. There was an older Italian lady in here, and while I was making pizza, I could feel this lady staring at me. I knew she was eating the scallopini, and I knew she wanted to talk to me. Whether it was good or bad, I wasn't sure."

"I went over and asked her how she was doing," he continued. "She screamed out, 'Oh my f—cking god!' in front of everybody. 'You brought me back forty years to my nonna's kitchen! That's what I feel when I eat this sandwich!' And that's what it's all about; no amount of money ever could replace the feeling I get when I hear that."[512]

And yet change is inevitable; whether it be El Chingon's cemitas, Huda's milk buns or just a slight modification to a traditional steak or hoagie, there will always be something different to experience. Even day to day, week to week, nothing is guaranteed.

In late 2022, I happened to see a social media post about Angelo's, DiGiampietro's South Philly mega-darling. The post author—a guy named

Brian—shared his disappointment after waiting forty-five minutes for a cheesesteak (further proof of how seriously sandwich fiends take this place) that contained, he reported, unevenly cut chunks of raw onion and barely any cheese.[513] In response, some weighed in with similar experiences, while others defended the place's quality.

The reason to share this, however, is not to make any inferences about Angelo's in particular. Maybe they had a bad hour, a bad day, etc. Perhaps they're just not for Brian. Or maybe, as one commenter suggested, their popularity had, by this point, risen to the level that quality began to slip. It can happen to the best of places. (I have had some great sandwiches at Angelo's since Brian's post, so this is probably not the case here.)

The point is, instead, that the details of Philly's sandwich scene are ever-changing. Shops open and close. Chefs come and go. Trends and fads evolve. Such is life. But on a grander scale, the sandwich endures. If someone is reading this book five years from now, twenty years from now, fifty years from now—a writer can dream—Angelo's may still be popular, or it might not exist. People might still be raving about places like Poe's, Woodrow's or Middle Child, or the new kid on the block might be having their moment in the spotlight.

As for the sandwiches themselves, they'll surely evolve, too. Maybe climate change will force us away from so much beef. Or to eat lab-grown beef. 3D-printed bread. Who knows? The only thing certain is that Philadelphians will still be eating great sandwiches—and arguing about who makes them best.

Appendix

# RECIPES

### Fish Cake and Combo Recipe

*Here's a technique to recreate the combo, sometimes called the Philly surf 'n' turf, poor man's surf 'n' turf, etc. This sandwich was popularized at Old Original Levis, as well as Lenny's Hot Dogs (where pepper hash was added, see next recipe).*

*There's much room for interpretation and customization when it comes to fish cakes. Various fish can be used. Some cakes are heavily breaded, others not. Some contain more fish than mashed potatoes, for example, while others have the opposite. Eggs and breadcrumbs can be added or omitted. A fair amount of this is personal preference. As such, here's a general overview of the technique and a basic recipe:*

## Ingredients

2 cups cooked fish (typically cod, though tilapia also works well), chopped, with bones removed
2 cups prepared mashed potatoes
2 tablespoons butter
2 tablespoons minced fresh parsley
2 eggs, lightly beaten
½ cup breadcrumbs, plus more for breading
Oil, for frying
Salt and pepper to taste

## Method

Mix fish with potatoes in a large bowl. Add butter and parsley (optional but delicious: fry parsley in butter first), along with eggs and breadcrumbs. Add salt and pepper to taste.

Form into flat cakes. Coat with breadcrumbs. Pan fry in shallow oil for about five minutes per side until nicely browned and warmed through. (This recipe can be halved or doubled easily.)

For the combo, spread mustard on a hot dog bun and fill with one cooked beef frank. Cut fish cake in half and mash into the top of the bun. Optionally, top with pepper hash. Grab plenty of napkins!

## Mom's Pepper Hash Recipe

*The Kravitz family started the Lenny's Hot Dogs brand in the 1930s—it was originally known as Mom & Pop's Hot Dogs—and Ida Kravitz added her soon-to-be-famous pepper hash topping shortly thereafter.*

*This Kravitz family recipe was shared by Tracy Kauffman Wood, with the "Mom" here being Lenny's sister Sylvia Kravitz Kauffman.*

## Ingredients

1 head of cabbage, minced
2 large green peppers, minced
2 large carrots, minced
1 cup white sugar
1 cup distilled white vinegar
½ cup water (or more if vinegar taste is strong)
Salt to taste

## Method

Prepare vegetables. Add dry and liquid ingredients. Mix and taste as you go. Smother hot dogs with this and other toppings.

## Notes

- This makes an enormous amount of pepper hash! Plan to share or consider halving.
- It lasts about a week in the fridge but doesn't freeze all that well.
- Many pepper hash recipes include other spices, most commonly mustard seed or celery salt. This basic recipe should allow for experimentation.

## Philadelphia Italian Hoagie Recipe

*Ben DeAngelis, the head chef at the Bellevue Strafford hotel, told this recipe to the* Philadelphia Daily News *in 1972.*

*Two keys to a real hoagie, according to DeAngelis, are (1) using Italian meats, and (2) oil instead of mayo. "A mortal sin," the chef said of the latter. "Some will pour oil on top of the whole product," he continued, indicating that he prefers to "marinate" the hoagie roll before he starts, dousing it with olive oil and then sprinkling on a bit of oregano.*

*Of the former, DeAngelis added that the Italian lunch meats "make the hoagie…[the] deli-type cut.…That's the secret." It's this delicate blend that makes the classic hoagie.*

*"Some don't like to use onion," DeAngelis continued. "They'll say onions will kill the flavor.…Then they'll use red hot cherry peppers, enough to blow your head off. After you eat them, you have no taste at all. Onion doesn't kill the taste. In fact, I think it adds to it."*

*(Personally, I'd never put raw onion on the hoagie, as I do believe it kills the taste, just like hot cherry peppers. But to each his own.)*

*There are, of course, many variations of the Italian hoagie, but this recipe gives a basic technique that can serve as a starting point.*

## Ingredients

Italian roll
3 slices each: Italian salami, prosciutto, capicola, coteghino, provolone cheese
Shredded lettuce

Sliced tomato
Shredded onion
Roasted red peppers (optional)
Extra virgin olive oil
Oregano

## Method

Marinate roll with oil and sprinkle with oregano. Place cheese, then layer prosciutto, salami, capicola and cotechino on roll. Top with shredded lettuce, tomatoes and onions. Add peppers if desired.

*As told to the* Philadelphia Daily News, *April 12, 1972, page 24.*

## Pat's King of Steaks Cheesesteak Recipe

*This recipe comes directly from the source: Frank Olivieri Jr., who shared his family's recipe with the* Philadelphia Daily News *in 2002.*

## Ingredients

24 ounces thin-sliced rib eye or eye roll steak
6 tablespoons soybean oil
Cheez Whiz
4 crusty Italian rolls
1 large Spanish onion, sliced
Optional: sweet green and red peppers sautéed in oil and/or mushrooms sautéed in oil

## Method

Heat an iron skillet or a nonstick pan over medium heat. Add three tablespoons oil and sauté the onions to desired doneness.

Remove onions, add the remaining oil and sauté the meat quickly on both sides. Melt the Cheez Whiz in a double boiler or microwave. Place six ounces of cooked steak into each roll. Add onions and pour Cheez

Whiz on top. Garnish with hot or fried sweet peppers, mushrooms and ketchup.

Put on the theme song from *Rocky* and enjoy! Serves four.

*As told to the* Philadelphia Daily News, *May 8, 2002, page 35.*

## Salmon Cheesesteak Recipe

*These sandwiches are not nearly as well-known as the beef or chicken cheesesteaks, but they are slowly becoming as popular in certain areas of the Philly region.*

### Ingredients

6–8 broccoli florets
1 pound salmon filet
Baby spinach, handful
(Other veggies that can be added: bell peppers, chili peppers, mushrooms, etc.)
Cheese (American or mild provolone)
2 6- to 8-inch hoagie rolls, or 1 12-inch roll sliced in half
Old Bay seasoning (or similar—get creative)

### Method

Lightly steam broccoli, cutting large florets in half. Rub salmon with seasoning. Add a small amount of oil to a large nonstick pan and then sear salmon over medium-high heat for a few minutes per side, until both sides are browned. (If skin is still on, remove after searing that side.) Add spinach and broccoli to pan. Cover until spinach has wilted. Then chop up salmon with a spatula and mix the vegetables and salmon together. Add cheese on top of mixture, and then cover again until the cheese melts. Scoop mix into a prepared roll.

This isn't as flavorful as a beef cheesesteak, so a sauce can also add some benefit here. Try, for example, mixing some Dijon mustard and mayo together for an easy winner.

(Remember, there are no rules when it comes to salmon cheesesteaks.)

## Less Bitter Broccoli Rabe Recipe

*Renowned for its bitter taste, broccoli rabe (also known as rapini) should be slow cooked in olive oil and water, as this mellows the flavor and integrates any herbs, garlic or other spices that are added.*

### Ingredients

3 tablespoons extra virgin olive oil
I clove garlic, minced (or more to taste)
I bunch broccoli rabe (rapini), thick stems removed and roughly chopped
½ cup water
Salt and pepper
Optional: I teaspoon Italian seasoning, pinch fennel pollen, pinch red pepper (feel free to experiment with similar herbs and spices)

### Method

Heat oil, garlic and spices in a skillet over medium heat. Cook, stirring occasionally, until garlic is aromatic, about two minutes. (Do not burn garlic!) Add broccoli rabe and water, reduce heat to medium-low—erring on the lower side—and cover the pan. Cook, stirring occasionally, until it takes on a sludge-like consistency, about ninety minutes. Uncover for fifteen to twenty minutes at the end to evaporate any remaining water.

Add salt and pepper to taste and serve. In addition to topping sandwiches, this makes a great side dish for grilled or roasted pork tenderloin.

## DiNic's Slow-Cooker Pulled Pork Recipe

*Joe Nicolosi of DiNic's shared this recipe with the* Philadelphia Inquirer *as an at-home approximation of the famous Philly pork sandwich shop's pulled pork recipe (which is different from the roast pork recipe).*

## Ingredients

10-pound pork butt, with 1 raw pound yielding about two sandwiches
1 medium onion, finely chopped
1 bulb fresh garlic, finely chopped
Salt and pepper
Pinch red pepper
1 handful dry or fresh rosemary
Fennel seeds or pollen
1 cup red wine
1 cup canned tomatoes, chopped

## Method

Rub outside of pork with salt, pepper and a pinch of red pepper.

If using dry rosemary, rub on the outside of pork. If using fresh rosemary, stuff into the center, along with three to five cloves of finely chopped garlic. If using fennel pollen, rub that on the outside. If using fennel seeds, place inside.

Heat oven to 425 degrees Fahrenheit and brown pork in a pan in oven for thirty minutes. Move the pan to the stove top, remove pork and sauté onions and remaining garlic in same pan until soft.

Transfer pork, onions and garlic to slow cooker. Add tomatoes, wine, one sprig of fresh rosemary if desired and enough water to go halfway up the side of the meat.

Cook on low to medium setting until the pork is easily pulled apart with a fork. The internal temperature should be at least 200 degrees Fahrenheit, and cooking should take about eight hours.

Serve on rolls with desired toppings. Makes about twenty sandwiches.

*As told to the* Philadelphia Inquirer, *October 4, 2018, page D4.*

## Willie's Tripe Recipe

*Joe Alvini, manager of Willie's Sandwich Shop—once a Philadelphia Italian Market mainstay—gave this tripe recipe to the* Philadelphia Daily News *in 1975; it is presented with only a few clarifications.*

### Ingredients

1 pound tripe, cut into 1- to 2-inch pieces, cleaned and washed
Medium onion, diced
Green pepper, diced
3 carrots, diced
28 ounces canned crushed tomatoes
Oregano (or Italian seasoning)
Salt and pepper to taste
Parmigiano Reggiano cheese
Olive oil (for browning)

### Method

Cook tripe, onion, green pepper and carrots in olive oil until brown. Season with oregano, salt and pepper. Add tomatoes. Cook until tender, about two and a half hours. Freshly grate cheese when serving. This can be served in a hoagie roll, on pasta or just as a stew.

*As told to the* Philadelphia Daily News, *September 24, 1975, page 34.*

# NOTES

For a full bibliography, visit https://lifeattable.com/phillysandwiches.

## Introduction

1. Craig LaBan, phone call with author, March 16, 2023.
2. LaBan, phone call.
3. LaBan, phone call.
4. LaBan, phone call.
5. Victor Fiorillo, "The Cheesesteak: An Oral History," *Philadelphia Magazine*, September 23, 2018, https://www.phillymag.com/foobooz/2018/09/22/cheesesteak-history/.

## Chapter 1

6. Robert Strauss, "Hot Dogs with Pedigree," *Philadelphia Inquirer*, July 21, 2005.
7. "Hot Dog's Birthplace Marks 75th Anniversary," *Warren* (PA) *Times-Mirror and Observer*, November 18, 1970.
8. Edward Mayover, "Abe's Ideas," *Philadelphia Inquirer*, November 4, 1951.
9. Thomas Stevens, "The Drinks of the World," *Tribune* (Scranton, PA), October 2, 1887.
10. "On the Flashing Steel," *Paterson* (NJ) *Daily Press*, December 31, 1892.
11. Mayover, "Abe's Ideas."
12. Strauss, "Hot Dogs with Pedigree."
13. Maria Gallagher, "It Won't Go to the Dogs," *Philadelphia Daily News*, September 1, 1982.

14. Levis Kochin, phone call with author, May 22, 2022.

15. FamilySearch, "Pennsylvania, Philadelphia Marriage Indexes, 1885–1951," https:// familysearch.org/ark:/61903/3:1:S3HT-DTF3-YSG?cc=1388247&wc=M6P3-R68%3A10548501%2C10788501, (citing clerk of the Orphan's Court, city hall); Kochman, phone call; FamilySearch, "United States Census, 1900," https:// familysearch.org/ark:/61903/3:1:S3HY-XXD7-P3X?cc=1325221&wc=9BW6-KX2%3A1030550501%2C1036056801%2C1036091801.

16. *Boyd's Co-Partnership and Residence Business Directory of Philadelphia City* (Philadelphia, PA: C.E. Howe Co., 1858).

17. "Real Estate Transfers," *Philadelphia Inquirer*, July 21, 1910; *Boyd's Co-Partnership and Residence Business Directory*.

18. Kathy Hacker, "Levis Fans: That's Not All," *Philadelphia Inquirer*, December 28, 1982; Gallagher, "It Won't Go."

19. Sallie Kochin Abelson, phone call with author, May 16, 2022.

20. Gallagher, "It Won't Go."

21. Hacker, "Levis Fans."

22. Hacker, "Levis Fans."

23. Mayover, "Abe's Ideas."

24. Gallagher, "It Won't Go."

25. Abelson, phone call.

26. Robert Lasson, "Beyond Hot Dogs," *Philadelphia Inquirer*, October 21, 1984.

27. Elliot Hirsh, phone call with author, February 4, 2022.

28. "Month of the Dog," *Authentic Philadelphia*, July 6, 2015, https:// authenticphiladelphia.wordpress.com/tag/old-original-levis-hot-dog-and-sandwich-shop/.

29. Ron Avery, "A Few Philly-isms Hang On," *Philadelphia Daily News*, May 6, 1992.

30. "Marsh Sailed for Brazil," *Philadelphia Inquirer*, June 23, 1891.

31. Foursquare, "Menu—Levis Hot Dogs (Now Closed)—966 Old York Rd.," https://foursquare.com/v/levis-hot-dogs/4f340599e4b0cd90f71e73ac/menu.

32. Alexandra Jones, "The Fish Cake Hot Dog Is a Taste of Old Philadelphia," *Philadelphia Magazine*, July 18, 2018, https://www.phillymag.com/foobooz/2018/07/18/johnnys-hots-fish-cake-hot-dog/.

33. Kochin, phone call.

34. Nels Nelson, "They'll Put on the Dog For 'Old Original' Faithful," *Philadelphia Daily News*, November 10, 1970.

35. Ron Avery, "Hot Dog! We're on a Roll!" *Philadelphia Daily News*, March 20, 1991.

36. Avery, "Hot Dog!"; Michael Klein, "Hot Dog! Philly Classic Is Back," *Philadelphia Inquirer*, January 26, 2012.

37. Avery, "Hot Dog!"

38. Joel Spivak, "JOEL SPIVAK—LEVIS," https://www.joelspivak.com/Levis50.html.

39. Nelson, "They'll Put on the Dog."
40. Nelson, "They'll Put on the Dog."
41. Nelson, "They'll Put on the Dog."
42. Nelson, "They'll Put on the Dog."
43. Mayover, "Abe's Ideas."
44. Kochin, phone call.
45. Marianne C., Facebook comment in "Vintage Philadelphia" group, August 16, 2020, https://www.facebook.com/groups/1434456940102314/posts/2767498713464790/.
46. Tracy T., Facebook comment in "Vintage Philadelphia" group, July 1, 2016, https://www.facebook.com/groups/1434456940102314/posts/1777137492500922/.
47. Peggy H., Facebook comment in "Row House Recollections" group, June 10, 2019, https://www.facebook.com/rowhouserecollections/posts/ pfbid02UEnwQ6V1Qf7GkdkfJfSgY1 4zRPgqa2CWAshkDDzXVVy8kQCSsKiezo2oQJT1kAmZl.
48. Delores S., Facebook comment in "Vintage Philadelphia" group, July 9, 2018, https://www.facebook.com/groups/1434456940102314/posts/2149817121899622/.
49. Joel Spivak, phone call with author, February 9, 2022.
50. Tracey Kauffman Wood, phone call with author, May 6, 2022.
51. Kauffman Wood, phone call.
52. Kauffman Wood, phone call.
53. Kauffman Wood, phone call.
54. Kauffman Wood, phone call.
55. Lari Robling, "Do You Have the Hots for a Sandwich?" *Philadelphia Daily News*, April 27, 2007.
56. William Woys Weaver, *Thirty-Five Receipts from* The Larder Invaded (Philadelphia, PA: Library Company of Philadelphia, 1986), 50.
57. Woys Weaver, *Thirty-Five Receipts*, 50.
58. Kauffman Wood, phone call.
59. Kauffman Wood, phone call.
60. Facebook comment in "Vintage Philadelphia" group, December 2, 2018, https://www.facebook.com/groups/1434456940102314/posts/1777137492500922/; Facebook comment in "Vintage Philadelphia" group, March 21, 2018, https://www.facebook.com/groups/1434456940102314/posts/1777137492500922.
61. Kochin, phone call; Abelson, phone call; Bryan Kravitz, phone call with author, May 2, 2022; Marc Polish, phone call with author, February 11, 2022; Hirsh, phone call.

62. "Leonard 'Lenny' Kravitz, 76, Celebrity Hot Dog Vendor," *Philadelphia Inquirer*, August 9, 1998.

63. "Celebrity Hot Dog Vendor," *Philadelphia Inquirer*; Kauffman Wood, phone call.

64. Kravitz, phone call.

65. Kauffman Wood, phone call.

66. Kravitz, phone call.

67. Kravitz, phone call.

68. Kravitz, phone call.

69. Kravitz, phone call.

70. Kauffman Wood, phone call.

71. Kochin, phone call.

72. John Corr, "The Busboy Is Home—With a Big Dream," *Philadelphia Inquirer*, October 12, 1979.

73. Hacker, "Levis Fans."

74. Hacker, "Levis Fans."

75. Gallagher, "It Won't Go"; Polish, phone call.

76. Lasson, "Beyond Hot Dogs."

77. Caroline Stewart, "Buzz," *Philadelphia Daily News*, January 23, 1990.

78. Stewart, "Buzz."

79. Hirsh, phone call.

80. Hirsh, phone call.

81. Clark DeLeon, "The Scene," *Philadelphia Inquirer*, September 16, 1992.

82. Donna Shaw, "The Bitter and the Sweet of a Juice Man," *Philadelphia Inquirer*, March 21, 1994.

83. Hirsh, phone call.

84. Kravitz, phone call.

85. Rosalie Longo, "Hot Texas Wiener Thrives in Paterson," *The News* (Paterson, NJ), March 8, 1982; "John A. Patrellis, Leader in City's Greek Community," *The News* (Paterson, NJ), December 3, 1969.

86. Texas Hot Dogs, "Our History," https://www.texashotdogs.com/our-story/.

87. Ron Avery, "'Secret Sauce' Was His Legacy," *Philadelphia Daily News*, March 12, 1993.

88. Avery, "Secret Sauce."

89. "Restaurant Critic Enters the Twitter World," *Philadelphia Inquirer*, May 5, 2011.

90. Avery, "Secret Sauce"; Scrapple TV, "Texas Wieners [Same as It Ever Was] Philadelphia, PA," YouTube, March 30, 2011, https://youtu.be/Y9RpsCv4dKc.

91. Avery, "Secret Sauce."

92. Avery, "Secret Sauce."

93. Avery, "Secret Sauce."

94. Scrapple TV, "Texas Wieners."
95. Yelp, "A.P.J. Texas Weiner," https://www.yelp.com/biz/a-p-j-texas-weiner-philadelphia.

## Chapter 2

96. "Angelo of the Sandwiches," *The Sun* (New York), December 19, 1908; Edwin Eames and Howard Robboy, "The Socio-Cultural Context of an Italian-American Dietary Item," in *Anthropology and American Life*, edited by Joseph G. Jorgensen and Marcello Truzzi (Englewood Cliffs, NJ: Prentice-Hall Inc., 1974), 505–16; Richard Gehman, "The Noblest Sandwich of them All," *Saturday Evening Post*, January 1, 1955; Amato's, https://amatos.com.
97. Eames and Robboy, "Socio-Cultural Context of an Italian-American Dietary Item," 505–16.
98. Bob Finucane, "Along the Streets of Chester," *Delaware County* (Chester, PA) *Daily Times*, January 24, 1947.
99. Finucane, "Along the Streets."
100. DiCostanza's, "How It All Started," https://dicostanzasandwiches.com/about-us/.
101. William Robbins, "About Philadelphia," *New York Times*, April 17, 1984.
102. Jim Quinn, "The Story of the First Hoagie," *Philadelphia Inquirer*, January 16, 1983.
103. Quinn, "Story of the First Hoagie."
104. "Letters to the Editor," *Philadelphia Inquirer*, January 30, 1983.
105. "Letters," *Philadelphia Inquirer*.
106. Robbins, "About Philadelphia."
107. Quinn, "Story of the First Hoagie."
108. Andy Wallace, "Antoinette Iannelli, Restaurateur and Pioneer of the S. Phila. Hoagie," *Philadelphia Inquirer*, April 8, 1992.
109. This can be concluded from visiting Amato's website (amatos.com), as well as searching newspapers of the time.
110. What's Cooking America, "Submarine-Style Sandwiches History," https://whatscookingamerica.net/history/hoagiesubmarinepoboy.htm.
111. What's Cooking America, "Submarine-Style Sandwiches."
112. "Treborian Tattler," *The News* (Paterson, NJ), July 1, 1931.
113. Donna J. Di Giacomo, *Italians of Philadelphia* (Charleston, SC: Arcadia Publishing, 2007), 81.
114. Ken Finkel, "The Hoagie Is Venerable (But Not as Historic as We've Been Led to Believe)," *PhillyHistory Blog*, November 12, 2018, https://blog.phillyhistory.org/index.php/2018/11/the-hoagie-is-venerable-but-not-as-historic-as-weve-been-led-to-believe/.

115. Herr Mann and Lucille Gaines, "Quaker City Daze," *Pittsburgh Courier*, July 20, 1940.

116. "Business Opportunities," *Philadelphia Inquirer*, November 3, 1940.

117. Finkel, "Hoagie Is Venerable."

118. "Two Fined in Fraud on Mayonnaise," *Philadelphia Inquirer*, October 9, 1946; "Jail Breaker Thumbs Ride with Police," *Philadelphia Inquirer*, November 26, 1951.

119. "From the Reader Mail" *New York Times*, September 2, 1950.

120. Johnny Roosevelt, "The Regional Italian and Submarine Sandwiches of America: Pennsylvania," *America Fun Fact of the Day*, January 23, 2014, https://affotd.com/2014/01/23/the-regional-italian-and-submarine-sandwiches-of-america-pennsylvania/.

121. John W. Lawrence, "Hog Island," *Encyclopedia of Greater Philadelphia*, https://philadelphiaencyclopedia.org/essays/hog-island/.

122. James J. Martin, "The Saga of Hog Island, 1917–1921: The Story of the First Great War Boondoggle," *Memory Hole*, https://web.archive.org/web/20110612140744/http://tmh.floonet.net/articles/hogisle.shtml.

123. Geoff Manaugh, "Hog Island," *BLDGBLOG*, October 2, 2007, https://bldgblog.com/2007/10/hog-island/.

124. "Answers to Queries," *Philadelphia Evening Bulletin*, October 7, 1953.

125. *United States Shipping Board Emergency Fleet Corporation: Hearings Before the Committee on Commerce, United States Senate, Sixty-Fifth Congress, Second–[third] Session, on S.Res. 170, Directing the Committee on Commerce to Investigate All Matters Connected with the Building of Merchant Vessels Under the Direction of the United States Shipping Board Emergency Fleet Corporation, and Report Its Findings to the Senate, Together with Its Recommendations Thereon* [December 21, 1917–January 30, 1919] (Washington, D.C.: U.S. Government Printing Office, 1918), 1,829.

126. Frederick S. Crum, *Restaurant Facilities for Shipyard Workers* (Philadelphia, PA: Industrial Relations Division United States Shipping Board Emergency Fleet Corporation, 1918), 9; *United States Shipping Board Emergency Fleet Corporation: Hearings Before the Committee on Commerce*, 2,179.

127. *United States Shipping Board Emergency Fleet Corporation: Hearings Before the Committee on Commerce*, 2,179.

128. *United States Shipping Board Emergency Fleet Corporation: Hearings Before the Committee on Commerce*, 1,434.

129. Mary Anne Hines, Gordon M. Marshall and William Woys Weaver, *The Larder Invaded* (Philadelphia, PA: Library Company of Philadelphia, 1987), 38.

130. *Philadelphia Times*, July 23, 1893.

131. hot dog: "Careless Venders [*sic*] Warned by City," *Philadelphia Inquirer*, June 1, 1925; doughnuts: "Great Fire Under Control Two More Big Explosions," *Philadelphia Inquirer*, August 22, 1901; hot waffle wagon, waterfront vendor of

catfish: "But We Liked 'Em: Dirt and All!" *Philadelphia Inquirer*, July 19, 1940; chicken sandwich: "South Jersey Negroes' Big Day," *Philadelphia Inquirer*, June 10, 1912; pretzels, etc.: "Ordinance Curbs Hokey-Pokey Men," *Philadelphia Inquirer*, April 18, 1941.

132. "But We Liked 'Em," *Philadelphia Inquirer*.
133. "Answers to Queries," *Philadelphia Evening Bulletin*, September 7, 1953.
134. "Answers to Queries," *Philadelphia Evening Bulletin*, September 23, 1953.
135. Ralph Vigoda, "How the Hoagie Started: Truth, or a Lot of Baloney?" *Philadelphia Inquirer*, July 2, 2009, https://www.inquirer.com/philly/food/restaurants/Hoagie_History_Truth_or_a_Lot_of_Baloney_.html.
136. "Hoagie Sandwich Researcher," *Courier-News* (Bridgewater, NJ), March 19, 1971.
137. Phyllis Stein-Novak, "Hoagie Lore and Allure," *South Philadelphia Review*, February 19, 1998.
138. John Scaltrito, conversation with author, March 4, 2022.
139. Stein-Novak, "Hoagie Lore and Allure."
140. Stein-Novak, "Hoagie Lore and Allure."
141. Scaltrito, conversation.
142. Scaltrito, conversation; *Philadelphia Inquirer*, June 17, 1945.
143. Robboy, phone call.
144. Stein-Novak, "Hoagie Lore and Allure."
145. "$400 Started 'King of the Hoagies,'" *Philadelphia Daily News*, June 12, 1975.
146. "$400 Started 'King,'" *Philadelphia Daily News*; Scaltrito, conversation.
147. "Local Briefs," *Philadelphia Inquirer*, May 29, 1951; "Church Sandwich Sells for $105," *News Journal* (Wilmington, DE), May 31, 1951.
148. Scaltrito, conversation; Robboy, phone call.
149. "Deaths," *Philadelphia Daily News*, June 14, 1975.
150. Becky Batcha, "His Hoggies Get an 'A,'" *Philadelphia Daily News*, February 17, 1992.
151. Batcha, "Hoggies Get an 'A.'"
152. Batcha, "Hoggies Get an 'A.'"
153. Batcha, "Hoggies Get an 'A.'"
154. Scaltrito, conversation.
155. Robboy, phone call.
156. Tom Baldwin, "Yo, Bring Back the Old Hoagie," *Philadelphia Inquirer*, October 6, 1993.
157. Baldwin, "Yo."
158. Stephen F. Friend, "Home Sweet Hoagie," *Philadelphia Inquirer*, April 9, 1972.
159. Tait, "Expert's Recipe."
160. LaBan, phone call.

## Chapter 3

161. Fiorillo, "The Cheesesteak."

162. Fiorillo, "The Cheesesteak."

163. Frank Olivieri Jr., phone call with author, January 18, 2022.

164. Sidney Hantman, "Steak King," *Philadelphia Inquirer*, July 22, 1951.

165. Hantman, "Steak King."

166. Danya Henninger, "Revealed: The Philadelphia Cabbie Who First Suggested Selling Cheesesteaks," Billy Penn, March 19, 2016, https://billypenn.com/2016/03/19/revealed-the-philadelphia-cabbie-who-first-suggested-selling-cheesesteaks/.

167. Henninger, "Revealed."

168. Olivieri Jr., phone call.

169. Tun Tavern, "About the Tun Tavern," https://www.tuntavern.com/about/.

170. William Woys Weaver, email to author, January 13, 2022.

171. Olivieri Jr., phone call.

172. Celeste Morello, phone call with author, August 18, 2022.

173. Ken Silver, phone call with author, January 27, 2022.

174. Olivieri Jr., phone call.

175. Carolyn Wyman, *The Great Philly Cheesesteak Book* (Philadelphia, PA: Running Press, 2009), 14.

176. These conclusions are cobbled together from a variety of sources. Carolyn Wyman's book suggests Michael sent his family to live in Italy for a time in the '10s and '20s, though Wyman also connects Michael's emigration to Mussolini, which is impossible from a timeline perspective. Harry Olivieri's 2006 obituary says he lived in Italy from the time he was three (1919) through the time he was seven (1923). Immigration records show Pat came to the United States in 1914 at the age of six, then in 1924 at the age of sixteen. And finally, Pat's U.S. naturalization record shows he was indeed born in Italy.

177. "Letters," *Philadelphia Inquirer*, December 7, 1980.

178. Zachary Crockett, "The Birth of the Philly Cheesesteak," Pricenomics, February 2, 2015, https://priceonomics.com/the-birth-of-the-cheesesteak/.

179. Wyman, *Great Philly Cheesesteak*, 14.

180. Wyman, *Great Philly Cheesesteak*, 14; John F. Morrison and Christine Olley, "Steak Legend Harry Olivieri Dies," *Philadelphia Daily News*, July 21, 2006.

181. Fiorillo, "The Cheesesteak."

182. Olivieri Jr., phone call.

183. Crockett, "Birth of the Philly Cheesesteak."

184. Olivieri Jr., phone call.

185. Olivieri Jr., phone call.

186. Hantman, "Steak King."

187. Crockett, "Birth of the Philly Cheesesteak."

188. John Corr, "More Than a Sandwich, It's Part of Philadelphia," *Philadelphia Inquirer*, July 27, 1985.

189. Olivieri Jr., phone call.

190. Wyman, *Great Philly Cheesesteak*, 85.

191. Morello, phone call.

192. Crockett, "Birth of the Philly Cheesesteak."

193. Joseph A. Gambardello and staff reports, "The Ultimate Guide to the Philly Cheesesteak," *Philadelphia Inquirer*, June 9, 2021, https://www.inquirer.com/philly-tips/philly-cheesesteaks-ultimate-guide-20210609.html.

194. Alyse Whitney, "The American Cheese I Grew Up Eating (and Haven't Stopped Since)," *Bon Appetit*, March 9, 2017, https://www.bonappetit.com/story/cooper-american-cheese.

195. Danny DiGiampietro, phone call with author, March 22, 2023.

196. DiGiampietro, phone call.

197. Wyman, *Great Philly Cheesesteak*, 17.

198. Library of Congress, "Pennsylvania—Yellow Pages—Philadelphia—June LOC through Z—Pennsylvania, 1947—Image," https://www.loc.gov/item/usteledirec08168/.

199. Ellen Kaye, "Beauty and the Feast," *Philadelphia Inquirer*, December 25, 1977.

200. Kaye, "Beauty and the Feast."

201. Silver, phone call.

202. Michael Klein, "Abner Silver, 79, Jim's Steaks Owner," *Philadelphia Daily News*, January 14, 2015; Fiorillo, "The Cheesesteak."

203. Fiorillo, "The Cheesesteak."

204. Wyman, *Great Philly Cheesesteak*, 58.

205. Gwen Florio, "Cheers to Donkey's Place, Still Kicking in Camden after 50 Years," *Philadelphia Inquirer*, June 16, 1993.

206. Michael Steed, dir., *Anthony Bourdain: Parts Unknown*, season 5, episode 5, "New Jersey," aired May 31, 2015, on CNN.

207. Wyman, *Great Philly Cheesesteak*, 28.

208. Tony Luke Jr., phone call with author, March 7, 2023.

209. Michael Currie Schaffer, "Joey Vento Is a Man of Many Parts," *Philadelphia Inquirer*, June 18, 2006.

210. Schaffer, "Joey Vento."

211. Schaffer, "Joey Vento."

212. Fiorillo, "The Cheesesteak."

213. Fiorillo, "The Cheesesteak"; Olivieri Jr., phone call.

214. Dennis Hevesi, "Famed Cheesesteak Pioneer Built Empire with $6 in Cash," *Honolulu Star-Advertiser*, August 31, 2011.

215. Silver, phone call.
216. John Bucci, phone call with author, February 2, 2023.
217. Nick Miglino, phone call with author, March 23, 2023.
218. Miglino, phone call.
219. Wyman, *Great Philly Cheesesteak*, 83.
220. Craig LaBan, "Epic Hoagies, Pizza Steak a Reminder of Family's Legacy," *Philadelphia Inquirer*, July 15, 2021.
221. LaBan, "Epic Hoagies, Pizza Steak."
222. Miglino, phone call.
223. Rusty Pray, "P. D'Alessandro, 97, a Cook for 35 Years at Family Steak Shop," *Philadelphia Inquirer*, August 24, 2001.
224. Theresa Stigale, "The Skinny—And Everything More—On 52nd Street," Hidden City, April 25, 2012, https://hiddencityphila.org/2012/04/the-skinny-and-everything-more-on-52nd-street/.
225. "'Foo-Foo' Ragan Given 3 Years," *Philadelphia Daily News*, December 11, 1979.
226. Jerry Blavat, *You Only Rock Once* (Philadelphia, PA: Running Press, 2011), 324.
227. Robboy, phone call.
228. Jillian Wilson, Craig LaBan and Michael Klein, "The Best Cheesesteaks to Eat in Philly Right Now," *Philadelphia Inquirer*, March 24, 2022, https://www.inquirer.com/philly-tips/best-cheesesteaks-philadelphia.html.
229. JL Jupiter, "'The Schmitter' Cheesesteak Sandwich at McNally's Tavern," YouTube, May 12, 2022, https://youtu.be/jbaAbVl64i8.
230. HillontheAvenue, "Biting into the Schmitter Story," YouTube, August 4, 2010, https://youtu.be/C4LTNArdxAE.
231. McNally's Tavern, untitled video, http://www.mcnallystavern.com.
232. HillontheAvenue, "Biting into the Schmitter Story."
233. Teresa Banik, "So Who Came First?" *Philadelphia Daily News*, August 24, 1994.
234. Banik, "Who Came First?"
235. Banik, "Who Came First?"
236. Banik, "Who Came First?"
237. Wyman, *Great Philly Cheesesteak*, 71.
238. Banik, "Who Came First?"
239. Banik, "Who Came First?"
240. Banik, "Who Came First?"; Wyman, *Great Philly Cheesesteak*, 71.
241. Banik, "Who Came First?"
242. Matthew Korfhage, "In North Philly and Beyond, Salmon Is the New Cheesesteak. But Don't Tell South Philly," *Courier-Post* (Cherry Hill, NJ), September 28, 2021, https://www.courierpostonline.com/story/life/2021/09/28/story-salmon-cheesesiteak-philadelphia-sandwich/5687208001/.

243. Korfhage, "Salmon Is the New Cheesesteak."
244. jason n. peters (@JPeters2100), Twitter post, February 17, 2019, https://x. com/JPeters2100/status/1097278890983215104
245. *Courier Post*, "Bella's Salmon Cheesesteak," video, September 28, 2021, https://www.courierpostonline.com/videos/life/2021/09/28/bellas-salmon-cheesesteak/8356465002/.
246. *Courier Post*, "Bella's Salmon Cheesesteak."
247. Cheesesteak Factory, Facebook post, August 29, 2009, https://www.facebook. com/permalink.php?story_fbid=pfbid0AQnpkAi85zNfgF4mHT2HkLHhFC H4CQX11ur7h2cnAJa6SoE7uZvRssPJqhGK93BEl&id=93013936563; AC (@MeenBean), Twitter post, September 1, 2010, https://x.com/MeenBean/ status/22738682251; Korfhage, "Salmon Is the New Cheesesteak."
248. Korfhage, "Salmon Is the New Cheesesteak."
249. JL Jupiter, "This SEAFOOD CHEESESTEAK Is to DIE For! Harvinskins Seafood," YouTube, January 2, 2019, https://youtu.be/pqbyibzaGqE.
250. Korfhage, "Salmon Is the New Cheesesteak."

## *Chapter 4*

251. Karen Heller, "Time to Retire the Cheesesteak," *Philadelphia Inquirer*, June 30, 2008; Karen Heller, "Toasting Warm Moments, Worthy Resolutions," *Philadelphia Inquirer*, December 31, 2006.
252. Rick Nichols, "Where's the Beef? Still at Nick's," *Philadelphia Inquirer*, December 30, 2007.
253. Tim Warren, "Gee Whiz, the Cheesesteak Isn't Philly's Best Sub," *Sunday News* (Lancaster, PA), April 6, 2008.
254. Craig LaBan, "Pork's Place," *Philadelphia Inquirer*, April 2, 2000.
255. Bucci, phone call.
256. C.F., "Per Celebrare Il Capo D'Anno," *La Libera Parola* (Philadelphia, PA), January 7, 1922 (translated by author).
257. LaBan, "Pork's Place."
258. Rose DeWolf, "Street Smarts," *Philadelphia Daily News*, April 4, 1997.
259. Bucci, phone call.
260. Danya Henninger, "John's Roast Pork: Big Stories from a Small Shack," *Philadelphia Inquirer*, March 21, 2016, https://www.inquirer.com/philly/blogs/ the_spot/Johns-Roast-Pork-John-Bucci.html.
261. Henninger, "John's Roast Pork."
262. Bucci, phone call.
263. Bucci, phone call.
264. Bucci, phone call.
265. Bucci, phone call.

266. Henninger, "John's Roast Pork."
267. Bucci, phone call.
268. Bucci, phone call.
269. Bucci, phone call.
270. Bucci, phone call.
271. LaBan, phone call.
272. LaBan, phone call.
273. Bucci, phone call.
274. Bucci, phone call.
275. Bucci, phone call.
276. Bucci, phone call.
277. Bucci, phone call.
278. Bucci, phone call.
279. Bucci, phone call.
280. Bucci, phone call.
281. Rick Nichols, "Dinic's Roast Pork Classic," *Philadelphia Inquirer*, July 22, 2004.
282. Nichols, "Dinic's Roast Pork Classic."
283. Murray Dubin, "A Family Affair Carries on South Philadelphia Tradition," *Philadelphia Inquirer*, April 26, 1975.
284. "Mystery Muncher," *Philadelphia Inquirer*, February 27, 1981.
285. Joe Nicolosi, phone call with author, February 10, 2023.
286. Nicolosi, phone call.
287. Jim Quinn, "On a Roll," *Philadelphia Inquirer*, February 19, 1995.
288. Nicolosi, phone call.
289. Nicolosi, phone call.
290. Nicolosi, phone call.
291. Bucci, phone call.
292. Nicolosi, phone call.
293. Quinn, "On a Roll."
294. Bucci, phone call.
295. Quinn, "On a Roll."
296. Quinn, "On a Roll."
297. Nicolosi, phone call.
298. Nicolosi, phone call.
299. Bucci, phone call.
300. Bucci, phone call.
301. Quinn, "On a Roll."
302. Miglino, phone call.
303. Betsy Andrews, "Philly Tastes," *Saveur*, April 2011.
304. Karen Heller, "Pleasures of the Flesh," *Philadelphia Inquirer*, February 10, 2005.

305. "They're Lining Up for Tony Luke's," *Philadelphia Inquirer*, October 2, 1992; Michael Klein, "Table Talk," *Philadelphia Inquirer*, December 4, 1994.

306. Luke Jr., phone call.

307. Luke Jr., phone call.

308. Luke Jr., phone call.

309. Luke Jr., phone call.

310. *The Best of Philly Guide* (Philadelphia, PA: Running Press, 1994), 39.

311. "Your Guide to America's Best Restaurants," *Gourmet*, October 2000.

312. Luke Jr., phone call.

313. Nicolosi, phone call.

314. Luke Jr., phone call.

315. Luigi Lemme, email to author, February 25, 2023.

316. Lemme, email.

317. "Chatting with Craig LaBan: The Top Sandwich (Pulled, Not Sliced, Pork)," *Philadelphia Inquirer*, November 4, 2010.

318. Nicolosi, phone call.

## Chapter 5

319. *Philadelphia Magazine*, "Best of Philly," https://www.phillymag.com/best-of-philly/?bestof_search=cutlet.

320. John F. Morrison, "Restaurateur Frank Perri, 57," *Philadelphia Daily News*, March 18, 1994.

321. Morrison, "Restaurateur Frank Perri."

322. Shank's Original, "Zagat Awards," http://www.shanksoriginal.com/awards/zagatawards.pdf.

323. Barbara J. Richberg, "Frank 'Shank' Perri, a Master Italian Cook," *Philadelphia Inquirer*, March 18, 1994.

324. Richberg, "Frank 'Shank' Perri."

325. Melissa S. Treacy, "Get the Best Sandwich in the City, Hands Down," *Philadelphia Inquirer*, August 23, 2010, http://www.shanksoriginal.com/press/clips%2020.pdf.

326. Ed Brennan, phone call with author, November 17, 2022.

327. Rick Nichols, "Transplanting Shank's," *Philadelphia Inquirer*, April 9, 2009.

328. Nichols, "Transplanting Shank's."

329. Luke Jr., phone call.

330. Nichols, "Transplanting Shank's."

331. Brennan, phone call.

332. Peggy Landers, "PR Maven Finds a Family Feeling in South Philly," *Philadelphia Daily News*, January 8, 1999.

333. "Mystery Muncher: Home Cooking Away from Home," *Philadelphia Inquirer*, January 26, 1990.

334. Michael Klein, "Shank's Moves Uptown," *Philadelphia Inquirer*, July 28, 2009, https://www.inquirer.com/philly/blogs/the-insider/Shanks_moves_uptown.html.

335. "The Best Sandwiches in America," *Esquire Magazine*, March 2008.

336. FooBooz, "Shank's Wine Sandwich Safari," *Philadelphia Magazine*, July 23, 2010, https://www.phillymag.com/foobooz/2010/07/23/shanks-wins-sandwich-safari/.

337. Treacy, "Best Sandwich in the City."

338. DiGiampietro, phone call.

339. DiGiampietro, phone call.

340. Craig LaBan, "Cutlet Lovers Rejoice: This Stack at Cotoletta Is for You," *Philadelphia Inquirer*, June 14, 2017, https://www.inquirer.com/philly/columnists/craig_laban/cutlet-lovers-rejoice-this-stack-at-cotoletta-is-for-you-20170614.html.

## *Chapter 6*

341. Craig LaBan, "The Classic Sandwiches," *Philadelphia Inquirer*, October 18, 2018.

342. Nicolosi, phone call.

343. Nichols, "Where's the Beef?"

344. Luke Jr., phone call.

345. Megan Rose, phone call with author, March 21, 2023.

346. LaBan, "Classic Sandwiches."

347. Nichols, "Where's the Beef?"

348. Rose, phone call.

349. Rose, phone call.

350. Nichols, "Where's the Beef?"

351. Jonathan Takiff, "Nick's Has Come a Long Way from Jackson Street," *Philadelphia Daily News*, June 18, 1971.

352. Rose, phone call.

353. Nichols, "Where's the Beef?"

354. Takiff, "Nick's Has Come a Long Way."

355. Nichols, "Where's the Beef?"

356. DiGiampietro, phone call.

357. Peter Genovese, "Taylor Ham (or Pork Roll): What the Iconic Meat Means to Jersey," *Thrillist*, March 31, 2016, https://www.thrillist.com/eat/new-york/taylor-ham-or-pork-roll-what-it-means-for-new-jersey.

358. Jersey Pork Roll, "The History of Pork Roll," https://jerseyporkroll.com/pork-roll-history/.

359. Marah, "Christian Street," track 3 on *Kids in Philly*, 2000.

360. John Vellios, phone call with author, March 13, 2023.

361. Vellios, phone call.

362. Vellios, phone call.

363. Vellios, phone call.

364. Chris Marino, director, *Bizarre Foods with Andrew Zimmern*, season 4, episode 2, "Pennsylvania," aired January 25, 2011, on Travel Channel.

365. Vellios, phone call.

366. Vellios, phone call.

367. Marino, *Bizarre Foods with Andrew Zimmern*, "Pennsylvania."

368. Vellios, phone call.

369. Vellios, phone call.

370. Vellios, phone call.

371. Vellios, phone call.

372. Vellios, phone call.

373. Vellios, phone call.

374. Carly Szkaradnik, "Chickie's Italian Deli Is Closing, Cruelly Taking Its Veggie Hoagies with It," *Eater Philadelphia*, April 6, 2015, https://philly.eater.com/2015/4/6/8353165/chickies-italian-deli-closing-veggie-hoagies-sandwiches.

375. Michael Klein, "Antonio's Deli Picks Up Where Chickie's Leaves Off," *Philadelphia Inquirer*, July 5, 2015, https://www.inquirer.com/philly/blogs/the-insider/Antonios-Deli-picks-up-where-Chickies-leaves-off.html.

376. Quinn, "On a Roll."

377. Craig LaBan, "Yo! Sandwiches Are Our Thing," *Philadelphia Inquirer*, October 17, 2019.

378. Rick Nichols, "A Sandwich Gets Around," *Philadelphia Inquirer*, January 3, 2010.

379. Jim Quinn, "South Vietnam Meets South Philly," *Philadelphia Inquirer*, April 28, 1985.

380. Quinn, "South Vietnam Meets South Philly."

381. Maria Gallagher, "Viet Huong Put Personality in Hoagies," *Philadelphia Daily News*, July 6, 1990.

382. LaBan, phone call.

383. Stacia Friedman, "A Dearth of Delis: In Remembrance of Philly's Jewish Eateries," *Hidden City*, September 13, 2022, https://hiddencityphila.org/2022/09/a-dearth-of-delis-in-remembrance-of-phillys-jewish-eateries/.

384. Allen Meyers, *The Jewish Community of West Philadelphia* (Charleston, SC: Arcadia Publishing, 2001), 72.

385. LaBan, phone call.

386. Craig LaBan, "Good Taste," *Philadelphia Inquirer*, June 22, 2017.

387. Derek Nunnally, "Local Hero: Norristown's Zep Sandwich," *Philadelphia Inquirer*, December 9, 2009.
388. LaBan, "Good Taste."
389. LaBan, "Good Taste."
390. LaBan, "Good Taste."
391. Nunnally, "Local Hero."
392. Nunnally, "Local Hero."
393. Nunnally, "Local Hero."
394. Nunnally, "Local Hero."
395. Robboy, phone call.
396. Nunnally, "Local Hero."
397. Peter Romano, phone call with author, March 6, 2023.
398. Romano, phone call.
399. Romano, phone call.
400. Romano, phone call.
401. Romano, phone call.
402. Romano, phone call.
403. Romano, phone call.
404. Romano, phone call.
405. Romano, phone call.
406. Romano, phone call.
407. Romano, phone call.
408. Romano, phone call.

*Chapter 7*

409. Olivieri Jr., phone call.
410. DiGiampietro, phone call.
411. Silver, phone call.
412. "No Bread, No Life," *South Philly Review*, March 19, 2004, https://southphillyreview.com/2004/03/19/no-bread-no-life/.
413. Olivieri Jr., phone call.
414. Jack McCarthy, "Bakeries and Bakers," *Encyclopedia of Greater Philadelphia*, https://philadelphiaencyclopedia.org/essays/bakeries-and-bakers/.
415. "Destruction of an Historical Relic.; THE 'OLD BAKE-HOUSE' ON THE DELAWARE BURNED," *New York Times*, December 10, 1865.
416. Benjamin Franklin, *The Autobiography of Benjamin Franklin* (Boston: Houghton, 1917), 35–39.
417. McCarthy, "Bakeries and Bakers."
418. McCarthy, "Bakeries and Bakers."
419. McCarthy, "Bakeries and Bakers."

420. FamilySearch, "United States Census, 1880," https://familysearch.org/ark:/61903/3:1:33SQ-GYB6-8GW?cc=1417683&wc=X414-K68%3A1589394781%2C1589410714%2C1589401700%2C1589395329.

421. Ernest L. Biagi, *The Italians of Philadelphia* (New York: Carlton Press, 1967), 58; *Gopsill's Philadelphia City Directory* (N.p.: various publishers, 1895).

422. Celeste A. Morello, *The Philadelphia Italian Market Cookbook: The Tastes of South 9th Street* (Philadelphia, PA: Jefferies & Manz, 1999), 28–29.

423. Morello, *Philadelphia Italian Market Cookbook*, 123.

424. Morello, *Philadelphia Italian Market Cookbook*, 123.

425. Olivieri Jr., phone call.

426. Miglino, phone call.

427. *Gopsill's Philadelphia City Directory*.

428. Eric Schroeder, "Longtime Philadelphia Bread and Roll Baker Closes," *Baking Business*, January 28, 2013, https://www.bakingbusiness.com/articles/23725-longtime-philadelphia-bread-and-roll-baker-closes.

429. ExcursionsTV, "Amoroso's Baking Company," YouTube, February 6, 2009, https://youtu.be/Od5Dss7oZd8.

430. Jesse Amoroso, phone call with author, January 20, 2023.

431. Amoroso, phone call.

432. Amoroso, phone call.

433. ExcursionsTV, "Amoroso's Baking Company."

434. ExcursionsTV, "Amoroso's Baking Company."

435. Cheesesteak Shop, "Our Story," https://www.cheesesteakshop.com.

436. ExcursionsTV, "Amoroso's Baking Company."

437. Victor Fiorillo, "31 Fun Facts Every Wawa Nerd Should Know," *Philadelphia Magazine*, December 14, 2018, https://www.phillymag.com/news/2018/12/14/wawa-statistics/.

438. Joseph DiStefano, "PhillyDeals: Wawa Hoagie Rolls Now from Vineland," *Philadelphia Inquirer*, July 27, 2008, https://www.inquirer.com/philly/business/20080727_PhillyDeals__Wawa_hoagie_rolls_now_from_Vineland.html.

439. DiStefano, "PhillyDeals."

440. Joseph N. DiStefano, "Wawa's New Boss Pledges a Bread Oven in Every Store: Update," *Philadelphia Inquirer*, January 16, 2013, https://www.inquirer.com/philly/blogs/inq-phillydeals/Wawas-new-boss-pledges-a-bakery-in-every-store.html.

441. Amoroso, phone call.

442. Amoroso, phone call.

443. Grace Maiorano, "Family Reflects on Louis Sarcone, Cherishes Bakery's 100 Milestone," *South Philly Review*, July 18, 2018, https://southphillyreview.com/2018/07/18/family-reflects-on-louis-sarcone-cherishes-bakerys-100-milestone/.

444. Kurt Smith, "It's All About the Bread," *JerseyMan Magazine*, https://agreatnumberofthings.com/wp-content/uploads/2020/08/Its-All-About-The-Bread.pdf.

445. Maiorano, "Family Reflects."

446. Rick Nichols, "The Flavor Also Rises: Baking Bread Takes Time at Sarcone's," *Philadelphia Inquirer*, July 4, 2018, https://www.inquirer.com/philly/food/the-flavor-also-rises-baking-bread-takes-time-at-sarcones-20180704.html.

447. Smith, "All About the Bread."

448. Smith, "All About the Bread."

449. Smith, "All About the Bread."

450. Nichols, "Flavor Also Rises."

451. Nichols, "Flavor Also Rises."

452. Michael Klein, "The Sons Also Rise at Sarcone's Bakery," *Philadelphia Inquirer*, August 17, 2017, https://www.inquirer.com/philly/blogs/the-insider/sarcone-bakery-louis-hoagie-south-philly-20170817.html.

453. Smith, "All About the Bread."

454. Smith, "All About the Bread."

455. Smith, "All About the Bread."

456. Klein, "The Sons Also Rise."

457. Klein, "The Sons Also Rise."

458. Smith, "All About the Bread."

459. Peter Mucha, "Why Philadelphia Hoagies Have Gone to Seed," *Philadelphia Inquirer*, June 26, 2009, https://www.inquirer.com/philly/news/breaking/20090626_Why_Philadelphia_hoagies_have_gone_to_seed.html.

460. Smith, "All About the Bread."

461. Mucha, "Hoagies Have Gone to Seed."

462. Mucha, "Hoagies Have Gone to Seed."

463. Mucha, "Hoagies Have Gone to Seed."

464. "The Effects of Hard Water and Soft Water on Baked Goods," *Bakers Journal*, September 2001, https://web.archive.org/web/20190226135804/http://www.triangularwave.com/bakeryeffects.htm.

465. "Effects of Hard Water and Soft Water," *Bakers Journal*.

466. Ian Romano, "Roll with It," *South Philly Review*, October 8, 2009, https://southphillyreview.com/2009/10/08/roll-with-it/.

467. Julie R. Thomson, "Debunking the Myth That NYC Water Is What Makes New York Bagels So Damn Good," *Huffpost*, May 11, 2015, https://www.huffpost.com/entry/new-york-water-bagels-so-good-nom_n_7242452.

468. Chris Opfer, "Is It Something in the Water?" *Narratively*, September 23, 2014, https://www.narratively.com/p/is-it-something-in-the-water.

469. Opfer, "Something in the Water?"

470. Gary Lane, phone call with author, December 13, 2022.
471. Lane, phone call.

## Chapter 8

472. Raymond Ricci, phone call with author, June 1, 2023.
473. Ricci, phone call.
474. Ricci, phone call.
475. Ricci, phone call.
476. Ricci, phone call.
477. Danya Henninger, "Cosmi's Deli: A 'Little Mortadell' Makes All the Difference," *Philadelphia Inquirer*, November 9, 2015, https://www.inquirer.com/philly/blogs/the_spot/Cosmis-Deli-mortadell.html.
478. Rick Nichols, "The Real Thing," *Philadelphia Inquirer*, June 27, 1999; Henninger, "Cosmi's Deli."
479. Steven Ujifus, "Campo's and Our Lady of Loreto (Part I)," *PhillyHistory Blog*, October 20, 2016, https://blog.phillyhistory.org/index.php/2016/10/campos-and-our-lady-of-loreto-part-i/.
480. Mike Campo Sr., phone call with author, January 20, 2023.
481. Campo's Deli, "Our History," https://camposdeli.com/our-story/; Campo Sr., phone call.
482. Campo Sr., phone call.
483. Campo Sr., phone call.
484. Ray Kirchdoerffer, "The King of Steaks," *Philadelphia Inquirer*, September 14, 1980.
485. Kirchdoerffer, "King of Steaks."
486. Len Lear, "A Half-Century of Comfort Food in South Philly," *Public Record*, http://www.shanksoriginal.com/press/clips%2027.pdf.
487. Nichols, "Transplanting Shank's."
488. Wyman, *Great Philly Cheesesteak*, 32.
489. Mary Martin Niepold, "A Calendar of Events for the Children," *Philadelphia Inquirer*, July 4, 1976.
490. Jim O'Brien, "Council Hopeful Eats Way Out," *Philadelphia Daily News*, April 17, 1967.
491. Joe Sharkey, "You Can't Leave the City Without a Steak Sandwich," *Philadelphia Inquirer*, June 11, 1971.
492. Friend, "Home Sweet Hoagie."
493. Fiorillo, "The Cheesesteak."
494. Silver, phone call.
495. Spivak, phone call.

496. Luke Jr., phone call.

497. LaBan, phone call.

498. LaBan, phone call.

499. Craig LaBan, "Phil Mancuso and Angelo Scuderi Upheld Philadelphia's Italian American Food Traditions," *Philadelphia Inquirer*, February 17, 2021.

500. LaBan, phone call.

501. LaBan, phone call.

502. LaBan, phone call.

503. LaBan, phone call.

504. Trevor Kerin, email to author, March 21, 2023.

505. LaBan, phone call.

506. DiGiampietro, phone call.

507. Miglino, phone call.

508. LaBan, "Epic Hoagies, Pizza Steak."

509. Miglino, phone call.

510. DiGiampietro, phone call.

511. DiGiampietro, phone call.

512. DiGiampietro, phone call.

513. Brian R., Facebook comment in "Cheesesteak Gurus" group, September 25, 2022, https://www.facebook.com/groups/1252670318457974/posts/1890081568050176/.

# INDEX

# ABOUT THE AUTHOR

Mike Madaio is a food and wine writer based outside of Philadelphia. His career began with the creation of *Main Line Dine*, a popular restaurant and dining blog covering the Philadelphia suburbs, and his writing has appeared in publications such as *Wine Enthusiast*, *VinePair* and *Edible Philly*. He has also achieved Italian Wine Ambassador certification from the Vinitaly International Academy. His previous book for The History Press, *Lost Mount Penn: Wineries, Railroads and Resorts of Reading*, covered the wine house scene in and around Reading, Pennsylvania, in the 1800s.

Follow Mike on social media @lifeattable.

Visit Mike's website at https://lifeattable.com.

*Visit us at*
www.historypress.com